ADVANCE PRAISE FOR

The New Partnership

"Pay attention corporate America. Stop trying to convince your-
selves that your company is unique and will not yield to Melohn's
wisdom. And do what he says. It works. He knows. He's been
there."

JAMES A. AUTRY
Author of *Love and Profit*

"This is a book to be savored, absorbed, and acted upon. . . . Why
wait another moment to start to transform yourself and ultimately
your place of work into one that brings out the best in everyone
with humor, heart, and basic values."

MICHAEL L. RAY
Professor of Creativity and Innovation
Stanford Business School

"*The New Partnership* is disarming in its simplicity and moving in
its faith in the ability of ordinary people to do great things. It should
be required reading at all business schools and at companies both
large and small."

DAVID E. GUMPERT
Author of *How to Really Create
a Successful Business Plan*
and a former editor of
Inc magazine and the
Harvard Business Review

"Tom Melohn explains, in vivid and heartwarming terms, how traditional values such as caring, trust, and respect for human dignity can be woven into the fabric of corporate culture. Tom doesn't ignore the bottom line. He simply redefines the real bottom line pathway to fun and productivity, and the profits take care of themselves."

ALAN R. NELSON, MD
Executive Vice President, American Society of
Internal Medicine and past President,
American Medical Association

"Tom Melohn's philosophy of life is evident in *The New Partnership*. If a job is worth doing, do it right. And listen to others advice along the way, just as he did at NATD."

PAUL E. SHEEHAN
Past President, American Production and
Inventory Control Society

The New Partnership

The New Partnership

PROFIT BY BRINGING OUT THE BEST

IN YOUR PEOPLE, CUSTOMERS,

AND YOURSELF

Tom Melohn

John Wiley & Sons, Inc.
New York · Chichester · Brisbane · Toronto · Singapore

To the gang at North American Tool & Die,
without whose help things like this
never would have been possible.

Special Acknowledgments

I wrote a manuscript; she showed me how to write a book. Dr. Sue McKibbin is a true Renaissance lady.

It was his idea and he kept the faith throughout—Jim Childs, publisher, editor.

Contents

Foreword by M. Scott Peck   **xv**

Introduction: What's Going On Here?   **xvii**
- Why the purchase of North American Tool & Die?
- Our strategy for growth and the results
- The *real* purpose of this book

Prologue   **3**
- One coworker stayed alone—in the dark—after the San Francisco Earthquake. Why did he do it?

CHAPTER I · IT ALL STARTS WITH HONESTY   **7**
- Walking our talk in the beginning
- Employees planning their *own* layoffs?
- No telephones in the plants?
- Corporate America and honesty (and other fables)

CHAPTER II · THEN COMES TRUST   **17**
- A new employee buys a $250,000 machine—on his own
- Trust your sales associates
- Caring by walking around
- The early days at NATD—how do you begin?

- Graveyard shift refuses extra overtime pay
- Mutual trust with customers
- Corporate America and trust (what's that?)

CHAPTER III · PLAIN TALK   31
- Setting company objectives
- How to handle pay and employee evaluations
- How to stop company politics
- Use plain talk with your customers
- Corporate America and plain talk (please, no snickering)

CHAPTER IV · DO UNTO OTHERS— TREAT OTHER PEOPLE JUST THE WAY YOU WANT TO BE TREATED   45
- Equality ("We're all bosses")
- No physical trappings of status
- A new kind of pay—mutual respect, dignity, self-worth, recognition
- The early days at NATD (employees . . . leading customer plant tours?)
- What's the Sick and Tired Award?
- Letters from your(?) employees after NATD featured on "In Search of Excellence" on PBS-TV
- Corporate America and the Golden Rule (sorry; it's not in the policy manual)—plush offices, yet rundown plants

CHAPTER V · IT'S CALLED FAMILY—BE CAREFUL, IT'S PROFITABLE   61
- Emotional security
- Happy employment anniversary—one silver dollar per year
- Family feelings between coworkers
- Be yourself (red pants and a pink lathe)
- Corporate America and family (that's not required by EEOC!)

CHAPTER VI · VINCE LOMBARDI WAS RIGHT—IT'S CALLED TEAMWORK   77

- Office personnel, working in the plant?
- Flip the organization chart upside down
- The people run the plants
- Job rotation increases teamwork
- Earning part of your coworker's paycheck
- Teamwork with your customers (Hewlett Packard and Apple letters)
- Corporate America and teamwork (okay, but don't expect us to play)

CHAPTER VII · HIRING THE EAGLES—FINDING, HIRING, MOTIVATING, AND KEEPING SUPER EMPLOYEES   91

- Develop an employee profile
- Finding good people
- Help wanted ads: they can work
- The selection process
- The job interview
- Determining pay
- Checking references
- Keeping good people
- Corporate America and hiring (by the book—rote and without feeling)

CHAPTER VIII · LET ME GROW, LET ME CREATE—HOW TO RELEASE EMPLOYEE CREATIVITY   109

- You gotta believe
- It's your ball
- There's no such word as no
- It's okay to make a mistake
- You can do it, I know you can
- You thought it up on your way home . . . and it *tripled* our production!
- A special check for "chewing me out"

- "The employees worked even faster than my new homemade machine 'cause I made it kinda like a game"
- Corporate America and creativity (sorry, just kidding)

CHAPTER IX · THANK YOU   127
- Super Person of the Month award
- Thank You, in a union shop?
- I'm helpless; my boss doesn't believe in this stuff (it's free, just go do it)
- Our company's just too big to say thank you (no way!)
- You don't have to say "thank you" to say thank you
- How many coworkers for dinner?
- Corporate America and thank you (I'm still waiting)

CHAPTER X · LESS IS MORE—A LESSON FROM ARCHITECTURE... FOR BUSINESS?   139
- Small is lean
- Small is efficient
- Small is fast
- Small is profitable
- Small is fun
- How small is small?
- Corporate America and size (big departments mean big power)

CHAPTER XI · "I'M IN CONTROL HERE"—THE PURSUIT OF POWER IS A DANGEROUS THING—DESTROY IT   153
- The promotion syndrome (now I'm better than you)
- Power to the People
- Setting up NATD University

- Power to allocate resources, make decisions, gain information, and act
- Corporate America and power ("If I'm not in control, it must be out of control")

CHAPTER XII · QUALITY: IN THE HEAD, IN THE HEART   169
- They came, they saw, but did not see
- Quality through people (even entry level co-workers can care)
- Quality—the customer's perspective (Hewlett Packard and a shiny yellow school bus; 4,636 pairs of gloves—for quality)
- Service departments and quality
- Corporate America and quality (they're getting the idea, finally)

CHAPTER XIII · THE CUSTOMER IS KING VERSUS HOWDY PARTNER   185
- Customers and suppliers as family (Hewlett Packard, Sun, Apple, Nummi)
- Keeping customer service in perspective
- Corporate America and their customers (smile and nod; tell 'em what they want to hear)

CHAPTER XIV · THAT'S ALL THERE IS— HOW THIS MANAGEMENT STRATEGY GENERATES IMPRESSIVE AND SUSTAINED PROFITS   199
- The joy of management (psychic income)
- Profit and our fellow employees ("Working here . . . it's like having your own business")
- I love to give away money 'cause we all win
- Subcontract to increase your profit
- Corporate America and profit (money is the biggest narcotic of all)

CHAPTER XV · ENTHUSIASM AND HUMOR—BOTH ARE KEY MANAGEMENT TOOLS   213

- Enthusiasm is a key element in sales
- Humor is an unfair competitive weapon
- Humor with the customer
- Corporate America and enthusiasm and humor ("Somewhere over the rainbow. . . .")

CHAPTER XVI · LEADERSHIP: FROM THE HEAD, FROM THE HEART   225

- Leaders are made, not born
- Everyone leads themselves
- Three tough choices
- Corporate America and leadership (I'm waiting . . . still waiting)

CHAPTER XVII · TOMORROW AND TOMORROW   241

- You are not alone
- Question authority
- A quiet revolution
- An unlikely ally for change
- For your kids' sake

Afterword by Distinguished Professor Warren Bennis, U.S.C.   **249**

Index   **251**

Foreword

This book is a description of how a person took over the leadership of a failing business and turned it into a hugely profitable success.

The person in question, Tom Melohn, asked me to write a foreword to his book, and I agreed to do so. Why? There are several reasons.

I have a passion for common sense as opposed to fashion. The books and manuscripts with which I am deluged are generally one part common sense and nine parts fashion. Only once every year or two does a book fall into my hands proclaiming with almost child-like clarity that "the emperor has no clothes." In this world of supposed sophistication where cynicism itself has become the emperor, we desperately need such voices. So I am writing because this is a book about such corny notions as "honesty" and "integrity" and "love." Be put off if you choose, dear manager, but you will be passing up a whole gold mine of very concrete—and surprisingly imaginative—suggestions about how to help people click and make business work.

We're still in a time and society of sellout. As a contrast to this general trend, the story of the North American Tool & Die Company reads like an account of a fluke of sorts—but I hope this is not the case. I write as a scientist. Essential to the scientific method is the replication of results in different laboratories. The future of our civilization depends upon the degree to which we can learn to replicate such unusual happenings. It will be the reader's choice whether to simply pass off the NATD story as a fluke—an accident of some kind—or assume the responsibility of attempting personally to replicate it in the most important laboratory we have: day-to-day business and commercial enterprise.

M. Scott Peck
Author of *The Road Less Traveled*

Introduction: What's Going On Here?

"Tom, you're fired!"

What a shattering experience!
What a blessing in disguise.
For almost twenty-five years I labored amid the arid fields of "Big Corporate." Slavishly adhering to the unwritten but inviolate precepts for success, I steadily climbed the corporate ladder. Senior Vice President of Marketing for a food company with $500 million in annual sales at age 42, I had arrived—only to find my victory to be hollow, flawed and without meaning.

The trappings of success were all in place—a big salary, bonus, company car, a generous expense account, two paid club memberships, a beautiful home, world travel, etc. Yet I found no personal satisfaction, no sense of accomplishment. Increasingly, I abhorred the ridiculous daily charades, the incompetence, the politics, the never-ending expediency and personal compromise required to survive in Big Corporate.

Each day I railed at the ever-increasing depersonalization at big corporations. I wasn't Tom Melohn; I was employee #510-524-4077. So was everyone else—a number, to be manipulated, to be exploited, and ultimately, to be expendable.

Human emotions had no place in big companies. Whenever decisions finally *had* to be made, it was always by the book—rote, precise, sterile, and uncompromising. There was no place for independent thought. Tradition and protocol reigned supreme. The system took care of its own—if you played the game by their rules. The consequences were clear if you dared to be different: to speak out for a better way, to challenge the traditional rules. Your tenure would be a brief one.

My earlier career was no different. Encrusted with the same barnacles, my prior employers—all big corporations—lumbered on day after day, choking in an ever more constricting environment of redundant management layers, play it safe, cover your butt, hide your true feelings, and don't make waves. Big Corporate was an absolute monarchy.

For years I just couldn't accept the notion that most of our major American corporations were the same, in both climate and operating procedure. Every three or four years (thanks to the executive recruiters) I'd change jobs, hoping to find the "Holy Grail"—a company where individual performance would be the primary yardstick, where politics was outlawed, where people could work together toward a common goal.

Somewhere in America there had to be a major corporation where each employee could be treated as an individual, a person of worth whose contributions, however small, could be recognized and appreciated; a company where people truly enjoyed their work and could live their values—every day. Over the years, I'd repeatedly query fellow executives who worked elsewhere in Big Corporate. Alas, they too were searching for the same Nirvana—with equally meager results.

After being fired, I decided to buy and then build my own company, running it the way I had always dreamed. There it was, listed in the business opportunities section of *The Wall Street Journal:*

FOR SALE
San Francisco
North American Tool & Die (NATD).

At first it made no sense. My entire business experience was in consumer packaged-goods marketing. There was little I could bring to this company. Let's face it, the manufacture and marketing of custom metal stampings and subassemblies to the electronics and automotive industries required totally different aptitudes and skills. Or so it seemed.

Yet upon reflection, I realized that the type of business I bought would make very little difference. Throughout my entire career I had come into totally disparate businesses, each with unique manufacturing, distribution, and marketing problems. In every instance, profits had subsequently increased dramatically. I knew how to make money.

One of my indictments of Big Corporate centered upon its callous treatment of employees. If my management beliefs were correct, they should be equally applicable in any business, whether manufacturing or service.

So we began. My lawyer introduced me to a silent financial partner. At the outset we each owned 50 percent of the company. My purchase price was funded by a bank loan, secured by our life's savings.

Here's what we bought. NATD was a company with:

- static sales

- marginal profit

- aged and second-hand capital equipment

- a dispirited work force with high turnover

- a haphazard customer list

- unacceptable quality

Yet I felt this company had great potential. In the nearby computer industry growth was exploding. This was a huge potential market. In addition, Nummi (a joint venture between General Motors and Toyota) had just reopened a massive auto assembly plant nearby. Our competition was fragmented. No one was serving the customer. Quality was marginal. Here was my opportunity—to build a company by managing the way I had always wanted to be managed.

During those twenty-five years in Big Corporate, I had—sometimes painfully—learned these truths:

- As Henry David Thoreau noted in *Walden*, in 1854, "The mass of men lead lives of quiet desperation."

- Good people really do want to do a good job.

- People value honesty—very much. Just tell it like it is.

- The people "on the line" are no different from you and me.

- Everyone's creative, in some way.

- The trappings of power in most corporations get in the way of working together.

- Trust is very fragile, yet we all yearn to trust each other, our company, and our leaders.

Distilling these beliefs into an action plan, I set three objectives for NATD:

- to grow the company profitably

- to share the wealth

- to have fun

The strategy to attain our goals came from our potential customers. At the outset I asked them what they wanted from NATD as a supplier. Their response was clear: quality, service, and price—and in that order. (By the way, is it any different in your company, whether manufacturing or service?)

Implementation at NATD centered around four basic principles:

- Hire only good people who care.

- These people are the same as you and me.

- Treat your fellow employees just the way you want to be treated.

- The person doing the job knows it better than anyone else.

All of this may seem mushy and soft. Forget it. This was no social experiment. It was a profit-making enterprise. Let's put it another way: North American Tool & Die was the only financial source of current income and retirement, for me and our fellow employees. We played to win, but in a different way.

Here's a summary of the results in twelve years:

• Sales	up 28% per year
• Pretax earnings	up 2,400%
• Return on investment	in the top 10% of the Fortune 500
• Company stock	up 47% compounded each year (happily, we're privately held)
• Productivity	up 480%
• Employee turnover	less than 4%
• Absenteeism	less than 1%
• Customer reject rate	0.1%; all parts, all year, all customers

Suddenly NATD was news. Certainly there were countless companies whose growth and profitability exceeded ours. The news value at NATD was different; here was a rare instance of a company whose success was the direct result of being nice to your fellow employees. It was a classic case study of how to improve employee trust, productivity . . . and profit. *We forged a new partnership with our coworkers simply by hiring good people who care and treating them just the way we want to be treated.*

The business community became intrigued. First the *San Francisco Chronicle* ran a major article, then the *San Jose Mercury-News*, *USA Today*, and *Inc Magazine* ("Screening for the Best Employees," January 1987, pp. 104–106). This was followed by countless other newspaper and magazine stories all across the country. They asked me to write an article about NATD in the *Harvard Business Review* entitled "How to Build Employee Trust and Productivity" (January–February 1983, p. 56–59). Tom Peters and Bob Waterman read it and chose NATD to be in their now legendary PBS-TV documentary "In Search of Excellence." Tom Peters also cited NATD in both *A Passion for Excellence* and *Thriving on Chaos. The Leadership Challenge* and the American Management Association's book *Winner Takes All* also noted NATD's "revolutionary" approach to management.

Soon the professional speaking circuit beckoned. It was ironic. Now Big Corporate across the world paid me to tell them how we transformed a marginal company into an industry leader.

Suddenly my wife, Holly, had a stroke. The first whistle of our mortality had sounded. Happily, she later recovered, but the message was clear. I had accomplished what I wanted to prove at NATD. It was time to move on, to spend more time with my wife and to share lessons learned at North American Tool & Die with others. I sold all my stock in the company to my coworkers through their ESOP (Employee Stock Ownership Plan) and also to the corporation itself. Although I severed all connection with NATD, I hear they are doing fine.

To my surprise, Jim Childs (publisher-editor) called, introduced himself, and asked me to write a book. At the outset I said no. Heck, I'm a businessman, not a writer. Yet as I thought it through, it seemed to me that there would be some value in contrasting what worked at NATD vs. Big Corporate's modus operandi. The lessons learned at NATD were equally applicable at companies both large and small, manufacturing or service.

We're in deep trouble today in American business. You know it first hand, where you work, right now. The "Band-Aid" solutions aren't working. They never have, not really. First, it was MBOs, then zero-based budgeting, then quality circles. Now it's total quality management, self-directed work teams, worker empowerment,

gainsharing, flat organization charts, and reengineering the corporation. They're an improvement, as far as they go. But they're not
addressing the real core problem: how to *truly* motivate your fellow
employees. What will be the next fad?

Each chapter in this book defines a basic business problem and
provides fresh and yet proven and pragmatic solutions. Specific
hands-on stories illustrate these new management concepts at work
at North American Tool & Die, Inc. These are in sharp contrast
with the traditional responses of big corporations. At the close of
each chapter, you'll see how you can build a New Partnership: steps
you can take right now, first thing in the morning, to make a
difference—for yourself, your job, your department, or your
corporation—regardless of size.

It may seem incredible, but every story in this book is true. Each
quotation of our coworkers is verbatim. Their comments were
unrehearsed and spontaneous, given in response to various TV
interview questions during recent years.

Finally, I want to explain two stylistic anomalies in this book.
First, it's written in the present tense. Obviously these were the best
years of my business life. The personal bond I and my coworkers
forged at NATD as fellow employees is unforgettable and still very
real in my mind. Hence the present tense. My second stylistic
deviation is the use of "we" throughout the book. There are several
reasons. First, I was raised to avoid the repeated use of "I." Bluntly
stated, that's boasting. The second reason for the use of the pro-
noun "we" is simple. It was true. *We* forged a new partnership
together.

The New Partnership

Prologue

Anybody remember what happened in San Francisco at 5:04 P.M. on Tuesday afternoon, October 17, 1989? There was a major earthquake—one measuring 6.9 on the Richter scale.

Here's what happened at North American Tool & Die that night. Eric Karlsson (Production) had come in at about 2:00 P.M., just before the start of the second shift. We ship just-in-time delivery to Hewlett Packard, San Diego, two trucks a day, every day, just like clockwork. The first truck arrived from HP about 3:00 P.M.. Thirty minutes later, loaded for the return trip, the driver left, mentioning that his buddy in the second truck was about two hours behind.

At 5:04 P.M., the world stopped at NATD. The earth truly rumbled; the building repeatedly shook; the noise was deafening; dust was everywhere. Then the lights and power went out. Everything stopped. One of our coworkers turned on her portable radio and heard that part of the Bay Bridge had collapsed. Raging fires had engulfed portions of the Marina district; several elevated freeways had fallen, trapping countless motorists in the debris. Even the World Series was postponed. Eric sent everyone home—with full pay for the entire shift.

But one person stayed—alone—in the dark—in a deserted plant—for almost two hours—after a major earthquake—waiting for that second truck to arrive (It showed up the next morning). It was Eric. He knew that HP needed those parts for their production line the next morning.

Why? Why did he do that? How can you possibly pay someone for that? How can you ever thank him?

You know something? There are Eric Karlssons all over this country, all over the world. They're at your company. They're there. We don't have any monopoly on them at NATD.

I'd like to sell you something today, something very special, something you may *think* you already own, something you can't ever buy with just money. I'd like to sell you your most important corporate asset: your fellow employees.

But you see, they're not for sale—not for just money alone. It takes a different kind of currency. It's called:

Honesty
Trust
Equality
Mutual respect
Self Worth
Dignity
Recognition
Teamwork
Caring

Most of all, caring.

How do I know?

Because these are the basic values we try to live every day, every night, at NATD. Some carping cynics would perhaps categorize this management style as Alice in Wonderland. But it works, my friend. As the kids would say, it works big time.

This is an enormously profitable strategy. It's also a fun way to work. NATD "honors" man; therefore, it is a great place to work. Finally, for us believers, it is a religious way to live. Take your choice, choose your motivation. But you've got to go do it. Just do it—now. The clock is running.

The central idea here is simple: Treat other people just the way you want to be treated. Remember, they're no different from us— the good ones who care. They care about the same things we value: ourselves, our family, our kids, our job, and our future. Therefore, they'll react to the same things you do in the same way. Incidentally, this "new" currency won't cost your company a cent. With few exceptions, it's all free. You can start tomorrow—without the need for any official approval.

Come on. See how you too can forge a New Partnership in your department, division, profit center, or company.

CHAPTER ONE

It All Starts with Honesty

"Tom, how come there's a shopping bag filled with dollar bills sitting on the lunch-room table?"

"That's our coworkers' weekly NFL football pool. Why do you ask, Ken?"

"I don't believe it! All that money just sits there unattended in your factory, twenty-four hours a day, all week, and nobody steals it?"

"You don't understand, Ken. The people here are honest. No one ever steals—money, tools, supplies, nothing. The women even leave their purses out, unattended, during the entire shift."

*From a conversation at NATD between
Ken Mudge, (buyer, Data Products Corporation)
and Tom Melohn (head sweeper, NATD)*

Seems like a dream, doesn't it? But it's true. We built a New Partnership at NATD—together with our fellow employees, and with our customers. Everybody won—including our bottom line, year after year. Our partnership was based on honesty, total honesty.

I didn't come into NATD preaching a bunch of words, passing out preprinted vision statements or corporate credos. I just tried to live my personal values, every day, every night, in every area, inside the company, with our customers, and with our vendors. It took time—a lot of time—probably about two years. But our fellow employees slowly realized that we tried to be honest, bone honest, in everything we did.

Stop for a minute and think it through. There are a couple of key elements at work here. First, all the pronouncements, all the pontifications, they just don't work anymore—if they ever did. We've all heard too many words, empty words. We need to believe, to really believe again, both in our business and in our personal lives.

Only actions count: consistent actions, every day, every night, every shift, every time. Then we'll believe again—slowly, ever so slowly. Funny, isn't it, but the little things really do mean a lot. It's like an Impressionist painting: a bunch of seemingly unconnected dabs or strokes, until you step back and view the completed painting. Then the pattern becomes clear. But remember, the pattern has to *start* with you. "Do as I say, not as I do" just doesn't work anymore.

WALKING OUR TALK

Shortly after the purchase of NATD, we stopped partial unaccounted cash payments from our vending machine service companies. The same arrangement was quickly ended with our scrap dealer. Historically, these payments totaled thousands of dollars each year. We told our associates why we had made these decisions at a plantwide meeting.

Our expense accounts were meticulously accurate. There was absolutely no largesse. Our choice of a company car for sales calls was very deliberate. The former owner had driven a Mercedes; we leased an Oldsmobile station wagon that could also handle small deliveries. This new symbol was easy for all to see.

Round-trip travel by car between my home and our offices became a personal expense. Fuel and maintenance for our personal cars at home were never charged to the business. We told our fellow employees this. Simply stated, we tried to be honest—totally honest.

We soon hired a "big six" accounting firm for our year-end audit. Perhaps this seems extravagant for a small company; their fee was a major expense. But we felt it would be a graphic and very public symbol of our honesty. Creative accounting was not allowed. We deliberately told each coworker our reasons.

As you know, honesty can't be applied selectively. You're either honest or you're not. Here's one seemingly trivial incident from our early days at NATD that had a lasting impact.

> "Tom, we just got a check from Diablo Systems for too much money. They must have transposed the price on our invoice. What should I do?"
> "Just call and tell them, Gloria. Why do you ask?"
>
> *A conversation between*
> *Gloria Bega (office worker)*
> *and Tom Melohn (head sweeper)*

At the time, this discussion didn't even register in my mind. Several days later, more than one coworker in the plant complimented me on our decision. The lesson was clear: Actions do speak louder than words.

About the same time, another situation developed that also helped establish a climate of honesty at NATD.

> "Hey, Tom, let's bid this job high. We can make a bundle. Our regular price is thirty percent lower than the current supplier's."
> "No thanks. Let's not get greedy, Joe. Besides, that's not honest."
>
> *From a conversation between*
> *Joe Rosario (machinist)*
> *and Tom Melohn (head sweeper)*

Soon I heard that Joe had related this story to others in the company. The word was out.

The most important tool to foster an atmosphere of honesty is simply to tell the truth, consistently, and in every area. Unfortunately, the first month after we purchased NATD there was a

sharp downturn in our business. I got the department heads together and opened the meeting this way:

> "It looks like a layoff's coming. Let's plan ahead together.
> Anyone who can take their vacation next month, please do
> it. Let's figure out how we can all cut back to a thirty-two-
> hour week. In that way no one will get too badly hurt
> financially."

I can still remember the reaction. There was shocked silence.
No one had ever honestly discussed an impending layoff with them.
No one openly planned with these people how best to minimize the
financial impact on them. No one had ever treated them as
equals—with brains—and sought their ideas . . . honestly.

Slowly, hesitantly, some suggestions came forth:

> "I guess I can take my vacation now. We didn't plan on
> going away anyway."

> "There are working moms here. They need the money more
> than I do. I'll go on layoff. It's just me and the Mrs. now.
> We'll get along."

> "To save the company money, we can pay for our own
> coffee."

> "There's not much work in our department. We'll work in
> another area of the company—if that will help."

Here's what we decided—together. We turned down the coffee
suggestion—though it was appreciated. Everyone worked a thirty-
two-hour week. Some associates took vacation. A few coworkers
volunteered to be laid off. And unfortunately, several more were
laid off. Happily, they were all rehired later.

At the time, I didn't think it unusual to talk honestly about
possible layoffs. We had a problem; we had to solve it—together.
Later on, our associates told me how appreciative they were—that
I was honest with them, that I told it just the way it was.

Yet, if you think about it, employees usually know about

an upcoming layoff anyway. They're not naive. They can see production going down and fewer shipments out the door. Who's kidding whom?

Two other incidents come to mind that further established the climate of honesty at NATD. Both were unplanned, spontaneous; perhaps that's why some of our coworkers still remember them. The underlying idea is straightforward. If you treat people as though they are honest, most often they will act in an honest way.

Here's a conversation held in front of several NATD employees, who later spread the word.

TELEPHONE COMPANY REPRESENTATIVE:	With your new system, we've capped the phones on the plant floor so no one can make unauthorized long-distance calls.
TOM MELOHN:	Thanks, no. Take all the caps off. Our fellow employees are honest. They wouldn't do anything like that.

Guess what? At NATD, there was *never* one unauthorized long-distance phone call from the plant floor—ever. The employees could have called Europe, the Far East, or Mexico, and we'd never have known who did it.

Not too long thereafter, Joan Wright, our purchasing person, told me about ten pounds of coffee were missing from the cafeteria. A few weeks later another ten pounds were gone. Joan reluctantly suggested that henceforth the coffee storage area be locked up. My response was immediate:

> "No way. These people are honest. I know they wouldn't do it."

Shortly thereafter, we fired our night janitorial service for poor performance. Perhaps it was a coincidence, but the theft stopped.

Again and again, our fellow employees saw ample evidence that I believed they were honest. As a result, most of our associates started to be honest—to themselves, to each other, and to me.

Remember one of those basic truths we discussed earlier? "The mass of men lead lives of quiet desperation." These people—our fellow employees and yours—have been lied to by masters. As a result, they're looking at you with a crooked eye, watching, waiting, for just one slip. You lie once, just once, and the credibility's gone— totally gone. And that's as it should be.

HONESTY—IN BOTH DIRECTIONS

Yet honesty can't be a one-way street, not for long. Our fellow employees also had to live their values every day, every time. At the outset at NATD, it was difficult, very difficult. We had to change a complete mind-set. Many members of the existing work force were not being honest. They were working, but not really. It was slow-paced. It was reactive: "Tell me what you want me to do and I'll do it." No one was reaching out, no one was trying to find a better way. They were just going through the motions, covering their butts, and protecting their turf. Their attitude was "Just let me put in my time, give me my paycheck, and I'm out of here."

Nobody took ownership. The inventory counts were incomplete and inaccurate. Scrap was high, our job costs varied wildly. Absenteeism was pronounced; turnover, disheartening. Nobody would level with me. Nobody really cared.

How do you motivate each coworker to do a full day's work? At NATD we live our values. We expect our associates to do the same. Putting out less than a full day's work is not permitted. It isn't honest. We tell our coworkers that, plainly, openly. Everybody knows what is expected and why. People with different values leave soon enough. They know there's little future at NATD for them.

The good people who care quietly encourage my actions to live our values. They work hard; they expect the same from their coworkers. There cannot be a double standard for performance.

Phony absenteeism is also not acceptable. It is dishonest. I can still remember one young man who was repeatedly absent—purportedly ill—always on Monday. After several pointed discussions together, he quit. Out he marched, stating that his life was rock music, not boring production work. Fine. He made a choice. NATD could not afford a weekend band member who slept in every Monday. Sick-leave days are just that, for those days when a coworker is ill. People who feel their sick leave is additional vacation are quickly and candidly disabused of this notion. There are no exceptions—including me.

Honesty's a funny word, isn't it? You can be honest and yet dishonest. We've all seen it again and again. Honesty's more than not cheating, stealing, or lying. It's living by the spirit as well as the letter of the word. We can skirt the line of dishonesty, but that doesn't make us honest.

When we queried some of our associates about excessive scrap or high production costs, vague and evasive answers were often forthcoming. It wasn't the truth and we told them so. We asked for their help in defining and solving our problems honestly. Over time we learned who was telling the truth. We encouraged those associates and applauded their candor publicly. Slowly, ever so slowly, other coworkers joined in, seeing that they too were safe in telling the truth. They were not blamed, nor were their ideas ridiculed or ignored.

Employees who persisted in lying were repeatedly warned and ultimately fired. Because we had already clearly set forth and lived our values, there were no surprises.

Incidentally, don't avoid the issue here. Any employee can be fired for inadequate performance. The procedures are in place, the protocol known. You know who the contributors are; you know who the malcontents are; you know which employees are not honest. So do your associates. Your coworkers are watching you. Your actions will speak volumes.

In retrospect, these actions built a cohesiveness, the start of a team feeling. Here was a group of people who worked together, living their common values every day, every night, every shift, every job.

We could count on each other.

BIG CORPORATIONS AND HONESTY

Now, let's contrast our stories from NATD with Big Corporate. Here's probably how these companies would react. See if you agree.

> "A new phone system in the plant? We'll need a lock on each unit to stop unauthorized calls. By the way, be sure to update the existing list of our executives who have authorization for an unlocked telephone."

What's the nonverbal message here for the employees, both on the line and in the office? That's right. You're dishonest. Only management is honest.

Is that truly what you believe? Is that the message you really want to convey? Does that create the best working climate for your company?

Here's another hypothetical corporate response. Let's lump the missing coffee and bag full of money together. They'd be handled the same way:

> "Coffee stolen? Gambling on company property? That's dishonest and against company policy. Get the legals and Human Resources over here this afternoon to witness an all-plant meeting. Somebody'll pay for this with their job."

Let's see if we're in agreement. Here are the messages conveyed by these actions:

All of you are dishonest.
We're adversaries.
We're going to punish you.

And we wonder why our fellow employees are often so guarded, so sullen, so resentful.

There's no reason to contrast the story about the upcoming

layoff at NATD with how big companies would handle it. We've already seen it—over and over.

And management sometimes wonders why their employees don't believe them—about anything.

At NATD it was critical to encourage all coworkers to be honest. Honesty was an essential underpinning to our future success. Only in that way could a New Partnership flourish.

THE *ESSENCE* OF A NEW PARTNERSHIP— HONESTY

1. Live your values. Don't just pontificate; no one will believe you.

2. Consistency—every day, every night, every situation— pays off in the long run.

3. Lying and deception are never acceptable.

4. Honesty means living by the spirit as well as the letter of one's word.

5. Honesty cannot be applied selectively. You're either honest or you're not.

6. Good people are honest. Treat them that way . . . and they will be that way.

HOW *YOU* CAN BUILD A NEW PARTNERSHIP BASED ON HONESTY

1. Which of your fellow employees aren't being honest? Why?

2. Are you being honest with your associates—consistently? If not, why? In what areas?

3. Reassess which "confidential" data about the company would help your fellow employees do a better job. Share this information and tell them why.

4. Ask your associates to come to a meeting with a list of sensitive questions and then candidly answer them.

5. Give the habitual liars plenty of warning. Then call them on it every time.

   If their dishonesty continues, fire them.

   They can contribute nothing of value in your new environment.

6. Be patient; good people will respond.

7. Start right now—don't put it off for even one more day.

CHAPTER TWO

Then Comes Trust

"Tom treats you different. He makes you feel like you're part of this company—that he trusts you."

Teresa Bettencourt (Production)

That's what it's really all about, isn't it? To build a solid relationship—whether in business or your personal life— there must first be honesty and then trust. Everything else stems from those basic values. Honesty means don't lie or cheat; trust means we have confidence in each other, that we can rely on our associates.

When we first bought NATD, there was little evidence that trust was in place between the owner and his employees. In my mind, building mutual trust was a critical underpinning for our future growth at NATD.

TRUST YOUR COWORKERS' COMPETENCE

Shortly after our purchase of NATD, our fellow employees told me we should buy an electronic discharge machine (EDM). This unit could be computer-programmed to cut through six-inch hardened steel blocks with unbelievable accuracy and within phenomenally close tolerances, all unattended. This was new technology and essential to becoming a progressive precision manufacturing company. No one at NATD had any experience in this area except Larry Vosner (Engineering).

Here's Larry's description of what happened:

> I had joined NATD only two months ago. One day Tom came up and said, "I understand you've got some background in EDM equipment. I want you to research different models and pick out the best one."
>
> We looked at four or five different brands. I presented all the facts and a recommendation to him.
>
> Tom said, "Great—go buy it."
>
> I was kinda shocked. It's a lot of money—about a quarter of a million dollars. Don't you want to hold my hand? Don't you want to lead me through it? It's not something you let a guy do on his own who's been here only two months.
>
> Tom said, "You know what you're doing. I've got confidence in you. Go ahead and do the job."
>
> It was a different kind of feeling. It makes you feel proud of yourself—uplifting—stuff like that.

In my mind this was a nonevent. Larry was a good human being, with our set of values. His competence was clearly evident. I trusted him.

Larry was a very popular coworker at NATD. His EDM assignment and personal reaction soon became common knowledge throughout NATD. This was an inadvertent but highly visible first step in building mutual trust.

TRUST YOUR COWORKERS' CONSCIENCE

Soon afterward, I told Allan Kemline (Engineering) to get out one day and go on home. He looked at me in shock. I think he thought I was firing him. In those early days, he didn't know me that well. In reality, it was simply a suggestion that he could get more done by working at home. His days at the office seemed particularly hectic. I also knew he had a major engineering design project due the following week.

This was unheard of in those days. Work at home? Unsupervised? No way! The employee would just goof off. In my mind, this was not the case—not with Allan. I trusted him. I knew I could rely on him. And it worked. Again and again, when he was really under time pressure, Allan would simply clear out, take his computer, and head home where he could work more productively. His fellow employees saw this visible sign of trust between us.

TRUST YOUR SALES ASSOCIATES

Trust? Trust a salesman? You must be crazy! But we did. If you hire good people who care, people with the same values, mutual trust is almost automatic.

When I first arrived at NATD, I hired a national sales manager. His charter was straightforward: personally build a profitable business for NATD; then build a sales force. Run it and "send money."

Shortly thereafter we abolished any sales call reports. Why not? I trusted him. I never checked his daily whereabouts or his expense account. The "house rule" was clear: Spend our company's money as if it were your own. His travel plans were also his business; he knew best when and where to go for sales.

Perhaps every other week, we'd have lunch or coffee together outside the office. In this way, he could give me a verbal overview of the marketplace and the sales status of specific accounts. Yes, the sales group had offices at NATD. But by mutual agreement, they were most often empty. You don't get new business sitting comfortably behind your desk. All our associates at NATD were aware of this working arrangement. I told them so. They knew I trusted our sales group.

TRUST: IN THE OFFICE, ON THE PLANT FLOOR

In my experience, an "open door" policy is self-deluding and ineffective. You know what I mean? The boss grandly proclaims: "My door is open at all times to any employee. Come in and visit with me at your convenience. Any subject is fair game, no holds barred."

That's baloney. How many times have you seen people use it where you work? That's right, almost never. People are afraid of the boss (I wonder why). Besides, they'd rarely get a straight answer anyway. In addition, it's often misconstrued by other coworkers. "There goes Joe again, in to butter up the boss."

At NATD, we reversed our "open door" policy. We moved it to the plant floor. In that way my visits were on the turf of our fellow employees, where they would be more comfortable, more relaxed and in familiar surroundings. Usually the end result was a more open visit together.

We also changed the subjects of discussion. Instead of talking about their work, we visited together about them and their personal well-being. If you're into initials, you could call this "caring by walking around" (CBWA). In this way, we got to know each other, to trust each other, to rely on each other—to care. Hear Teresa Bettencourt's observation:

> "Everyone here knows everyone and you trust the people you work with. When Tom comes around and tells us something, we trust his word because we know he's trustworthy. If he tells you something, you know that you can trust him."

The comments of Fred Weiser in Maintenance provide an additional perspective on CBWA:

> "Tom is caring. He has a personality that—he cares for his people. And he wants to make sure that everybody feels the same way. Caring and feeling that way for the company. He comes around often, and he is always in a good mood with the people."

CBWA is an essential means of building trust between our associates and me.

There is a hidden benefit here. Over time, my respect for these people grew almost exponentially. Our coworkers are truly exceptional human beings. Oftentimes instead of my doing CBWA with them, I become the beneficiary. Here's how I phrased it:

> "Sometimes—very selfishly—when I'm right up to here with problems, I've got to get out and take a breath. Every time I come back from the plant floor, I feel stronger. They're such incredible people that they give me strength."

Mutual trust? You bet!

THE EARLY DAYS AT NATD

In the beginning, many of our fellow workers didn't believe us. They didn't trust us and I don't blame them. Building trust doesn't happen overnight. It's only my surmise but here are some of the thoughts that probably were in our associates' minds, early on:

> "Organize our own work? No way. I'll wait for them to tell me . . . like always. Then I can't be chewed out if there's a mistake."

> "Help them to define and solve our problems together? Forget it! That's their problem."

> "A better way to do it? How would I know? You're the so-called expert."

> "Trust my fellow employee? What have you been smoking? I'm hunkering down, covering my tail, guarding my turf. I don't trust anybody here. Then I won't be hurt."

So we reached out to those people who seemed to believe that we really trusted them. And we tried to live our beliefs consistently.

Remember, for a long time after, your employees will be watching to see if you mean it—every time. Put it in perspective. How long has it been since anyone in management trusted them?

Together we picked out one or two key problems in the plant, and they went to work. Sure, we stumbled, we screwed up—but we kept trying. I was in awe of their technical skills. I became their cheerleader, their patron, their believer. They had to do it! And they did. Here's a typical example.

Every year it was the same routine with one of our customers. The buyer would call and order X sets of parts for NATD to manufacture. Located in the Sierra Mountains of California, his company built peach-pitting machines. There was only one problem. Every year NATD would lose money on the job.

Obviously, I hadn't the slightest idea of where or what the problems were. But I had a good idea of who did know—our fellow employees. So I got the gang together to sort it out. Slowly, haltingly, and with great apprehension, our associates pawed through all the relevant cost information. This was a new experience for them. They had never seen a cost analysis on any job—ever. They laboriously compared our bid to our actual cost for every step in the production process. Finally, our associates identified the major loss areas.

Now came the dilemma. How can we improve our production flow to avoid another financial loss? This was the point when I left these group sessions. There were four reasons. First, I knew my presence would inhibit them. Second, they'd turn to the owner for the solution as they always had with my predecessor. Third, I had faith in them; I knew our associates would come up with the solution. Fourth, I knew these people were intelligent. Perhaps Rene McPherson, former chairman of the Dana Corporation, said it best at the first of Tom Peters's "Skunk Camps" in 1985: "Do you think those people on the line are dumb? They can raise a family of four on three hundred forty-seven dollars a week. I don't have one vice president who can do that."

Sure enough, deciding among themselves and still with great hesitation, our fellow employees improved production on the next run. There was no profit but we were now headed in the right direction—for the first time ever.

Once we had a few wins, it became easier. Our fellow employees lived these beliefs:

- He trusts us.

- He respects us.

- He can't help us technically.

- It's our job.

- It worked—our ideas worked.

- He sure is proud of us.

- This is fun; let me try it too.

Then it spread. First one department, then another. First one problem, then a number of problems being solved concurrently, in different departments.

And away we went.

Not everyone jumped in. A number of our associates did their jobs well but nothing more. That's okay. Not everybody can drive the bus.

Those people who sneered at us, who thought it was just more "smoke from the front office," soon went elsewhere. The idea of mutual trust was not important to them.

We were forging a team at NATD, a team of pros who shared the same values: first, honesty, and now, mutual trust. Soon we would develop a new partnership.

TRUST WORKS BOTH WAYS

You'll find this next example of trust working both ways to be incredible—but it's true. We had a happy problem; we were swamped with new production orders. The only solution was a third shift, the infamous "graveyard."

At NATD, overtime is always voluntary. You just can't arbitrarily tell your coworkers that they must work this Saturday or else. That's not fair. The same premise applied to staffing the third shift. Jim in Production volunteered to head up that group. But what should their overtime pay premium be? I asked the plant manager and other shift supervisors; they finally agreed upon twenty-five cents per hour. Yet some thought fifty cents per hour was more appropriate. Even that seemed insufficient—to ask someone to turn his family's daily routine upside down for $20 a week.

We finally decided to resolve it by asking Jim his opinion. After all, it was his pocketbook. When we called him into our meeting, his answer was clear and to the point.

> "Twenty-five cents an hour is okay. It's fair. Fifty cents an hour? That's too much."

In that moment, Jim cemented a trust that would go a long way in building a new partnership at NATD.

Remember when you were a kid? Remember the first time someone trusted you as an adult? What a great moment. How proud you were. How grown up you felt—and acted. You were confident because you knew implicitly that your parents, teacher, coach, or whoever would have faith in your actions, regardless of the outcome. Whatever the assignment, you were very careful to complete the task properly—as an adult. They trusted you. They relied on you.

Certainly these same emotions and motivations can still be effective in our daily lives. Use them, for everyone's benefit. Trust your associates, collectively and in their individual efforts to improve, to create. Once your coworkers know they have your trust, win or lose, they'll be more apt to reach out, to try the unknown.

Once I relearned this truth the hard way at NATD. Year after year, I trusted our coworkers. Win or lose, they had my vocal and active support. About three years ago, our engineers came up with an innovative way to build a customer's dies. There was a possibility of failure but we were all enthusiastic. As the days and weeks went by, it became increasingly apparent that the project would fail.

We hadn't done enough engineering homework. Unfortunately, I showed my frustration and disappointment. Larry Vosner, a key engineer on the project, subsequently quit to take another job (*the Larry Vosner of EDM fame*). When he told me, I was stunned. He was our kind of person and slated for much bigger things at NATD. I tried to dissuade him but to no avail. He quietly told me that my apparent loss of faith in him on that major project was the primary reason for leaving. If he couldn't count on unstinting trust from his boss, the job had little appeal. He was right. I never forgot it.

MUTUAL TRUST WITH CUSTOMERS

Trust? Trust a customer? You must be crazy. They're the adversary. They'll take you for all you're worth.

You're right—in some cases. You know who the bad ones are and you deal with them appropriately, the ones who lie, who cheat, who take advantage. Don't even sell to them. But how about all the others? We found the same situation prevailed among most of our customers as it did with our fellow employees. Trust them, and they'll act in a trustworthy way.

It is common for NATD to take major verbal purchase orders and spend our own money—big money—without any formal written customer purchase authorization. That comes much later. We trust our customers. And for the most part, they never let us down. Again and again, buyers like Wayne Knittle, Ken Mudge, Paul Alvarez, and David Cannon, all from different companies, place tooling and production orders, each well over one million dollars, by telephone, year after year. There's never a problem. There is a bond of mutual trust between our companies. Confirming purchase orders always arrive weeks later.

Remember, trust works both ways. Delivery dates at NATD are inviolate—not to the month promised, nor the week, but to the day. In many instances, our customer's trust in us is defined by our delivery schedules—to the hour. Long before it became the norm we were doing just-in-time delivery to our major accounts. Oftentimes our customer has only three or four hours' inventory of our parts on hand. They trust us to deliver on time, every time. Even one hour late is not acceptable. Sometimes we even "eat" the expense and air-freight our parts to a customer—just to be on time.

We just can't let them down. It's a matter of principle and good business.

Our associates saw all of this, they saw that our actions reinforced our beliefs—in this case, trust. And they knew. We were on our way to building a New Partnership.

CORPORATE AMERICA AND MUTUAL TRUST

Now, let's play "Big Corporation." How would the people there react to the EDM story?

MANAGER: That's fine, Larry. Let's write up your recommendation in triplicate and submit it to our Corporate Capital Appropriations Committee. If and when they sign it off, I'll route it through our standard one-over-one signature system for approval. Then we can charge.

LARRY: Charge? By then, the bus will be long gone. Corporate Capital Appropriations Committee? What in heaven's name do they know about our needs and the appropriate EDM equipment? The one-over-one signature system is nothing but a corporate CYA technique.

It's so frustrating. They just don't trust me. They don't think I know what I'm doing. Forget it; why should I even try?

How sad, how really sad. And what a waste of human talent! Here are a few more examples of Corporate America and trust:

> "Eliminate all sales call reports? There's no way we could ever do that. We'd lose control" (i.e. we don't trust them).

> "Of course we do routine checks of all expense accounts. Just a precaution, you know" (except for V.P.'s and above; we trust them).

> "Check proposed travel plans of our sales people? Certainly—to better coordinate all our efforts."

One day after a speech I was chatting with a manager in a big corporation. He was bothered by the mutual trust we have at NATD. When asked why, he said, "Because if I'm not in control, the organization must be out of control." That's a common reaction to the notion of mutual trust, of shared power with your fellow employees. If you don't trust your associates, the organization has to feel out of control. Think about it. The traditional role of the boss is to serve as a control mechanism. The workers have to be controlled because you don't trust them to work independently. And that's a tragedy!

Let's give credit where credit is due. Corporate America has come a long way in recent years in its attitude toward employees who work at home. The advent of the personal computer and fax machine was the turning point. Key employees recognized the mutual benefits of such an arrangement and "moved out."

CBWA also has no place in Corporate America. Caring for employees is simply not in its purview. If the underpinning of trust doesn't already exist, there is no way for caring to flourish.

Remember the adage outlined earlier, the one we learned while in Big Corporate:

> Trust is very fragile, yet we all yearn to trust each other, our company, our leaders.

We put it to work at North American Tool & Die, gently at first, carefully—living our values consistently, in every situation, both inside and outside the company.

THE *ESSENCE* OF A NEW PARTNERSHIP— TRUST

1. Trust your fellow employees, and in turn, they'll trust you.

2. Trust your customers, and they'll usually act in a trustworthy way.

3. Hire only good people who care. Fellow employees have the same values and will soon trust each other.

4. Live your values every day—and be patient. They'll be watching.

HOW *YOU* CAN BUILD A NEW PARTNERSHIP BASED ON TRUST

1. Determine which of your fellow employees you don't trust. Figure out why.

2. Do your employees really trust you, consistently, in all areas?

   • Develop a list of "sensitive" issues that may have been misconstrued by your associates and may have led to mistrust.

   • Discuss these together, candidly.

3. Pick out one or two of these issues (better yet, ask your coworkers).

   • Jointly decide who's qualified to solve them.

   • Let them go do it their way. Show your trust by providing support and encouragement.

   • Keep the "experts upstairs" out of their way.

   • Act on their recommendations—promptly.

4. The people you don't trust because of their repeated actions, call them on it—every time. Have a candid discussion. If they persist, fire them. They aren't part of your new partnership.

5. Once mutual trust is flourishing, work with your associates to eliminate the signs of mistrust: time cards, attendance records, rule books, job descriptions, etc.

6. Start now—don't wait. The results will stun you.

CHAPTER THREE

Plain Talk

"Tom's honest. He'll tell it the way it is. This is the way I like to hear it and most of the people here do too."

John Vitti (Production)

I n today's increasingly complex world we strive to simplify our lives, to reduce things to a manageable, intelligible level. Yet we're bombarded on all sides with new information, new situations, new problems that have to be assimilated and solved—fast. As a result, we're starting to abhor verbosity, obtuseness, and sham. Let's be sure we're communicating here. Plain talk is different from honesty. Obviously you must first be honest. But then you've got to tell it straight—no embellishments, no qualifiers. Straight ahead. Plain vanilla.

PLAIN TALK AND COMPANY OBJECTIVES

Plain talk at NATD is a critical element in our success. All our fellow employees know that "no rejects" is our number one objective. Our group understands this because we define it simply, clearly, directly, again and again—and again—and then prove it with our actions. We put it in their terms: "One tenth percent customer reject rate—all parts, all year, all customers." We keep it simple and straightforward, using a number, 0.1 percent, to symbolize our goal—and our achievement. This solitary objective never changes, year after year. Parenthetically, it's interesting to note that our only corporate goal is in natural alignment with a basic human trait: to do our best.

Perhaps the best measure of the efficacy of our plain talk on "no rejects" comes from our coworkers.

> "Quality is there. It has to be. Otherwise we're not here; otherwise we don't have any customers."

> *John Vitti (Production)*

PLAIN TALK AND PAY

It's the same old story wherever we go, isn't it? Management rarely wants to talk about compensation with their "subordinates." And yet it's ever present, on everyone's mind. At NATD we try to defuse the issue by meeting it head on—with plain talk. Six months after we bought the company, we told our associates three things regarding pay. These innovations were shockingly novel:

- NATD would *always* pay the *entire* cost of medical, dental, and life insurance for each employee and his or her family.

- The total plant payroll would *always* be increased once a year to reflect inflation.

- Each employee's pay would *always* be reviewed at least annually for a *possible* merit increase.

It was clear and straightforward—no hedging. Everyone knew where they stood. For twelve years it never varied, never changed. That's how we built trust: with consistency, one step at a time.

Sometimes plain talk can be painful for all parties. But that's never a reason to avoid it. How do you tell a long-time fellow employee not to expect any more automatic pay increases? The answer? With plain talk.

Tom Parrnelli's tenure was amazing. In Quality Control, he was one of NATD's first employees, with over twenty years at the company. He had received regular pay increases year after year. Tom's work performance was fine.

Yet sooner or later his automatic merit pay increases had to end. Tom's base compensation was about 50 percent more than that of his counterparts in the marketplace and we told him that. Tom knew the facts; it was no surprise. Yet he was rightfully upset. It hurt his pride and self-respect.

In our discussion, I tried to reassure him of his worth to the company. I tried to point out specific self-improvement projects that would result in his future career growth. Further technical education was the key. It was up to him. Even today, Tom is a valued associate at NATD.

PLAIN TALK AND EMPLOYEE EVALUATIONS

In our experience, most people want to do a good job. Yet nobody is perfect (except corporate vice presidents). As a result, people truly appreciate a thoughtful and specific assessment of where they can improve at work. The key is to encourage your coworkers to learn, to grow, and then provide the proper tools to help them accomplish their goals. Then instead of being in a critical and adversarial role, you're now a coach, a cheerleader and helper. If your coworkers know you want them to succeed, if they know you're there, ready to help—that's a whole different climate.

Plain talk is also a staple in our employee evaluation sessions at NATD. Everyone in business knows that plaudits are easy to hand out (but in reality, so rarely used) in recognition of an employee's contributions. Yet when it comes to a discussion of how a co-worker's job performance can be improved, we suddenly go mute. We carefully avoid any discussion of a possibly sensitive subject. This just isn't fair.

On one occasion use of plain talk at NATD in employee evaluations paid wonderful dividends. In my opinion, Allan Kemline in

Engineering is a superb coworker. His contributions to the success of NATD are manifold.

About three years ago, it seemed that Allan was slowing down. There was nothing specific, just a general malaise. Several months passed and there was no change in Allan's "pace." It was obvious we needed to chat. After our frank discussion, Allan had a complete medical exam and got a clean bill of health. In typically thorough Kemline fashion, he also joined a health club and worked out regularly before work each day. That regimen, coupled with multipurpose vitamins, did the trick. Allan soon became his former vital self. Plain talk was the key.

Ever had less than a perfect day at work? You know what I mean—the alligators swarming about, snapping at your heels all day. Nothing seems to go right. Sure, we all have. And that's what led to the "three strikes and you're out" policy.

Whenever we notice a coworker's job performance slipping, we make sure it isn't just a bad day. After a period of time, we sit down with him or her and talk plain. What's wrong? We both know your work's been slipping. Is it poor instruction? Is your machine not running correctly? Is there a problem at home? How can we help?

Once we get a definition of the problem, then we try to help fix it. But make no mistake, the ultimate responsibility to improve is clearly the employee's. Each coworker at NATD is aware of this procedure. If we sit down together three different times over a reasonable period of time and there is no marked improvement in job performance, the employee is fired. It does not come as a surprise.

Your coworkers know who's putting in a full day's work and who isn't. If you allow marginal producers to continue, the message is clear to all: Do just enough to get by; you can get away with it. As a manager, if you overlook it, guess who'll be next? "Why should I bust my butt when Joe goofs off all day and gets the same pay?"

Have you ever fired someone?

It's tough, isn't it? There's little sleep the night before, sweaty palms all day, and a dry parched throat just before the meeting. And that's as it should be. After all, our actions will have a major impact on the person, family, kids, and future. Can there ever be a fair and humane way to do it?

Here's what we learned at NATD. First, hire only good people who care. Be as sure as you can be. That should sharply reduce the incidence of possible terminations. Second, care about your fellow employees—really care about them as human beings. Be sure they're happy, growing in their jobs, and, most of all, appreciated, sincerely appreciated for their contributions. Third, talk with them, visit with them, get to know them. Then if a problem develops, at least there's an underpinning of candid communication and understanding. And that's the key. Plain talk is critical.

PLAIN TALK AND COMPANY POLITICS

Internal politics can wreck a company. We all know that. The insidious jockeying for advantage, the little games of one-upmanship, the subtle innuendo to disparage a coworker, and the unending currying of the boss's favor—all of these ridiculous bits of gamesmanship are debilitating. These endless charades only divert your coworkers' attention from their real jobs. Did you ever think of what could be accomplished if we took all the human energy expended in corporate politicking and focused it in the marketplace? We'd probably double sales and triple our profit!

How can you ever stop internal politics at your company? Some cynics will say, "You can't, that's just human nature." I disagree. Think about it for a minute. Politicking usually increases as you move up the corporate ladder. However, if you want it stopped—and stopped for good—it's really simple. Don't put up with it—not once—not ever! Here again, plain talk is the key.

About nine months after we bought NATD, our plant manager, George Slippery (obviously, not his real name) came into my office and closed the door. He started to severely criticize Allan Kemline, our chief engineer. My response was almost instinctive: "Whoa, wait just a minute, George." I picked up the intercom phone and asked Allan to come in and join us. Once my office door closed behind Allan, I had only one request: "George, would you please tell Allan what you just told me about him—behind his back?"

There was a long, long pause, one increasingly red face, followed by guttural noises, and then silence. I closed the meeting with this request:

> "Look, George, you're entitled to your opinion. But if you have a problem with someone, sit down with him and talk it through—in plain English. If you still can't reach an understanding then come on in here—together. I'll try to adjudicate. But don't you *ever* come back in here alone and talk behind someone's back."

When George started to disparage Allan behind his back, he was stopped in his tracks by simple and direct action and communication. He never did it again, nor did anyone else in either the office or the plant. You know why? I deliberately leaked the episode to our associates in the office and plant. No names were used but the message was clear. The Head Sweeper didn't want any politicking. The Head Sweeper won't put up with any politicking—*ever*. You *can* stop it cold if you use plain talk and action.

PLAIN TALK—IN BOTH DIRECTIONS

By the way, don't forget the obvious. Plain talk can and should work both ways, between you and your employees and vice versa. When it does, life becomes so much easier and simpler for everyone. Then all of us know where we stand. We can concentrate on our jobs. It almost becomes fun—the start of a team of equals doing a job together.

Here is one memory of two-way plain talk that's still vivid in my mind. We had just finished a heated session on potential manufacturing improvements at NATD. Larry Curtis (Engineering) was insistent upon buying a robot for experimental purposes. He felt we should stay ahead of competition with new technology. I was in agreement with the concept but felt it inappropriate to spend significant capital dollars just "to experiment." Our discussion became heated. Finally, in exasperation, I berated Larry in front of his peers. The session slowly ground to a halt. We all dispersed.

Frank Blasques (Production) followed me to my office. Standing in my doorway, his comment jolted me to rapt attention: "Tom, you were wrong. The way you treated Larry in that meeting was unfair." I had screwed up badly and, worse, didn't even realize it. "You're right, Frank. I blew it. Get the same group together again. Right now. I've got to apologize. Frank, thanks for leveling with me."

Larry graciously accepted my apologies in front of his peers. My ineptness had not caused any lasting damage—thanks to Frank Blasques and his plain talk. You can say that Frank's actions took guts. It did. Yet there's another reason that this kind of candor is commonplace at NATD. The group knows I want their help, their expertise, and their plain talk. They know it because I tell them again and again—and repeatedly prove it with my actions.

PLAIN TALK WITH OUR CUSTOMERS

Candid two-way communication is also an asset when dealing with your customers. So often today managers hesitate to level with their clients for fear of losing—the order, the account, or the check.

At NATD, we find that plain talk works to our advantage. Whatever your business, there are three constant elements when you take a customer order: price, terms, and delivery. Let's examine each point to see how plain talk becomes a competitive advantage.

PRICE. There are two ways of dealing with unexpected cost increases. First, you can remain silent and absorb the loss in your profit margins. Another alternative is to wait until just prior to delivery and concoct some scheme to try to justify an increased price. Or you can use plain talk. The more often you use it in every phase of customer relations, the more effective it becomes. Your resulting credibility bank should stand you in good stead when a real problem develops.

Sun Microcomputer, a major customer, asked us to manufacture an extremely complicated part. In the process of designing the tooling, we found a way to manufacture it at a much lower price than our original quote. When we lowered the price, the client was understandably pleased.

Alas, we were far too optimistic! Both the final tooling and production costs exceeded our quotation. As soon as we knew this, we called our customer—immediately. In our subsequent meeting together, our coworkers in Sales and Engineering painstakingly went through the entire tooling and manufacturing sequence in a simple unembellished way. We told the client that we would honor the lower-priced contract. But we also asked for his help, his sense of fairness. Let's split the cost overrun. He agreed. Much later we learned that their largesse was due to our plain talk—everything was up-front, simple, and to the point. There was no deception, no cute ploys.

TERMS. Some may think that slow-paying customers surface only in a recession. Forget it. It's unfortunately widespread in business. Given this general truth, you'll think it unbelievable but our overdue receivables average about thirty-seven days, year after year. Our customer payment terms are 1 percent discount 10 days, net 30 days. How do we do it? Plain talk. Whenever we get a new customer, we review our payment terms, up-front, at the start of our relationship. We also point out very clearly that unless their check is in our bank by the thirty-fifth day, their shipments from NATD will stop. I can't prove it but I'm confident that plain talk makes the difference. We candidly discuss the critical importance of cash flow. NATD is not a bank.

Some of our clients have tested our convictions—but only once. We actually refuse to ship to the offender, without exception. We've heard all the excuses, all the pleas, but we have to "hang tough." And it works. We have proved that our word is our bond. The confrontations have been heated, the threats ominous. In twelve years, NATD has never lost a customer by holding firm on our thirty-day terms. You can be sure this policy's success is also the result of our outstanding quality and service record.

DELIVERY. It's the same thing here—plain talk always works. It's a terrible feeling when you realize you're not going to make the promised shipping date to your customer, isn't it? But it happens to all of us. Incidentally, these infrequent delivery lapses can be almost eliminated if you practice plain talk with your associates in the plant and with suppliers; don't accept any vague promises, no "I'll try for that date," etc.

Tell the customer right away that it looks as though that shipment will be late. Tell him why—in detail, without blame, and in plain talk. Pose each alternative to remedy the problem. Usually the customer will understand. Between the two parties, some interim solution can be found. Your status in the customer's eyes will be enhanced. He'll see first hand—from the inside, in plain talk—how your company really functions and how hard you try to be on time, always.

What's the alternative? To put your head in the sand and hope the problem somehow will magically go away? As you know, hell hath no fury like a buyer who's been surprised with an out-of-stock—at the last minute.

CORPORATE AMERICA AND PLAIN TALK

Plain talk is still a rarity in many corporations. Read the press releases, the annual report, the minutes of meetings with securities analysts—they're all the same. Avoid confrontation, duck the hard question, muddy the water, stonewall sensitive areas, deny any blame. The most recent personification of this evasiveness came from the CEO of a giant money-center bank. He blithely reported a second and *unexpected* billion-dollar loss in earnings in the same fiscal year. What was staggering to behold was his measured pronouncement that his bank was proceeding on schedule—according to plan—executing the strategy for recovery carefully devised some time ago.

And my cat has wings.

Think of the feelings of most of his coworkers at the bank, when they heard their leader engaging in such double-talk. Who's kidding whom? And yet there undoubtedly are the fast-trackers, the upwardly mobiles at this bank who think they should emulate their leader and think his performance put "the best possible face on a difficult situation."

And so it goes, the next generation of the bank's top executives unconsciously assimilating the traits of their mentors—their role models.

How often have you read an annual report that includes meaningless and vague phrases like:

> XYZ Corporation is well positioned to maximize the many growth opportunities in the future. (This tenuous generalization is usually a tip-off that XYZ has just announced a substantial write-off.)

> Your management wishes to thank our dedicated employees and loyal shareholders during this, a most trying year. . . . Respectfully submitted.

Perhaps "nolo contendere" is the best example of Big Corporate's deliberate "Stengelese." "We admit to no wrongdoing. After due deliberation, we think it best to put this isolated instance of our purported minor illegality behind us [and pay the government-imposed fine of $10 million]. Otherwise, many of our key officers would be diverted from their pressing daily duties."

One recent marketing ploy is low-cal, low-fat, low-cholesterol. In every product class, from cereal and yogurt to salad dressing, marketers are stumbling all over each other in a frenzy to "help" the consumer. Hyperbole has become the norm. Plain talk? What's that? The attorney general of New York State investigated the advertising and labeling claims of three brands—*each one a household name*—in three different segments of the food business. In announcing the settlement, the attorney general stated that each company had agreed to stop its false claims and also to pay $25,000 to cover the state's legal expense. Yet what do we hear? Self-serving excuses from the mouths of the guilty, as reported by Marion Burros in *The New York Times* (October 30, 1991, Section B; p. 1).

COMPANY #1

A company spokesman said the attorney general's office had nothing to do with the [product's] name change. "We signed the agreement because we didn't want to have to go to court, to spend the money we would have to have spent to win what we'd obviously win."

Yogi Berra, you just lost your title. This guy's beaten you hands down for gobbledygook.

COMPANY #2

"The ad campaign was discontinued weeks before the Attorney General began his investigation. Our ads are truthful; the only question is, there was confusion about the no-cholesterol claim."

That's deliberate stonewalling. Think of the nonverbal message of hypocrisy emanating from this corporate charade. What must their coworkers think? And how must they feel?

If you think these examples are farfetched, then ask your neighbor who works in a big corporation. If you're nodding your head in sad concurrence, I know where you work. I've been there—for twenty-five muffled years.

Just today I was asked to be the keynote speaker at a top-management meeting of a multi-billion-dollar corporation. After reviewing the agenda, I couldn't believe it. See what you think.

DAY ONE—VISION

8:00 A.M.   The CEO will share with us his vision

9:00 A.M.   Separate breakout sessions—by function
            (marketing, finance, production, etc.)
            Objective: to optimize the CEO's vision

9:30 A.M.	Separate breakout sessions—by profit center *Objective*: to maximize the CEO's vision
10:15 A.M.	Coffee Break [My addition, *Objective*: to relieve management's vision]
10:30 A.M.	Group session—all functions, all profit centers *Objective*: to synthesize and coordinate the CEO's vision
12:00 noon	Lunch
1:30 P.M.	Golf
6:30 P.M.	Cocktails
7:00 P.M.	Dinner

Can you believe this exercise in gossamer? The only time any vision will be maximized here is on the first tee—or looking for the opening cocktail. What an intellectual insult. Did management really believe the attendees couldn't see through this facade?

Contrast that corporate charade with the plain talk at NATD. Every day each of us clearly understood:

- our objectives
- our assignments
- our relationships
- our responsibilities

THE *ESSENCE* OF A NEW PARTNERSHIP— PLAIN TALK

1. Always talk straight—not only honestly but in plain English.

2. Your word is your bond. It is pivotal in building trust with your fellow employees.

3. The hard questions and difficult situations won't go away. Answer them directly and clearly.

4. Obtuseness is not a substitute for diplomacy or tact. It's just a convenient excuse to avoid a tough scene.

5. Plain talk is most effective when it works both ways— from you to the gang and vice versa.

HOW *YOU* CAN BUILD A NEW PARTNERSHIP BASED UPON PLAIN TALK

1. Do you deliberately talk vaguely about sensitive subjects? Which ones? Why?

2. Ask each of your associates to bring a list of critical problems to a work session.

    •   Speak to each one directly, candidly, without waffling.

    •   Ask your coworkers if your answer was clear. If necessary, do it again in plain talk.

3. Ask the group to talk plain with each other about the same subjects outlined above. Make sure the same ground rules apply with one another: plain talk.

4. Whenever B.S. occurs, stop it immediately. Be gentle at first, but if it persists, be ruthless in calling your coworkers on it—in every meeting, in every situation. Ask them to do the same with you.

5. Eliminate politics now. Don't tolerate it another day.

    •   Call the offenders on it at the time—every time.

    •   If they persist, have a closed-door review of their performance.

    •   Be specific in your criticism. If it continues, fire them.

    •   Politics is a disease and can eat away your firm's health.

6. Start now—tomorrow. Don't wait, just go do it.

CHAPTER FOUR

Do Unto Others

Treat Other People
Just the Way You
Want to Be Treated

"There's very little feeling of 'boss' here. Nobody feels like somebody's watching us. We all work together and because we're a team, I guess we're all bosses."

Tom Parrnelli (Quality Control)

Isn't that what you want where you work—for your employees to be boss, to think and act like a boss, to take ownership? In my experience, at least four conditions must be present for this attitude of "we're all bosses" to flourish: equality, mutual respect, dignity, and self-worth. These are some of the "currencies" that helped to create a new partnership at NATD.

It's no accident that I refer to NATD's employees as coworkers, associates, or fellow employees. These are not merely glib titles. I'm no better than they are. If you want the whole truth, I'm in awe of them. Their steadfast values, their unswerving use of plain talk, their quiet competence—these constitute the real core of our success.

EQUALITY

Equality at NATD is implicit in all our relationships with our fellow employees. If, indeed, this is family—if, in fact, the group and I are equals—then we should all be treated in the same way, in every area.

That's why I insisted upon an office (10 by 12 feet) no different from that of any other department head. That's why I deliberately refused the big suite in the corner (we use it for storage). That's why my office walls are of cinder block; the desk and chairs, used metal; the carpeting, indoor/outdoor—just like everyone else's. Incidentally, we have no private secretaries, for the same reason.

I feel I owe our coworkers a clean plant. Their residences are neat and clean; their "home away from home" should be no different. And it isn't. I make sure of it. The same holds true for the lunch room and coffee areas. Sure, we hire a cleaning service. Yet we expect each fellow employee to clean up after himself, just like at home. This is true throughout the company.

Once, early on, several die makers complained that cleaning their own work area was demeaning—beneath their status as craftsmen. After listening to their lament, I dropped to my knees in front of them and started to sweep up their work area of sharp metal remnants with my bare hands. They immediately began saying, "Get up! Get up! Don't cut yourself. Be careful!" They got the message. And so did the rest of our fellow employees, throughout the entire plant. We're all equals. No job is demeaning. We're all in this together.

Go ahead and laugh. Perhaps I have a fetish. But I'll tell you this: Visit any corporation's bathrooms—in the office and in the plant. That will tell you more about management's real attitude toward themselves and their employees than any motto, vision statement, or corporate credo. Sound silly? Don't forget, the key to the executive washroom is still a prominent symbol of corporate attainment. And it is still ridiculous.

As a result, all the bathrooms at NATD are available to everyone. I make it a point to check their cleanliness almost daily. Our group sees what I'm doing and why. They know.

Preferred parking is taboo—for everyone. First come, first served. Before we moved into Plant 20, the first thing we did was to paint out the names of our predecessors on their preferred parking slots.

Perhaps this conversation between Al Kronheimer, a buyer at Hewlett Packard, and me illustrates the symbols of equality at NATD:

> "Tom, how come NATD's offices are all so plain? Frankly, I expected more from a world-class company. You guys are famous."
>
> "Al, that's just us—downtown and plain pipe racks. We don't believe in big offices, preferred parking and all the rest of that status trip. It just gets in the way. We're all equals here.
>
> "Same for my clothes. See these slacks? Twenty-nine ninety-five, mail order."
>
> "No way, Tom. You didn't pay that much—for those things!"

This Head Sweeper's pay is deliberately designed to reinforce the premise of equality. My base compensation never exceeds eight times that of an entry-level unskilled coworker. My bonus formula is tied *solely* to profit: The more we earn, the more I make. If the company makes no profit, I earn zero bonus. And everyone knows it. The same is true for our associates: The corporation's contribution to their ESOP is directly linked to our total profit.

Sure, I use a leased company car for customer visits. But any time the group needs it to run errands, it's theirs. And they do—frequently. It's no big deal. It is, after all, a *company* car, not mine. This attitude of equality permeates the entire company. No artificial lines of demarcation are allowed in any area—department heads, front office, engineers, or die makers. We're all equals; we're all bosses. Fellow employees know my feelings; they see the proof every day.

These physical symbols of equality are only the first step. The real key comes from actions—consistently, every day.

MUTUAL RESPECT

Each fellow employee—from a janitor or a parts packer to department head—knows I respect his or her work. Often it's more important to show your respect for the people on the line than for your associates in the office. Because you're in less contact with the group in the factory, there's less chance to observe their work and compliment them.

Some people may think Emilia DeSerpa's job at NATD is inconsequential—packing and shipping our finished parts. Yet if your objective is 0.1 percent customer rejects, Emilia's role is critical. I still remember walking into her area early in the mornings. Our conversation often went something like this:

> "Good morning, Emilia. How are you?"
> "Fine, Tom. Thank you."
> "That's a beautiful circular pattern you're using to pack those parts. Arranged in that way, they look like a lady's fan lying in a carton wrapped in silk. Did our customer require that we pack them in that way?"
> "No. These parts are very delicate. I thought they should be protected in this way."

Respect her? You bet! And I told her so—repeatedly. When she first joined NATD, this same lady was terrified of using our forklift truck. Yet several months later, she was driving it through the plant like an old hand. I asked her how she overcame her fears. Emilia's answer said it all: "I just wanted to help."

An isolated instance? You be the judge. Here's another story that also illustrates why my respect for our coworkers is so strong.

It's Monday morning about 9:30 A.M., coffee break time.

TOM: Where's John Vitti? He was here earlier this morning.

JODDY: That guy's unbelievable! Know what he did, Tom? His mother died yesterday. She lived with

them. Yet this man came in this morning for
two hours just to finish his work on these
parts. He knew we needed them today to
finish the job on time. Then he left to complete
her funeral arrangements. That's called
dedication.

A conversation between
Joddy Lam (Quality Control)
and Tom Melohn (head sweeper)

These stories occur again and again at NATD. Perhaps now you can
better understand why I respect the gang so much—as human
beings, and in their work. Events like this can happen in your
department, division, or corporation if you'll just give it a chance.
Remember, NATD doesn't have a monopoly on good people who
care. They're there in your company.

Why do these people behave this way?

How do we possibly thank them?

How can we ever repay them?

Remember that special currency mentioned earlier? That's one
of the ways we "pay" our fellow employees—with respect. Because
they earn it, every day.

Simply stated, the group at NATD behave in this way because
they inherently take pride in their own work. They want to do it
right, for themselves, for their own self-worth. If someone else
recognizes their achievements, so much the better. If their boss
acknowledges it, great. If their peers see it as an accomplishment
that benefits everyone, that furthers everyone's sense of (and, in
fact, need for) teamwork—of family. By meshing these basic beliefs
and human needs with the goals of their company, we all win—
spectacularly. Besides, it is fun—exciting, neat to watch, to be a
part of. For me, the psychic income alone is enormous.

These comments are typical at NATD:

"My father always told us that when we went out to work to
feel that you were going to work for yourself. You're working for a company but you're really working for yourself. If

you feel you're working for yourself, then you're going to strive to do the very best job you can. Always do a good job. In that way the company will end up with more profit. And if they have more profit, then we've got better job security."

Teresa Bettencourt (Production)

"It's stress-free here and others feel the same way, because your bosses are terrific. There is nobody always on your back, pushing. They know you're going to do the job and they know you're going to do it right. So nobody really bothers you."

Tony Cabral (Quality Control)

"There is pride here; people put their heart in it because of the kind of people they are. The environment brings out a lot of that good stuff, too. When you work *with* somebody like Tom, he's a good person to be *with*. He's never bugged anybody—and I have been here about eleven years" (author's italics).

John Vitti (Production)

"He's never bugged anybody. . . ."

Know what that means? It means I trust them to do a good job. It means I respect them—their values and their work skills—and leave them alone to do their jobs.

We built a new partnership—together. You can too.

DIGNITY

Dignity in the workplace means the same as dignity anywhere else: "to honor." At NATD, you can watch dignity at work in four different dimensions—from me to our fellow employees, inside each coworker, between members of the group, and finally, perhaps surprisingly, from our customers.

Here, again, be sure your words and actions are sincere. You can fool these people only once. And then you're dead.

You value dignity in your own career and personal life, don't you? Well, your coworkers are no different. Remember how you felt when someone—in truth, anyone—recognized you as a person of value or for some accomplishment in business? Sure, you felt great. We all do. It doesn't have to be a big deal, either, does it? In fact, oftentimes it's the little things that mean the most and that provide lasting fond memories.

Let me share with you an incident that's still fresh in my mind:

> "Hi, Karl. Rumor has it that your relatives from Germany are coming over to visit you."
>
> "We're really excited, Tom. They raised me after the war."
>
> "Why don't you and your wife take them out for dinner? It will be NATD's treat. You pick the restaurant. And enjoy!"
>
> *A conversation between Karl Adam (machinist)*
> *and Tom Melohn (head sweeper)*

Imagine their feelings of pride—both Karl and his wife's, as well as his relatives'—that his company honored him in that way. Think of the lasting "return on investment" from that sincere gesture. From time to time we do the same for one of our other associates to recognize a special achievement. What would his wife think, of her husband, of "their" company? Dignity? Honor? Absolutely. It is sincere. And everyone knows it.

Some people may criticize my gesture toward Karl Adam. "Playing favorites, aren't you, Tom? You talk about equality. That's bunk. You'll cause nothing but dissension." Perhaps, with certain people—but not with good people who care. This is family, a team; when one wins, we all win. We celebrate together, for each other, with each other.

Perhaps once or twice a year, we'll send all our coworkers home about a half hour early—with full pay. Ostensibly, the reason is simple: "Enjoy. It's a beautiful day." In truth, I'm honoring our associates, thanking them for all their contributions. And I tell them so.

Our fellow employees often honor each other. More than once, Ling Supelario in Production would work her day shift, drive home, spend about three hours cooking delicious Filipino egg rolls called lumpia, and return to the plant. The lumpia were her gift to our night shift. And that's what it was, her tribute. Family, people working together who respect one another, treating their fellow employees with dignity.

The last dimension of dignity often comes from our customers. Over the years, we have received Vendor of the Year awards or special recognition of outstanding performance again and again. The morning after an awards banquet, I always get our coworkers together. I give *them* the plaque—because they earned it. Every time, every award.

David Lopes in Maintenance summed up the feelings of all his associates with this observation: "The customers we deal with, they tend to look highly on us. They think we are the greatest thing on earth. We try to be that way for them."

There's little question that dignity is a powerful "currency" to pay your fellow employees. The results are both spectacular and lasting.

SELF-WORTH

This currency comes in several denominations, each with enduring value. Your colleagues respond the same way we do. You long for self-worth in your own life, both in business and at home. So do they.

Have you ever been asked for advice? What's your reaction? How do you feel? Flattered, right? "Somebody thinks enough of me to get my opinion." This same reaction is equally applicable in business. Only we do it a bit differently at NATD.

If you think someone's capable of doing the job, give him the assignment. Be sure the problem's clearly defined, the tools are available to solve it, and there is an agreed-upon due date for completion. Then leave him alone—let him solve the problem in his own way. Isn't that what you want in your own business life? There's nothing worse than getting an assignment, and shortly thereafter your boss stops by to tell you how he'd solve it.

If you don't think someone is capable of doing the job, then don't give her the assignment. If you do, then let her go do it—in her own way. Usually, the results will be impressive. Of equal import will be her resulting feelings of self-worth. In a way, you're asking for her advice. Each time you seek her counsel, the better she gets and the more she grows, in knowledge and in self-worth. And that is not a bad place for you both to be.

After a few years, NATD happily expanded into a second plant. Guess who did the entire plant layout? That's right, the employees. And you know why. The person doing the job knows it better than anyone else. We live that belief every day at NATD. The group did it all: layout, production flow, machine locations, electrical connections, storage, shipping, everything. Why not? Our associates know more about it than anyone else.

Think that was an aberration? We soon expanded into yet another plant. The same assignment was given—with the same results. Think of the group's feelings of pride, of self-worth.

Not long after, we bought millions of dollars' worth of new capital equipment—a number of big punch presses, computer-operated feed lines, and ancillary equipment. The value was equal to our entire net worth. That's called betting the ranch. You know what I got to do? I picked out the color of the punch presses—and I was overruled. Our fellow employees did it all. Everyone got involved: Purchasing and Engineering, of course. But we didn't stop there. The die makers, die setters, Quality Control, the foremen—they all had a voice in the decision. And this was very sophisticated stuff—sensors, built-in computers. Why not? They knew more about it than anyone else. Think of our associates' pride, their feelings of self-worth. Imagine what you could accomplish in that working climate.

You probably think this is too good to be true. Yet NATD is a business that requires hard work and has lots of pressure (and lots of profit). Conventional wisdom decrees that this quichelike stuff—equality, mutual respect, dignity, and self-worth—is antithetical to the workplace. Horse hockey! That's all there is! That's what life's about—human emotion! Remember the last time you got "turned on," truly excited about something at work? What caused it? It wasn't some sterile decree, memo, or vision statement. It came from another human being who recognized your worth, who shared your pride, who "honored" you.

IN THE BEGINNING AT NATD

Before my arrival at NATD, people had been hired helter-skelter—as they came in the door, as needed, and as cheaply as possible. There was no template of the ideal employee. "Just get the bodies in here to man the machines."

People were treated as cannon fodder—expendable. They were treated with no respect—bullied, yelled at, put down, and humiliated. The results were predictable. We all know that working climate: guarded, cynical, indifferent, calloused, rote—and detached.

Slowly, ever so carefully, we changed all this. Sorry to sound like a Gregorian chant, but you've got to start with good people, people who care. What did Tom Wolfe call it?—*The Right Stuff*. If you don't get good people, two things will occur. First, your employees won't respond to these new values and the daily example you are setting because they have different beliefs. Second, you won't respect them—and they'll know it. There will be little or no teamwork because there's no mutual respect among the employees. In truth, in that climate, the employees themselves probably have little self-esteem.

An early indication of our respect for our fellow employees probably came about during prospective customer visits. When new prospects came to visit the plant in those early days, I panicked. There was no way I could take them through the shop and explain our technical capabilities and production system—not with my lack of mechanical aptitude.

But I sure knew who could: our associates. And they did. As we walked through the plant with prospective clients, I introduced each key employee and asked him to explain his work. The results were startling. For the first time, perhaps in their entire careers, the employees were treated as equals, as professionals, with dignity and self-worth. They responded just the way you and I would—with pride and feelings of self-esteem.

Oftentimes I'd leave our visitors to talk with our associates alone. Deliberately. Think through the dual impact of that action. Our coworkers saw that I really trusted them, respected them, and knew they would be honest with our future customers. In turn, our prospects saw the competence and pride our fellow employees had in their own skills. They wanted that in their purchased parts. Our new orders started to grow.

Can you imagine the employees' feelings of pride, of self-respect, of self-worth? They had never been allowed to talk to a customer, ever. It was unheard of. And now they were introduced by the "big boss" and asked to tell about their skills and how they organized their own work. Ed Nordhausen (die maker) later told me of this conversation with his wife:

> "Do you know what Tom did? He introduced me; he asked me to tell the prospect what I did. . . . And then he left. He left me, alone, to talk to these people. He didn't come back for five or ten minutes. I guess he trusts me. I guess he respects me. I guess he knows I'll tell the truth."

You can be sure it wasn't always that easy. Not every fellow employee responded. Many of them had different values—not wrong, just different. In time these people gradually left the company. They knew their days were numbered. Again, I keep going back to our basic truths learned through experience in Big Corporate: "Hire only good people who care."

Back in the early days of NATD, I spent an entire week on the road calling on potential new customers. Silicon Valley, Los Angeles, San Diego, Phoenix, Tucson, Dallas, and Houston—everywhere I went, the buyer/engineer response was identical: "The quality of your tooling is outstanding. Your die makers really know what they're doing. Those are really difficult parts." Again and again the story was the same.

I was elated and wanted to share this feedback with the group—but in a memorable way. Late that Friday afternoon, I called in and set up a meeting with all the die makers first thing Monday morning.

Here's what transpired:

> "Everywhere I went last week I heard the same thing about your work," I said. "Over and over, the buyer reaction was the same. And I, for one, am sick and tired of hearing it.
>
> "They said your work was outstanding.
>
> "They said your work was outstanding.
>
> "They said your work was outstanding.
>
> "I'm sick and tired of hearing it.
>
> "So here's a check for an extra week's pay for each of you.
>
> "Let's call it the Sick and Tired Award."
>
> Have you ever seen true incredulity before? Have you ever watched a kaleidoscope of real emotions register on a man's face in a fleeting instant? The group was stunned— silent.
>
> Finally Clare Stevens, the department head, croaked, "You're crazy. I've been in this business over thirty years. Never heard of anything like this. You're crazy."

And out they went. The word spread like wildfire throughout the entire company. Their feelings of pride, of self-worth, soared. You could see it. Our coworkers knew that I respected all of them, that I thought they were pros. And they are.

Try that working climate.

You'll be stunned with the results.

CORPORATE AMERICA AND "DO UNTO OTHERS"

Now let's examine how most corporations pay their employees, in contrast with the NATD currency of equality, mutual respect, dignity, and self-worth.

Going to be a short segment, isn't it?

How can we expect companies to recognize their fellow employees in these ways when the basic underpinnings of mutual honesty and trust are not in place—and lived—every day, in every situation? The result would be complete hypocrisy.

And yet, in actuality, that's exactly where we are throughout most of corporate America today. All the moves are there, all the right words, but their fellow employees know the underlying reality. They know Big Corporate speaks with forked tongue.

In my experience, the physical symbols of power get in the way of truly working together. The plush executive suite, the limousine, the corporate jet, the bloated paychecks—these unnecessary trappings signify a clear demarcation: I'm better than you.

As a result, management feels superior. They feel more important than other employees. And it shows. It shows again and again, throughout the corporation. It's visible down the corporate hierarchy, level by level, as managers emulate their boss. After all, he is their role model. He got promoted with that attitude, those actions, so "I will, too." The corporate financial and physical cocoon is neatly and proportionately dispensed level by level. The end result is that the average working person on the line is looked upon as inferior, not educated, not very bright . . . a low-paid and easily replaced commodity.

We work in a two-class system in big companies. Walk through almost every major plant in America and compare the front office to the plant area. Try to guess where the power is. Look at preferred parking only for management in company after company across the country. You may think this insignificant until you have to walk two blocks from the parking lot in the driving rain or freezing cold just to get to the plant door. Every day, twice a day, every shift, you live with this reminder that you're second class. Dignity? Partners? Forget that drivel.

Several years ago, I spent the day at a major manufacturing company in the Detroit area as a guest of the CEO. This company is a supplier to the major auto companies. My host was really concerned. Employee morale was at a low ebb, their quality slipping, their profit nil. My host couldn't put his finger on the problem.

The contrast was striking as we walked from the recently refurbished and plush executive suites into the plant, where the cement floors were cracked and often broken. More than once, the CEO warned me to be careful and don't trip. When I started to enter the bathroom in the plant, this CEO sharply admonished me: "Don't go in there; it's probably a mess." He was right.

We continued our tour carefully avoiding the small puddles of water on the floor that were scattered throughout the entire plant. The ancient roof regularly leaked during the rainy season.

Ever so gently, I tried to suggest that his workers might be disgruntled with the double standard that was so evident. The CEO was quick with his retort: "But we just can't afford to spruce up the plant too." My host then voiced his high regard for his labor force. "Read this," he exclaimed. "This memo is proof that I care." It read:

> Employees will pick up turkeys in the lunch room at the end of the shift on Wednesday. Line up by department in alphabetical order. Bring proper identification or no turkey. Happy Thanksgiving.

The blatant hypocrisy here is disheartening. There was certainly enough money to refurbish the plush executive suites but not enough to fix even the leaks in the roof or the broken floors or regularly clean the employees' bathrooms. What message is conveyed to the employees every day by these symbolic actions (or inactions)? What will the employees assume? That's right. "They think they're special. They don't care about me. I'm just another cog in the production line. They throw me a bone at Thanksgiving with a lousy turkey. Even then it's rote, like everything else around here. They don't even know who I am. Imagine having to show my I.D. after thirty-seven years here."

An isolated instance? Here are two of the hundreds of letters we received after the showing of the PBS-TV documentary "In Search of Excellence":

"Dear Mr. Melohn,

Too many jobs in this country are a source of drudgery and boredom instead of pride and accomplishment. Management appreciation and recognition of the individual and his work environment must drastically improve if we are ever going to eliminate the schism between management and labor.

I am looking forward to the time when business people don't merely pay lip service to the phrase 'people are our most valuable resource,' but actually put such philosophy into practice as well."

I still treasure the following letter (with original spelling):

"Dear Mr. Melohn,

My hat's off to you. I watched you on PBS-TV on Sunday, 'In Search of Excellence.'

An was I impress with you. My husban worked for——— Inc. for 27 years at the end of it all he didn't even have a pension.

So when I seen you on T.V. I was so moved. I just had to write & tell you. You keep up the good work & always have feelings for your people. When you give a person recognition & an Pat on the back you get better work & more work out of that person.

I wish my husban worked for someone like you years ago.

You gave me my faith back in management."

"You gave me my faith back in management." When I read that, I got choked up. I had to call her. I had to . . . to tell her I understood . . . to thank her. We had a joyous visit, chatted together as longtime friends. She was one of us, just like the family at NATD. You can be sure a copy of her letter was prominently posted on our bulletin boards for several months.

Let's stop here and try to summarize this chapter. Then we'll delineate specific action steps to "give me my faith back in management."

THE *ESSENCE* OF A NEW PARTNERSHIP— DO UNTO OTHERS

1. The NATD currency can be paid only after honesty and trust are already in place.

2. All men are created equal. Only mankind has tried to make them unequal.

3. To believe yourself superior to your associates—in business and in life—is a delusion.

4. The physical trappings of power are ludicrous. They reinforce a perceived inequality and impede open communication, teamwork, and true problem-solving.

5. Mutual respect has to be earned—every day. It feeds upon itself and grows—at a joyously exponential rate.

6. We all long for a sense of self-worth. If it's so important in our personal life, why not in business?

7. Dignity may seem incongruous on the plant floor—or in the office—but it's an integral human need, both in the workplace and at home.

HOW *YOU* CAN BUILD A NEW PARTNERSHIP BASED ON THE GOLDEN RULE

1. Don't make any changes until both you and your associates are consistently honest with each other and have developed mutual trust.

2. Eliminate all symbols of status and superiority in the office and in the plant.

3. Encourage your company to align personal compensation with corporate profit improvement.

4. Use the NATD currency. It's accepted all over the world. Use it sincerely, use it often. It works wonders.

5. Now—do it now!

CHAPTER FIVE

It's Called Family

Be Careful, It's Profitable

"It's like family. Everybody cares about each other. And we really try to do the best for each other. It's just a good place to work in. The owner, he cares about the people."

Teresa Bettencourt (Production)

Feelings of family—in business? What's this all about? I'm in business to make a profit, not to hand-hold a bunch of relative strangers. Besides, I'm too busy to experiment with all this mushy, golly-you're-nice-too gobbledygook. What good will it do anyway? They will think I'm too soft and try to walk all over me.

You are right. If you just experiment with this "stuff" and don't truly believe, then forget it. If you think it's mushy and stupid, then don't do it. If you use family as a manipulative device, don't. Your associates will see right through you.

Let me challenge you. Is family important in your personal life? Of course. Then why not in business? To allow personal values to flourish at work does not impede making a profit. Remember what we learned at NATD early on: When we meshed the goals of our company with the values of our fellow employees, the results were spectacular. It isn't faked, nor forced. It is real. And so are the profits—year after year.

I'm no sociologist or expert on family relations. But it would seem that feelings of family involve a number of elements: security (both economic and emotional), companionship, caring (and showing it openly, unashamedly), sharing, teaching, freedom, and feelings of cohesiveness, of togetherness, of unity.

Let's take them one by one. Let's see how each element was evoked at NATD, how each was encouraged, how each flourished. In contrast, we can analyze how most corporations regard feelings of family in the workplace. Then let's try to outline specific areas of application in your department, division, or corporation.

FAMILY VALUES AT WORK

Providing economic security for your business family is fairly straightforward. It is our job to increase sales and earnings, consistently. Note that it's our job—not my job, *our* job. My task is to point the company in the proper direction (overall strategy) and hire the right people. It is our job to ship 0.1 percent customer rejects—all parts, all year, all customers. That accomplishment provides the basis for our sustained economic growth. In turn, such growth generates economic security for everyone. No one's job is guaranteed, including mine. The pithy comment of John Vitti's in Production summed it all up: "The quality's there—or else we're not here." But if we all do our jobs, then the company will grow and provide economic security for each of us.

EMOTIONAL SECURITY

Emotional security for our business family is much harder to define—and certainly difficult to provide to others. But let's try. Again, analyze your own personal life. Then simply apply the findings and action steps to your business day. To me, personal emotional security involves feeling wanted, needed, able to contribute. All of us must have self-esteem and that comes from believing in ourselves. It can certainly be reinforced by our associates.

That's what we do at NATD—reinforce each other's intrinsic value as a human being. Here are some examples that illustrate the three dimensions of emotional security at NATD: from me to the group, from the group to me, and between fellow employees.

Back in the early days of NATD, we hired an outstanding Korean coworker, Kim Duk (Production). Several months later we noticed that he was losing weight. Since he wasn't a sumo wrestler in size to start with, any weight loss was significant. We finally determined that Kim's local doctor didn't speak Korean and thus couldn't understand Kim's problem. We searched the entire San Francisco Bay Area to find a Korean-speaking physician. Happily, the problem was soon solved. We didn't have to say a word. Kim knew we cared—our actions spoke for us. So did his ever-increasing proficiency at NATD.

Here's another example. Lydia Nunes in Production had her home robbed during the day while she was at work at NATD. The house was stripped of everything of value. We all offered to help. About six weeks later, I was visiting with Lydia and discovered that the insurance adjuster had offered ten cents on the dollar for all her stolen valuables. She didn't know where to turn. I sure did, and quick. We went into my office and called our company's attorney. I introduced Lydia to Pete Whitman by phone and left—after telling Pete that NATD would pay for his legal counsel and help. You know the outcome of this story. Her claim was paid in full. She was grateful—but then, so was I. She was a super employee.

Any employee can borrow our company trucks over the weekend to move or haul trash. Can't you hear the insurance types now? "No way! Think of the potential liability!" Wait a minute . . . wait . . . that's right. That's what insurance is for. What are we trying to say to our associates by doing this? I respect you; I trust you; I admire you; I want to help you. Know what? You'll get the same feelings in return from your coworkers, one hundred–fold. In twelve years, times fifty-two weekends, there has never been one accident—not one.

Every month I buy doughnuts for our coworkers. We celebrate the last Friday of the month—payday, the end of the week, start of the weekend, whatever. I order and pick them up personally, for two reasons. First, I want our coworkers to know they are important,

important enough for me to take the time to get their gift. Second, it is fun. Have you ever walked into a bakery at 6:00 A.M. to get two hundred assorted doughnuts? The clerks go wild.

In addition, in an emergency we lend any coworker a week's pay. We know each one will pay it back. These are good people. We send flowers to every employee or spouse who is in the hospital, whether for a happy or sad occasion. We want them to know we are thinking of them, that they are missed. If one coworker is home sick for over a week, often I'll call to see how he or she is doing, to see if I can help. It isn't to check on the person, and they know that. I care about each of them. I respect them. NATD will send flowers to any coworker who gets married—plus a check for fifty dollars.

What you do doesn't have to be a big deal. It doesn't have to cost money. All that's needed is respect—respect for your coworkers and their worth. And then show it, in any way you can—sincerely.

One time Teresa Bettencourt (Production) asked for an unpaid four-week leave of absence to be added on to her two weeks' paid vacation so she and her husband could take a trip. I never gave it a second thought. She was an outstanding coworker and had been with us a number of years. Besides, it was the trip of a lifetime for her and her husband. Later on, she told me how much this gesture meant to her—how much it was appreciated.

Your company would have done the same thing . . . wouldn't it?

Perhaps Teresa's observation expresses it best:

> "I think caring is one of the biggest things. The man—Tom—cares about his people. And in return we care about what we do. To me, we care—and we take pride in what we do. If you care and take pride, then you have quality. It's just a good place to work."

FEELINGS OF FAMILY BETWEEN COWORKERS

The people at NATD take care of each other as well. Eric Karlsson, second-shift foreman, stopped me one evening as I was in the plant and asked for my help. After we moved into our new facility, the night shift discovered that the parking lot overhead lights were inoperative. It was not only difficult for people to wend their way to their cars at 11:00 P.M. but also scary—alone in an industrial neighborhood. Eric arranged pairs to walk to their cars, but that wasn't enough.

Eric then asked the folks in maintenance to fix the lights, but nothing happened. Evidently there were higher-priority items. Eric gently kept prodding, but to no avail. Finally, in exasperation, he came to me for advice. The solution—as usual—was simple. Eric asked the head of maintenance to stay over several hours after the day shift ended. Then they "happened" to go out to the parking lot together in the dark. They had difficulty finding their way. The maintenance folk got the message. Soon after, the lights were fixed.

Here's yet another example of people helping people at NATD. Lydia Nunes (Production) cut her finger badly one day on the job. One of the group rushed her to the hospital, waited while she was stitched up, and drove her home. It could have been serious. The last person anyone expected to be at work the following morning was Lydia. But there she was, at 6:00 A.M., ready to go. She said she "forgot" the doctor's release and would bring it in the next day. She did the best she could but by midmorning several coworkers took her home. She was wobbly and pale. The next day, there she was at work again. But this time we wised up. Without a doctor's release, she couldn't come to work. Happily, her finger soon healed and she returned to work—with the doctor's signed release.

But why? Why did Lydia do this? It wasn't the pay. She qualified automatically for paid sick leave. What was it? I was incredulous. Shortly thereafter, I stopped to chat with her. When asked why she had come back to work so soon, Lydia's response touched my heart: "Because I didn't want to let my friends down."

A few years ago Frank Blasques in Production was about to retire. One Saturday morning, at home reading the sports section of the newspaper, I suddenly knew what one of Frank's retirement gifts would be from NATD. There was a mail-order ad for a plaque commemorating the 49ers' Super Bowl victory. The plaque also contained a real piece of 49er grass turf (they were installing a new synthetic surface at Candlestick Park). It was perfect. Frank was a fanatical fan. About two months later, we recognized Frank's retirement at the close of one of our regular monthly Super Person meetings. The entire group was there. We made sure Frank's wife was invited, unbeknownst to him. When he unveiled his 49er plaque, Frank choked up—absolutely choked up. We all did, together. We knew we'd miss him—his competence, his humor, his caring, his sense of family.

Everyone in that plant, the entire group, saw and felt a sense of caring, of companionship, of family, of closeness. Each of us felt it personally. I remember the outpouring of affection and respect for him. His coworkers were clustered around him, clapping him on the back, giving him hugs. It was an unforgettable moment—together. It's called building a family.

Happenings like this can't be planned or quantified. I can't sit here and tell you that one spontaneous event had a positive effect on our P&L. But I know this—we built a great sense of family. And we won big at NATD—year after year after year. And so can you.

Maintenance's Dave Lopes summed up the climate at NATD:

> "Everybody is like brothers and sisters and everybody is a friend. It's great to come to work where all of your friends work. It makes you want to be there. Everyone gets along very well and I like that. I haven't heard that from anyone else at another company. There is always someone that they don't like: their boss, supervisor, or foreman. They don't even want to go to work. But everyone gets along well here."

Christmas is a big event at NATD. It's important to our families at home—why should it be any different where you work? Everyone pitches in. Both the plant and office are decorated throughout the entire holiday period by the group. Master Chef Melohn (dressed all in red—toque, ski parka, and slacks) broils sirloin steaks outdoors for all of our fellow employees every December 23. We cook them on a homemade barbecue that the group made from splitting a fifty-five-gallon steel drum, just like in the Caribbean.

In the beginning NATD bought all the trimmings, too—potato salad, cold vegetables, snacks, dips, desserts, etc. Soon the women insisted on bringing their favorite dishes from home. They'd have been insulted if I had offered to pay for them.

One of our colleagues gets a Santa Claus suit and parades about during lunch and the subsequent party. Yours truly buys each foreman or department head an inexpensive, humorous present. We all try to guess whom each gift is for. It always turns into a lively, fun, and vocal game of charades. No business is discussed. This is Christmas. It is time for family. And I make sure everyone leaves the plant about thirty minutes early, at full pay. (By the way, I never give out turkeys at the holidays. In my judgment, it's an impersonal and therefore meaningless gesture.)

ENCOURAGING A SENSE OF FAMILY

There are other gifts that build a sense of family, of belonging. But they, too, must come from the heart. One such gift is time—your time, away from your other family at home. Here are several examples. Once, early on at NATD, I learned through CBWA that Jack Hawk (Production) had built a scale-model midget car, which his young son actually raced. His boy was the apple of his eye. Building the car was obviously a labor of love. Their homemade car was entered in a "beauty" contest. Sure enough, their midget racer won first prize and was exhibited at the Oakland Coliseum, along with many full-sized "exotic" cars.

My idea of a restful Saturday afternoon is not to visit a customized car show. But I knew it was terribly important to Jack—and his young son. So I went and saw his car. I saw the time spent, the painstaking detail, the obvious devotion involved in a handmade gift. And I told Jack so the following Monday night at work at NATD. His eyes got misty as he talked about his son. Jack was appreciative that I went—that I cared. I can't prove it but I think a bond was started—a tentative link that developed into a feeling of family. And Jack knew; he knew that I cared about him as a coworker. From time to time, I'd mention his car and my visit while CBWA. Some of his associates were openly amazed that I took time to go. But I think they knew why and shared my respect for him.

Another weekend, years later, my wife and I drove six hours round trip up into the mountains of California to see die maker Clare Stevens's future retirement home. Perhaps it doesn't sound special. But it was. He and his wife built it by hand themselves, over three years, every weekend. They camped out until they built the garage and then lived in it for over two and a half years on weekends until they moved into their two-bedroom dream house. They built a two-story natural fieldstone fireplace indoors, along with a beautiful outdoor redwood deck with a barbecue and hot tub. And they did it all themselves. As they proudly showed us through, I was openly in awe. For me, a guy who is a mechanical klutz, this was really something. My already high respect for him soared.

I went because I knew it was important to Clare. His pride of accomplishment showed during our frequent conversations on the plant floor. I wanted to share his pride, his achievement. Maybe I imagined the whole thing, but I think we felt a bit closer afterward. Clare certainly knew my respect for him, my admiration. His fellow employees knew it also. I sincerely raved about it with them— again, through our CBWA chats.

Some may think my perception of cause and effect is exaggerated. Perhaps you believe my conclusions are invalid. All I know is that over time the group and I developed a bond, a feeling of family, because I sincerely cared about them and their well-being as individuals of worth. And I showed it.

BE YOURSELF

For over twenty years, my daily corporate "uniform" was muted— either dark gray, brown, or navy blue suits. Conform, be dull, rote, inconspicuous, anonymous. Be interchangeable; don't be yourself. Play it safe. That's what I wore and that's what I did. As a result, I became a senior vice president. I was a success?

When we bought NATD, two symbolic changes occurred, one deliberate, one by chance. While I was working in Big Corporate, time was always my enemy. You've got two years to turn this division around; you've got eighteen months to make three acquisitions; you've got twelve months to introduce two new products. At NATD, I made time my friend. I decided to do any task right, regardless of time. Later on we called it "Long Ball." So I simply took my watch off. To this day, I have never worn it again.

The other and more meaningful symbol occurred purely by chance. During those initial months following our purchase of NATD, we asked the former owners to stay on as consultants to help this mechanical neophyte try to understand a totally new business. By habit I brought one of my old corporate uniforms to the office. When we made a sales call on a major corporation, I'd change into my uniform to be dressed appropriately—to be accepted.

As you may have surmised, the former owner was even more of a Type A personality than I. Once too often, he sat in his Mercedes out in front of our plant and honked the horn incessantly for me to hurry up and change clothes. In exasperation, I left my corporate uniform on its hanger and ran out to his car dressed in loud red golf slacks, a white polo shirt, and blue blazer—my daily "uniform" at the plant. He was aghast and told me so in no uncertain terms. "You can't go to Xerox Corporation dressed like that. You just don't look like a company president." That did it. Silence prevailed as we drove to the customer's office for our sales appointment.

The former owner stood at more than a discreet distance when I confirmed our appointment to the receptionist of this major corporation and our then largest customer. While waiting in the lobby, somehow the word of my garb spread like wildfire among the buyers. Heads started popping up over the three-quarter-height partitions that sectioned off individual offices. They wanted to see for themselves. There were slack jaws and stares of disbelief at my outfit. Slowly, almost imperceptibly, sporadic applause was heard. By the time we reached our buyer's open office cubicle, the clapping and cheers were in happy unison, definitely out of place in the somber atmosphere of Big Corporate. Dumb, yes. Stupid I am not. My "costume" became an instant symbol of NATD. Then I tried it elsewhere—at other customers', at other prospects'. The response was the same. We had inadvertently discovered NATD's logo. The gray-suited buyers loved it (I wonder why). Even today, in video training films and on the lecture tour throughout the world, Melohn wears that outfit.

When our associates at NATD heard about it, they started to kid me. They asked, "If you can wear what you want, why can't we paint 'our' equipment the way we want?"

"No problem," said Melohn, ever unsuspecting. Some weeks later, Clare Stevens asked me to come out in the plant. There, in front of all the die makers (and, surreptitiously, the entire group), he proudly displayed for the world to see: a shocking pink lathe. The die makers had secretly painted it—on company time—while I was out of the building.

I thought it was a riot. I was laughing like a kid. It was great. Success in business just doesn't result from always being so serious. Our colleagues' reaction was interesting to watch. It was a synthesis of relief, coupled with surprise, blended with satisfaction. This is pure hypothesis on my part but I think I inadvertently passed a test that day, a test that showed them what I was about, a test that said "he's okay," a test that genuinely illustrated the surprising fact (to them) that he's just one of us. In my mind that incident was an initial embryo of family—from them to me. A few days later, the lathe was repainted to its original color—again, unbeknownst to me.

Years later, in the same genre, Frank Blasques in Production had painted a two-foot-high 49er football team logo and helmet on the front of our brand-new three-hundred-ton press. I had enthusiastically endorsed his suggestion to commemorate a second Super Bowl victory. It was important to Frank. Besides, it blended beautifully with the fire-engine red punch press, the color specialordered secretly by me from the factory.

What were we doing here? "Playing with paint and Play-Doh? "Harumph! Sounds to me like a bunch of kids fooling around, goofing off—on company time." Perhaps. But in another sense, we were spontaneously building a unity, a bonding, a sense of family just by being ourselves. In these instances, fun was our common denominator—not deliberate and not contrived. These events just happened. And a sense of family grew, from them to me.

Does it seem strange to you that I put such emphasis on building this feeling of family at NATD? I hope not. Again and again, in sports, in war, in life, astonishing things have been accomplished, great victories have been won, by groups of people—in fact, entire nations—who bonded together with common values to win. We won very big at NATD for the past twelve years, together, as a family. You can, too, in the same way, doing the same things—as long as you are sincere.

In the final analysis, the greatest sense of family comes from giving. Everyone at NATD gives to each other (including me) *the* most important "gift" at NATD: 0.1 percent customer rejects, all parts, all year, all customers. What was it that Teresa Bettencourt (Production) said earlier? "Tom cares about his people. And *in return* we care about what we do. . . . If you care and take pride, then you have quality. . . ." It's as simple—and as complex—as that. And quite profitable.

CORPORATE AMERICA AND FAMILY

Stop, you say! That's not fair! How can we analyze and compare Big Corporate's efforts to build a sense of family among their employees? They don't. It's as simple as that. They won't. They just don't believe it's important.

Most corporations have extensive internal communications departments and wide-ranging media vehicles. These include periodic newsletters, closed-circuit TV, and E-mail. Tragically, most communications are sterile, impersonal pontifications—earnings statements, news about staff promotions. Precious few large companies have the desire to build a sense of community internally. The exceptions are painfully rare: Mike Walsh at Union Pacific (now at Tenneco), the late Sam Walton at Wal-Mart, and Ken Iverson at NuCor Steel. These CEOs stand out like bright but solitary beacons in a very dark and increasingly lonely night.

Many corporations would argue that a sense of family is not important. Even if it were, that objective is simply unattainable, given the massive size of today's major corporation, numerically or by geographic area. Yet Walsh and a few others do it, with both lasting and telling results. In my judgment, the principle of their success is relatively straightforward. They "touch" people, literally and figuratively.

The lore and legend of how Sam Walton often wandered into a Wal-Mart store unannounced is well known. A pilot, he would just "set" his small plane down at a local airport and go over "to visit a spell" with his fellow employees. This occurred two or three times a day, day after day. Even with their mammoth size (Wal-Mart is America's largest retailer), Sam's stated goal was to visit every one of their stores—in person. He wasn't there to check up; he was there to visit, to encourage, to "touch" his associates in person.

He also touched his associates in a figurative sense, having spread the gospel according to Sam. This gospel included greeting the customers at the store door, welcoming them sincerely, making them feel at home, helping them, so that they'd return. And do they ever. Wal-Mart's sense of family encompasses not only their employees but also their customers.

While at Union Pacific, Walsh held town meetings throughout the entire rail system—and in relatively small groups. The purpose: to explain Union Pacific's goals, its business plan and, perhaps equally important, to "schmooze," to see and be seen by his fellow employees. In the open forum portion of the town meeting, the ground rules were simple: no holds barred. No question or subject was taboo, off limits. Walsh's answers were equally clear—simple and straightforward. Both Walton and Walsh knew it was absolutely essential to get out and meet the people "on the line" and in turn, be "touched" by their associates. By the way, Walsh is now doing the same thing at Tenneco.

Contrast those philosophies and action steps with the following short story. Not long ago I spoke at a division of a major competitor of one of the companies described above. It was a three-day event for this division's three hundred top managers held at a resort away from the office.

On the first day, the general session was opened by a thirty-minute video-taped monologue by the CEO of the parent company. The usual verbiage oozed forth: "I regret not being with you today but due to the press of other business, blah, blah, blah." What jolted me to rapt attention was the CEO's next statement: "Congratulations on your stellar performance during the first nine months of this fiscal year—twenty-seven percent or 1.1 billion dollars above budgeted sales."

Over *one billion dollars* in sales over budget—that's an astonishing achievement! And this guy is too busy to come out of his corporate cocoon and congratulate this group in person. All it would cost is his time. The allocated cost of his corporate jet for the 1,500 miles round trip would probably offset the video production cost. In a larger sense, who even cares about the cost? What a record performance, what an achievement—obviously by a group of dedicated employees. Yet this CEO doesn't even think it worthy of his presence. What a mistake! What a lost opportunity to sincerely congratulate his fellow employees—to be a part of their feelings of pride, of attainment, of winning. What an opportunity to build a sense of family.

What do you think Sam would have done? Or Mike?

To cap this astonishing video performance, his monologue continued: "Don't let up in the final three months of this fiscal year. Keep pushing yourself. That's what it takes, you know." Do you think it is productive, appropriate, or inspiring to be (albeit gently) admonished at this juncture?

My frustrations boiled over later during my question-and-answer period with the audience. I made pointed reference to the verbiage in the video. I blurted out my true feelings: Rather than pontificating from the safe confines of the TV studio, it would have been a lot more meaningful if the corporate parent CEO had shown his face, live, to you people, particularly to mark such a great achievement. The burst of applause was both loud and sustained. Obviously, they weren't clapping for me. They were endorsing my sentiments as their own—in safe unison.

In stark and graphic counterpoint, here's a letter NATD got from Greg Watson, a buyer at Hewlett Packard, after he toured our plant with his teenage son. I shared this letter that he sent to our quality control manager with our coworkers, posting copies with my note on it on our bulletin boards for all to see. I still have it. Here it is (☺ is my signature within NATD):

To: The Gang
From: Me

This is what this place is all
about.

Thank you!   ☺

Dear Joddy:

There is nothing more precious for a father to give his
son than understanding about life. As you guided Andy
through "World Headquarters," he learned a most valuable
lesson. You are an exceptional young man and were able to
communicate dedication and caring in a way that I never
could have. As you introduced my son to each of the unique
folks there, they also opened his eyes to the underlying
atmosphere that makes North American Tool and Die not
only a top performer from a business perspective but also
from a personal one.

At the end of the day Tom asked Andy what he liked most
about the tour and your company. His answer was priceless.
"Your people love you and you love your people." Thanks.

Sincerely,

Greg Watson
Hewlett Packard
San Diego Division

THE *ESSENCE* OF A NEW PARTNERSHIP— FAMILY

1. A sense of family is an enormously powerful force—in business, in life. Family perpetuates basic values and gives people a sense that they are not alone.

2. In business (and at home), feelings of family should be multidirectional: top down, bottom up, and between family members.

3. The actions to engender this spirit must stem from a sincere belief in the value of each of your family members, as fellow human beings and as coworkers.

HOW *YOU* CAN BUILD A NEW PARTNERSHIP THROUGH FAMILY

1. Do you truly respect each of your coworkers? Do you really know each of them well enough even to make a judgment? If in doubt, spend time with them, get to know them and their work.

2. Then if you still don't respect them—as coworkers, as human beings—tell them why.

   • Develop a joint dialogue and plan for improvement.

   • Set firm dates for review.

   • If they don't meet the jointly developed criteria for their improvement, fire them. They'll never be family.

3. Build and develop this sense of family every chance you get. Its underpinnings are self-worth; recognition of this trait must emanate from each family member—sincerely.

4. Provide your coworkers with both financial and emotional security.

   • Identify specific actions you can take to reinforce the idea that the company is there to help its employees— before, during, and after work.

5. Show your sincere feelings and subsequent actions unabashedly.

   • This will evoke the same spirit from your coworkers.

   • Then the unity builds, the cohesiveness grows; petty animosity and jealousy will disappear between coworkers and departments.

   • You'll all be family.

6. Have fun.

7. Start now—right now. You can't afford to wait.

CHAPTER SIX

Vince Lombardi Was Right

It's Called Teamwork

"People love each other here. I don't know why but they really do. They work with each other, and they are willing to help each other. A person will stop at any time to help his fellow worker. If he's got a problem, they'll share any of their problems."

Frank Blasques (Production)

The late Vince Lombardi, the legendary coach of the Green Bay Packers, was right when he said, "Teamwork is key." I never met him but I'll bet we'd have been in agreement. See if you are. Here are my beliefs:

- Most people like other people.

- Most people like to work with other people.

- Most people like teamwork. They feel good working to-gether to achieve a common goal. They value a sense of belonging, of purpose, of unity.

- Most people know you can accomplish more by working together rather than alone.

- Most people don't like feeling alone.

If you can fill these human needs, you can win big—in profit, in providing your coworkers with a better working life, in promoting meaningful values, in rebuilding a better America.

Besides, it's a fun way to work.

ONE BIG TEAM

Teamwork is a wonderful word—with lots of meanings, shadings, and applications. In our experience, teamwork, at its best, encompasses the entire company. As Dave Lopes (Maintenance) phrased it: "It's one big team that works here."

It's a lot easier to attain this broadest level of teamwork if all your fellow employees have the same basic values. Then, almost by definition, you have the makings of a team. At NATD the people share the same perspective. "Everybody helps everybody." "A person will stop at any time to help his coworker." "Everybody wants to be together to work together." "Everybody is close to one another."

The employees at NATD also melded into an overall team because we meshed the only goal of the corporation with one of *their* inherent beliefs: to do their best (0.1 percent customer rejects). Everything we do—*everything*—focuses upon that single objective. No, it is not today's vision or this month's corporate credo; it is a very real daily fact of life.

After we started our winning streak (0.1 percent customer rejects), our spirit of teamwork grew, it took hold. A steady stream of customer recognition awards and customer compliments all further reaffirmed our accomplishments and, in turn, our overall team spirit. All of us, together—working toward a common goal.

Here's one instance that played an important role in dispelling the ageless notion in business that the women in the front office were better than their counterparts on the plant floor. As I've said, overtime at NATD is strictly voluntary. If you don't want to work extra hours, you don't have to. Late one week in the early days at NATD, there were not enough volunteers from the plant for overtime on that Saturday. Happily, several women in the front office—Lori Thomasy, Janie Johnson, and Gloria Bega—spoke up: "What about us? We'd like to help and always can use the extra money!" Fred Ferrari, plant manager, said, "You've got a deal. Try the assembly area. You don't need as much experience there."

The next Monday morning I heard about it and thought, "That's not right. They're front-office personnel, not production people." It's a good thing I kept my mouth shut. After discreet inquiry, I learned four things: The front office women did a great job in assembly; the plant women went out of their way to compliment their front-office peers ("They're just like us"); everyone saw the value of teamwork; and finally, I realized how foolishly hidebound I was.

"WE'RE ALL BOSSES HERE"

Let's step back for a minute and think. Who actually gets the work done at your company? No, not fair. Who *really* does the work—not the strategy, not the managing, the *work*? Sure, it's your coworkers. If that's the case, why not recognize that fact? When you do, the entire concept of the organization changes dramatically.

> "What they've done at NATD is to flip the traditional organization chart upside down. By doing that, the workers know that [Tom] trusted them. He turned the group loose and created a climate where the person on the line is boss."
>
> *Narrator,* The New Partnership *video training program filmed at NATD**

---

* All rights owned by Enterprise Media, Cambridge, Mass.

We simply recognized who does the real work—who achieves a 0.1 percent customer reject rate—year after year. It's our fellow employees. As a result, they became the boss, on the top, and I became Head Sweeper, on the bottom, doing everything I can to support them, to encourage them, to help them achieve our only objective: No rejects.

Listen again to Karl Adam, who works in the machine shop:

> "In this work, we're on our own, basically. It's all up to us because we've got the freedom to do it."

Hear Frank Blasques:

> "Our plants are run by the people. Nobody interferes. We don't need people looking after us. In fact, the front office hardly ever knows what's really happening in the plants because we're doing our thing. We're running the plants."

Please don't confuse the foregoing with "employee empowerment." By definition, empowerment is given, in the traditional instance, by the boss or manager. It's quite a different story at NATD. Since the employees are *all* bosses, they *already* have the power to shape their own working lives, be it selection of shift, choice of department, even starting times and holidays. The employees do it all: purchasing, production scheduling, die construction, part production, shipping, delivery, quality control, accounting, etc. Everything—themselves. They utilize teamwork—but on their terms.

If the employees do it all, what's my job? Football provides an apt analogy here. My job is coach. I recruit (hire) the best players, develop the game plan (strategy), and guide (coach) the players and build a team. My assignment also includes cheering when the team wins and boosting their self-esteem after a loss.

The team members at NATD run many different "plays" each shift, day and night. Just like football, the team members regularly call a huddle on their own—without the coach—to execute the game plan.

NATD HUDDLES

Every week there's a hot sheet meeting (a huddle) with all department heads to review the status of every order in process. The game plan is always the same: no rejects—none. The purpose of this meeting is just like a huddle in football—to call the plays, and to communicate. This coach is not in the huddle.

Calling the right plays requires information and feedback. Here are some typical questions in a hot sheet meeting:

> "Joan, will the delivery of the screw machine components be on time this Thursday? We'll need them in our final assembly operation for Job Seven on Friday morning."

> "Pat, will you finish up your stamping operation on Job One hundred twenty-three this Wednesday—per plan? I'd like to start on the tapping machines that evening."

> "Lori, can we have the computer printout by Wednesday so we can begin production on Job Two-fifty-four?"

Like on a winning football team, there's no bickering in the NATD huddle—no finger pointing over a broken play. The team members at NATD are pros; they respect each other and know the value of teamwork.

At any one time, there are about one hundred different production orders in process at NATD. Each order usually requires six or eight different manufacturing operations to complete. As a result, our coworkers are actively involved in perhaps seven hundred different production steps. Why isn't there complete chaos? Somebody has to be in charge.

"IF I'M NOT IN CONTROL, IT MUST BE OUT OF CONTROL"

Somebody *is* in control: our associates.

Because they are all bosses, they form their own teams, but with a difference. Their teams are continually forming, solving the problem, and then evaporating—on the plant floor, and in the office. Each day, each shift, there are small problems, perhaps not in themselves earth-shattering but in total they could spell disaster—and quickly—for all of us. Almost instinctively, the group seeks out those fellow employees who can help and get things done, whatever the department, whatever the skills.

Here's how Dave Lopes in Maintenance describes our system of problem-solving at NATD:

> "When there is a problem, everybody gets together. We put all the heads together and we create a top-dog guy out of each person, and they develop a solution. How can we solve this problem? Let's try this, let's try that. And everybody works together pretty well on that. So problems get solved well and very quickly with that kind of teamwork. Whatever it takes to get it done, we do it."

Oftentimes I observe these huddles as I CBWA and have to resist the temptation to get over there and find out what's going on. What's the problem? Solve it. That's my job. But it isn't; that's our fellow employees' job. They know more about it than you and I do.

While CBWA one night, I stumbled into a typical NATD huddle. It was fascinating to see. Ruben Ruiz runs NATD's parts-cleaning area—an important step in our production process. Our manufactured parts have to be clean, free of oil, dust, and minuscule nicks. Ruben is super at his job, always trying—to do better, to learn more, to grow. That evening I saw Ruben and Fred Weiser from Maintenance walking out the back door of the plant into the dark. I wondered why but minded my own business. Later, during dinner, Fred and Ruben were deep in conversation. My curiosity grew. Leaving the plant about nine o'clock, I noticed light streaming through the open door at the back of the plant.

As I drove toward the light, I saw Ruben shining a large flashlight on the control panels of our water-filtration unit outside the plant. Fred pointed animatedly to various dials and switches. I waved and drove on.

During CBWA the next afternoon, Fred cleared up the mystery. Ruben wanted to learn how to clean (flush) our water-filtration unit on his night shift. He wanted *absolutely pure* water for use in *his* cleaning equipment. Fred, who is on day-shift Equipment Maintenance, had come back to our plant during the night shift to teach Ruben the filtration system.

Huddles are also used to improve our production. Here's how Teresa Bettencourt (Production) described it:

> "Say I'm running a machine and I thought maybe we can change something to make it easier for us, or the job could be done better or in a shorter time. Say one of the die makers will go by. Maybe I'll call him over and I'll say, 'Hey, Clare, or Ken, or somebody else, I was thinking, suppose we change this or that. What do you think?' And they'll say, 'Hey, that's not a bad idea. We can do it!' And they do—right there and then."

JOB ROTATION INCREASES TEAMWORK

At NATD, teamwork flourishes because most coworkers don't have a regular job. What am I getting at?

Bang. Bang. Bang. Bang. Bang. Bang. Bang. Know what that is? That's a punch press. And that's boring! How would you like to run that machine eight hours a day, five days a week, fifty weeks a year? (You've got the same problem at your company: rote, repetitive, simple tasks that are boring—stultifying—numbing).

A happy worker is a more productive worker. To minimize boredom, we move people around. We vary their job content. Today on the punch press, tomorrow in assembly, the next day shipping, then the machine shop, etc. This regular job rotation provides four lasting benefits for all of us. First, job rotation minimizes worker boredom and increases efficiency. Second, this flexibility allows us to balance our work load in various areas of production. Third, we develop a more skilled work force that can, in turn, earn more money because of cross-training. Finally, this "policy" of regular job rotation not only breaks down the almost generic tension between departments, it practically eliminates even the concept of separate departments. We all are teammates—working together—rather than a series of enclaves, of cliques, each with its own turf, its own agenda.

The observation of Engineering's Larry Vosner is apt:

> "There's not a bunch of cliques here. It's not 'Oh, they're in Engineering, so they are up here on a pedestal and we are down here.' It's more of an even thing. We do a lot of back and forth. We are not aware of any structure."

As a result, teamwork flourishes because there are fewer barriers to overcome, traditional notions like "That's not my job," "They screwed up, it's their fault," "We were late because X department was late," and the ageless classic, "That's their problem, not mine." These excuses disappear because almost no one has a regular job. Their allegiance is to their company, to one another—not to a department.

The few people at NATD who are specialists have only one purpose in their daily business life: to support production—with a 0.1 percent customer reject rate. Die makers, engineers, front office—all of us clearly understand this goal. As a result, an overall team spirit has happily evolved.

Take it from me. Don't charge out first thing in the morning and tell your group that they're in charge. First of all, they won't believe you. Second, you can deploy this management style only if you have good people who care. Again, my one admonition: This philosophy doesn't work with employees whose values are different from yours. You've got to winnow out those other people—and fast. Once that's done, once honesty, trust, plain talk, and equality are in place, then there's only one other requisite for success with this way of life in management. And that's respect—respect for their competence, respect for them as human beings. Then you can fly.

It takes time—a lot of time; and patience—infinite patience; and finally, faith—faith in your fellow worker. But the results are worth it.

EARNING PART OF YOUR COWORKER'S PAYCHECK

Have you ever seen that poster that shows two identical side-by-side photos of a big gorilla? There are two captions, one under each photo. The first reads, "Sometimes I sits and thinks." The other caption states, "Sometimes I sits." Clare Stevens gave it to me years ago. It occupies a prominent place on the cinder-block wall in my office. One day I was just sitting and got an idea. It turned into one of the most moving symbols of teamwork at NATD.

In my mind, every coworker earns part of each other's weekly paycheck. Here's what I mean. If I don't produce a perfect production part at my machine and it's passed along to you, then you can't do your job correctly. Our quality will suffer, our customer rejects will rise, our sales will decline, and our profits will plummet. Obviously, the converse is equally true. In that way, I earn part of your pay—but only if we all are successful together. I also earn part of your pay if I stop and help you do your job. I want to encourage these latent feelings inherent in the group's psyche at NATD.

From time to time, perhaps once every six months, I hand-deliver everyone's paycheck, making it a point to thank each person individually for his or her help. Payday at NATD is always on Thursday mornings. But on one particular payday, it was different. The checks weren't handed out. Everyone started to wonder. Some of them made polite inquiry. They were told not to worry. Tom had everyone's check. They would be disbursed at the monthly Super Person meeting early that afternoon. (We talk more about these meetings in chapter 9.)

At the close of that meeting, I told our coworkers that each one of them had earned part of everyone else's wages. I told them why. Then I walked around the lunch room and handed each coworker someone else's paycheck (each check was in a sealed and addressed envelope). And I told them to give the other person his or her paycheck—because they had earned part of each other's pay.

For a few moments, everyone just stood there—until the concept sank in. Then slowly, hesitantly, each fellow employee sought out their coworker whose name appeared on the envelope. In a few minutes, "the joint was jumpin'." Clare Stevens (die maker) was yelling, "Frank, get over here. I earned your pay—as usual." Kenny MacMillan called out to Mark Valente (both die makers), "Here's your damn check. I'm tired of carrying you." It became fun, kidding, and lighthearted—perhaps to make light of the truth. We did, in fact, earn part of each other's paycheck—including mine. We had to—to survive, grow, and prosper. Each of us could sense the underlying feeling of teamwork.

TEAMWORK WITH CUSTOMERS

Another dimension of teamwork is with our customers. At NATD we treat the customer as though he is another fellow employee—another coworker in the NATD family. We are honest; we are open; we call it straight (plain talk). And we are equals—working together to fill the customer's needs—at a meaningful profit for both of us.

Not long ago Digital Equipment Corporation (DEC) came to NATD with a challenging invitation. Buyer Bill Lee outlined it succinctly: "We've chosen NATD to be our only assembly supplier on this important new computer disc drive. There will be no competitive bidding. Our decision to award NATD this assignment is based on your outstanding prior performance. Let's determine a fair price together."

This was our kind of customer—straight-ahead, open, honest. Our values meshed; we formed a new partnership. Bill and his associates in Engineering worked alongside our gang every step of the way—as equals, as teammates.

One example is still fresh in my mind. NATD was stymied; we just couldn't figure out a cost-effective way of clamping the four-piece outer assembly together prior to spot-welding. Again and again, trial after trial, nothing worked.

Rather than jealously guarding our proprietary production processes or hiding the fact that we were having problems, we opened our entire plant to Bill and his engineers. We trusted them—they were teammates, family. We asked for their help.

For several days, their engineers and Allan Kemline (Engineering) went back and forth through our plant, from our engineering offices to the welding area. We did not hide any NATD proprietary innovations.

Late one afternoon, our joint team whipped the problem—together. They used special clamps, a concept borrowed from the aircraft industry. Although I'm glad we solved the bottleneck, that's not the point. We did it together—openly, in a spirit of mutual trust, respect, and teamwork.

From a different vantage point, Greg Watson's observations are equally pertinent. Greg is a buyer at Hewlett Packard.

> "He [Tom Melohn] really wants his people to be the first line of relationship with the customer. You become almost part of the North American family. . . . You'll feel like it's a big family and you—as customer—are just a part of that family. You'll feel a closeness with them. It's very different."

Listen to Tom Curtis, an engineer at Apple Computer:

> "I've got freedom at NATD to go anywhere I want, talk to any people I want; it's almost like I own the plant. It's great. There's nothing to hide. We can communicate freely. It helps. It makes doing the job easy."

By the way, this isn't a bad atmosphere in which to do business—and to increase sales . . . profitably.

CORPORATE AMERICA AND TEAMWORK

Believe it or not, I'm not going to castigate most corporations on the subject of teamwork. Many companies have taken major steps to recognize the significant competitive advantage of an unfettered work force. Certainly phrases like "worker empowerment" and "self-directed work teams" are bandied about with great pride in the corporate suite.

Yet there are two concerns. This too may only be a fad and will go the way of MBOs, zero-based budgeting, and quality circles. If this is, indeed, a momentary management fashion, the eventual withdrawal of empowerment from the work force will result in even further disillusionment and resentment.

Unfortunately, most managers regard teamwork merely as an adjunct to their regular job. These executives exhort their underlings only to do their regular work; teamwork is almost an afterthought. As a sop, perhaps there's a weekly staff meeting for one hour, purportedly to improve communication and teamwork.

Instead, teamwork should be an ingrained and ongoing part of each coworker's job—a daily management tool for the bosses, and for our associates. It can be formal, such as the work accomplished by cross-functional teams. But teamwork can also involve informal on-the-spot sharing—NATD style.

THE *ESSENCE* OF A NEW PARTNERSHIP— TEAMWORK

1. Teamwork is a natural result of our instincts. We like other people, enjoy being with them, and know that a team can often accomplish more.

2. The impact of a team can be extended geometrically if the group has the same values: hopefully, honesty, trust, and the other NATD currencies.

3. An attitude expressed by an inverted organization pyramid fosters teamwork by providing each coworker with the freedom to do his or her best.

   • Workers are secure with the knowledge that their boss trusts and respects their competence.

4. The traditional format of teamwork includes a leader and associates.

   • A team in which everyone is a leader is even more effective.

   • Teamwork, at its best, ignites an entire organization of equals.

5. Teamwork is not an adjunct to your job. It should be an integral part of your working day—every day.

6. Teamwork is a great sales tool with the customer.

   • Treat your customers honestly, with trust, and as equals.

   • Include them as coworkers in your company.

HOW *YOU* CAN BUILD A NEW PARTNERSHIP BASED ON TEAMWORK

1. Let your people be themselves. Give them the latitude to solve problems on their own—both in the office and on the plant floor.

2. Have each associate come to a work session prepared with a prioritized list of problems in each area.

   • Urge your coworkers to choose their own team members—hopefully, from different departments.

   • Once they are in agreement on the problems and priorities, encourage them to go ahead and work out the solutions—on their own.

3. Provide the group with all the sincere emotional support they need. Cheer when they win, support them when they don't.

4. Each day invert the organization chart.

   • Ask your coworkers what you can do to help them.

   • Be ruthless in clearing away the bureaucratic underbrush that stifles their problem-solving: committees, management layers, traditional procedures.

5. Guide your fellow workers toward regular job rotation and cross-training to dissolve departmental walls.

6. Unite your associates as one. It is, in fact, one company. And together you can all win.

7. Get started now. Right now.

CHAPTER SEVEN

Hiring the Eagles

Finding, Hiring, Motivating, and Keeping Super Employees

"What's it like to work here? It's really great! It's the people here. When you first come in, you are a little nervous. But everybody makes you feel just great. It really is like one big happy family here. And that's no kidding."

Vera Ornellas (Production)

How does that song by Hal Green go? "A good man's hard to find . . . you can always get the other kind." It's exactly the same in business, isn't it?

Think of the number of times we've all bemoaned the fact that as managers we just can't find good people. Yet that's *the real key* to survival, growth, and success at both your company and mine. No matter how hard we try, we just can't do it alone. We've got to seek out, develop, and keep qualified and motivated co-workers.

At NATD, hiring the right people is my most important job. Without good employees, the best business plan will be only marginally effective. Without good people, the most revolutionary new product idea is doomed to mediocrity. With that in mind, I personally interviewed and hired almost every employee throughout our explosive growth years.

DEVELOPING AN EMPLOYEE PROFILE

Early on, we realized that our business philosophy of absolute honesty and trust would function best with fellow employees who shared these same basic values. As a result, we increasingly focused our recruiting efforts to find these people. It didn't happen overnight. It wasn't a sudden revelation. But it soon became apparent that the people we wanted had certain common traits, certain characteristics that we could identify in the hiring process.

First, good people care—they care a lot. They care about themselves, their families, their friends, their jobs, and their futures. It seems stupid now, in retrospect, but we were surprised to "discover" that these people were no different from us. As a result, we developed a mental profile of our kind of associates. Neither gender, color, age, nor religion has any bearing here. Basic human values also transcend national boundaries. The group at NATD looks like the United Nations.

Do you know the phrase "barn raising"? We search for people who are willing to be good neighbors. They will help you raise (build) your barn this year. Next year you'll help them put in a new fence. These people do it not as a quid pro quo, but to truly help each other. This spirit is an integral part of our American heritage. These are the same people who take pride in their work, who are craftsmen—however menial the task. They like working together and enjoy a team effort. They quietly and unobtrusively search out a new way—a better way—to do a job for the benefit of everyone.

I'll bet you'd give a lot to hire just one person with these values. They're out there—the Eric Karlssons (of earthquake fame at NATD) are out there. It's hard work and time-consuming to find them, but it's worth it!

Here's how we do it.

FINDING GOOD PEOPLE

First of all, we try to hire well ahead of the "crunch." At NATD, the search starts about 60 days ahead of our anticipated needs. Normally, it takes about 30 days to hire new employees. Then add another 30 days for them to learn the ropes, once on board. Our timetable may seem to add an extra "time cost of labor," but we've found it to be a profitable form of investment spending. At NATD, our new coworkers are in place, trained, and comfortable before increased production begins. If you need 100 new employees, interview the day before the start of production, and hire the first 100 bodies who come through the door, you deserve everything you'll get.

Once we've determined our staffing needs, there are two sources of new hires: personal referrals and newspaper classified ads. Obviously, if you're happy with your current coworkers, it's only logical to turn to them for referrals. People with the same values tend to associate with each other. Therefore, I ask our associates, one by one, in group meetings and on the bulletin boards, if they know of anyone who would fit in at NATD. Each time I remind them that their name and reputation are etched on the back of anyone they might recommend. Again and again I ask, "Are they our kind of people?" It's pointless to recommend someone for a job just to be nice. It's a real responsibility to refer someone to work at your company, a responsibility our fellow employees take seriously at NATD. I make sure of it.

"HELP WANTED" ADVERTISING

Advertising in the newspaper "help wanted" section is very competitive. To stand out, to be read, and to get reader response is a real challenge—and vitally important to your future growth.

Here are some lessons we learned. First, your ad must stand out—to be seen, to be read. To accomplish that with small space ads, we often use a black border around it. We always ask to be the first ad listed in our category, at the top of the column.

The job title is always in our headline with capital letters and white space around it for emphasis. The body copy is deliberately designed to start to attract our kind of people—with our values. We use phrases like "a neat place to work" or "a fun place to work." We emphasize our fixation on quality with statements like "0.1 percent customer reject rates." "Free company stock" is mentioned in the ad to illustrate our financial commitment to our fellow employees. (We instituted an Employee Stock Ownership Plan within one year of our purchase of NATD.)

Incidentally, we use the same themes to advertise all positions, whether they are for office jobs, production workers, or engineers. The people we want have the same values, regardless of background or training. The good ones who care—they're the same kind of people, no matter what their collar color is.

Perhaps of greater import is what we *don't* say. We don't use stereotyped words and phrases such as "self-starter," "highly motivated," "exceptional professionals," "strong analytical abilities," "excellent communication skills," "challenging opportunities." Words like that are phony and everyone knows it. Every big company seems to be looking only for people who can leap a tall building in a single bound and walk on water. That's ludicrous.

In our "help wanted" ads, we very deliberately include only our address, directions, and office hours. No phone number. We ask respondents to stop by and fill out applications or mail them in. We don't want the telephone jammed with callers who only ask about the pay. We can't answer that question anyway. It depends upon their skill level.

We also carefully avoid another traditional employment criterion in our "help wanted" ads. We could care less about formal education and degrees. It just doesn't matter. If the applicant shares our values, he or she can learn the necessary skills on the job. If the job requires specialized training, such as engineers, tool makers, or computer folk, it doesn't matter where the person got this experience—on the job or in the classroom. If we required a college degree, we would have to disqualify all but one of our department heads!

THE SELECTION PROCESS

When we advertise for production workers, we generally receive about three hundred applications. I personally read each twice, quickly culling the group to about ten to twelve people. After personal interviews, I generally hire only one or two candidates.

Here's what to look for in the applications. Generally, I avoid any applicant whose daily commute is more than forty minutes each way. That can quickly become an onerous chore. The result will be an unhappy employee who will shortly be looking for another job closer to home. And I don't blame him—I'd do the same thing. We don't want good people to leave, so why run that risk?

Another criterion is prior job tenure. Generally, we avoid any applicant who has changed jobs every year. Odds are they'll do the same thing again. We don't want employee turnover. It works against our concept of teamwork and family.

Incidentally, it is very rare for us to hire anyone who has to take a major pay cut to join our company. In difficult economic times people will take a job at lower pay just to make ends meet. Once the economy improves, they'll leave for a job at their old pay. So what have you gained? Some people argue that at least you can benefit from their skills in the interim. My experience suggests that "underpaid" employees usually become bitter, thinking that they're being financially exploited. And you know who ultimately gets blamed for that.

I prefer older coworkers. No, there is no reverse age discrimination at NATD. We just find that older associates have more clearly defined values. They know the worth of a good job, of being treated as equals, of working in an apolitical climate where they can contribute and be part of the group. They also act as a stabilizing influence upon their younger coworkers. It's almost like an extended family.

In addition, I look upon a job application as a mini-Rorschach—a tiny window inside the person's being. To me, if the application is messy, incomplete, and crumpled up, it reflects the same traits in the person. At NATD we can't afford that. Our business requires close tolerance work and the systematic building of complex metal subassemblies. Accuracy and completeness are mandatory. Incidentally, our job application forms are very straight-forward: one sheet, printed on both sides—a standard office-supply item.

Perhaps the most important part of the application is the section for extracurricular activities, hobbies, and outside interests. That is key. Most prospects either skip this segment or put down a cursory answer: watching TV, golf, etc. Yet here is an area of real insight into the prospective employee's true personality. We really probe hard in this area.

Here's a good example. Would you hire the Soccer Coach?

> "What are your hobbies, Manny?"
> "I'm head coach of a girl's soccer team in an after-school league."
> "What a great hobby. Why do you like it so much?"
> "Because I like people. I like to teach; I like the team-work."
>
> *A segment of a job interview at NATD between*
> *Manny Ortiz (job applicant)*
> *and Tom Melohn (head sweeper)*

His work experience was appropriate. But what set Manny apart was his hobby. To me, the traits of teaching and teamwork were indicative of success at NATD. He became a valued coworker.

It is reasonably predictable that applicants who reach out in their personal lives will do the same at NATD. We look for future coworkers who are active in their community, church, or syna-gogue. We look for people who are volunteers—Red Cross, Community Chest, or the P.T.A. These are people who want to put down roots, people who care, people who want to be part of something larger. These are the potential coworkers we really covet.

THE JOB INTERVIEW

A personal interview is a critical screen in our employment process. But first, here are some ground rules. We always interview with blocks of time, scheduling appointments for two or three consecutive days from 3:00 to 8:00 P.M. That way it is easier to make personnel comparisons and minimize my faulty memory. Besides, a significant portion of the business day is still available.

It's only considerate to interview at night. Think about it for a minute. If the candidate is already working, either he or she will have to lie and report in "sick" or else take a day of vacation to interview with you. That just isn't fair. Thus the evening interviews.

Each session is thirty minutes. In the first five minutes, the objective is to get the candidate to relax. I offer to get a soft drink or coffee, then we just visit for several minutes. After all, the interview is important to both of us. I truly want each person to do his or her best.

A job interview is a two-way street. Each party wants to learn about the other. The most effective way to get to know the person you are interviewing is to *listen*.

Have you ever changed jobs? Ever had a job interview? Ever prepped for your interview ahead of time? Ever developed pat answers to the predictable questions that were forthcoming? Well, these people are no different. They have their correct answers, too. But I want to get behind this veneer and find out their true feelings—their real values. And the way to do that is with silence.

After the first introductory five minutes, I ask each candidate if he or she has any questions about our company or the job opening. Then I just listen. Sometimes the silence is deafening. But I keep quiet. Sooner or later, they'll speak up. And that's when I learn, really learn about the other person.

Usually the interviewees' queries will fall into one of three categories: none, money, or sincere career questions. Let's look at each one. If the applicant has no questions, that in turn often signifies either fear of raising any inquiries or lack of interest and/or preparation. The key here is to discern the difference. Once again, the solution is silence. Just wait. Those who don't really care, those who just want a job—any job—will just sit there. But those human beings who are by nature a bit shy will slowly come forth with their questions. And then you can tell what they're about. Hopefully, they are sincere; they want to work.

Finding the right people is my *most* important job. It is critical that we hire people with our values. Remember that old adage: One rotten apple can spoil the entire bushel. That is equally applicable at NATD.

Besides, I have an obligation to our fellow employees. I can't let them down. It wouldn't be fair. If I hired one malcontent, one "dogger," then the burden of picking up the work slack would fall on the shoulders of the rest of the group. And that just wouldn't be right.

Here are the interview questions from two hypothetical job applicants. Which candidate would you want to interview further?

Candidate #1:   "What's the pay?"
                "What's the vacation policy?"
                "How long are the daily work breaks?"
                "How many sick days do I get?"

Candidate #2:   "What do you make here?"
                "Who are your customers?"
                "Is there a training program?"
                "Do you promote from within?"

That's easy—Candidate #2. Obviously #1 is concerned only with pay and benefits, and that's not the basis of a long-term relationship. On the other hand, Candidate #2 illustrates his interests and intelligence by his questions. And it's that kind of curiosity that will also make him a better employee—one who's searching for a better way.

A discussion of prior jobs can provide another clue about each candidate's inner workings. Rather than ask just what they did, probe what they liked most or least about their previous work. Usually this is predictive of their future success. We find that a happy employee is a more productive employee. As a result, we try to let people perform those tasks they most enjoy doing.

For factory workers, we ask in the interview whether they prefer running a machine or working with their hands in assembly. Once you get beyond the phrase "I like both" (i.e., "I need a job"), the answers can be quite helpful.

The same premise holds true in interviewing for office personnel. Concentrate on their likes and dislikes in prior jobs. Find out why. Then mesh their preferences with your job requirements. Usually everybody wins. The new employee's happier and her productivity is up.

Incidentally, we always offer each new employee her choice of shift. Why not? Again, a happier employee . . . At first, the interviewee is incredulous. "I'll take any shift. It doesn't matter." But you know it does. It certainly would make a big difference in your life—why not in hers? Once she realizes you mean it, once she realizes she has some voice in her own work life, her attitude change is quite noticeable. Incidentally, over time we've found that day and night shifts are equally popular.

One evening I interviewed a wonderful person. She had it all: attitude, values, experience, everything. I offered her a job with a choice of first or second shift. When she finally realized that she *truly* had a choice, that she had some control over her work life, she started to sob. Suddenly a young boy about eight years old came tearing into my office. Unbeknownst to me, he had been waiting in the lobby nearby. He hugged his mom and tried to console her. Slowly the lady explained to him that everything was going to be all right, that she just got a good job, that she got the night shift. Now she could be with her son during most of the day. Dad would be there with him at night. (Incidentally, she was so impressive that I offered her a job on the spot without checking with her former boss.) She became a solid member of NATD.

So it is: Even in the initial interview, future NATD employees can sense that this is a unique place to work. They see the differences in our "help wanted" ads, in the interview itself, and in the actual hiring—with both choice of job and shift.

Once I know I've found a person with NATD's values, I start to develop the themes that are the underpinnings of our company, even in the initial interview. I point out our low personnel turnover rate, our minuscule absenteeism, and discuss why. I chat about how important honesty is at NATD, citing specific examples as proof: the women's purses left unattended, the football pool money sitting out all week on the lunch table, etc. I talk about our need—no, *requirement*—to tell it like it is. If there's a better way to do the job, please tell us. If they see us making a mistake, I encourage them to speak up—and quickly.

We chat about trust, and reinforce it with true stories about our coworkers: the "open" phones on the shop floor, and the missing coffee episode. All of this is discussed openly with each potential new employee.

Finally, we talk about pay. Incidentally, I never bring it up until the very end of the interview, for two reasons. First, I want to see where pay is in their list of priorities. In addition, I want them to know what is of greater import to us—those critical values discussed earlier in the interview.

DETERMINING PAY

Want to know a secret? Each of your fellow employees generally knows about how much you make. Think about it. You have a pretty good idea of your coworkers' salaries, including your boss's and even his boss's. It's no different in the plant. So why not use this information to everyone's advantage?

Each current employee's name and hourly pay is on a list in my desk. During a successful job interview, I try to judge the prospect's job skills in comparison to those of current employees at NATD. Then I show the interviewee this list and point out the actual pay of those of our people who are comparable. That would be the compensation they'd make if they were subsequently hired. The rationale is straightforward. If I paid Jim, the new employee, more than Peggy, the incumbent, she'd be upset—rightly so. If the converse occurred and Jim was hired at less than Peggy, even though their job skills were roughly comparable, then Jim would be upset. Neither scenario would be good for the company. And don't deceive yourself for one second. They find out, sooner or later. Besides, arbitrary pay inequities aren't fair. You know how long it sticks in *your* mind, don't you? A long, long time.

CHECKING REFERENCES

There is another critical step in this hiring process: the reference check. As usual, we do it in a different way at NATD.

Do you know of anyone anywhere who ever listed a reference who would not speak well of the candidate? I don't either. Again, these people are no different from us. As a result, we just ignore their list of "cousins." If we are impressed with the candidate, we ask these questions during the interview: First, her former boss's name and office phone number; then her assessment of the former boss. Finally, we ask what that boss would probably say about the candidate—when we call him.

The answers are often surprising. Remember, at this stage hopefully we have winnowed out all those who don't share our values. As a result, the applicant usually speaks the truth. When they do, it further reinforces our instinct to hire them.

One future employee told me his former foreman would be critical of his attendance. Yet he probably wouldn't take the time to discuss a terminal illness in the applicant's family. Sure enough, when I chatted with the foreman by phone he was true to form. When I asked whether the candidate had a history of spotty attendance, the answer was yes. That told me all I needed to know. Yes, I know. My inquiries should be restricted to the personnel office. But we need more than name, rank, and serial number. It is just too important for us to be stonewalled.

Most people tell the truth. That's why I call their former supervisors directly. I ask him or her to rank the candidate on a scale of 1 to 10. The answers are crystal clear. A rating of 8.5 was unambiguous. Compare that to the current gobbledygook of "above average," etc., so prevalent in Big Corporate today.

Finally, I ask if the former boss would rehire the candidate. All of this information is melded into our earlier instincts and impressions gathered from the personal interview and completed application. Hopefully we will then telephone the applicant and offer her a job.

Incidentally, one other technique has proved to be very effective—the half- or whole-day job trial. If we have an opening that requires special skills, such as an engineer or computer programmer, we invite the top candidates to work at NATD for a half day and pay them. This gives each of us an opportunity to see if we like the candidates, and vice versa. If they are employed elsewhere they can come in on Saturday mornings. In this way, we can see first hand their specific job skills. Equally important, we can judge the applicant's character by his or her interest and questions.

In one instance, there were three finalists for a key office job— sales service manager. Each took a half-day paid job trial. It was readily apparent that two of them thought they knew the job already and acted that way. The third candidate asked all kinds of questions about our philosophy and procedures. Clearly she wanted to understand the nuances of our business. She was also able to handle complex tasks and seemed genuinely excited at the end of the half day. Needless to say, she got the job.

KEEPING GOOD PEOPLE

At this point you may think the hiring process is complete. Not at NATD. During the first thirty days, the new employee *has* to be verbally evaluated by his supervisor each Friday for four weeks. It isn't a long, formal procedure—just a summary of how the person is doing and a short discussion of strengths and weaknesses. (We called the first month of employment an "engagement" party.) Remember your fear and insecurity the first few weeks on your new job? Remember how you wished you knew how you were doing? How concerned you were? We try to alleviate this tension, to our mutual benefit. Besides, it is only the fair thing to do. Incidentally, after the "engagement" party, each new employee gets a token pay increase.

If you stop and think about it, you're "hiring" your current employees every day. Once you've expended the effort—in time and money—to attract the best coworkers, then it only makes sense to be sure they're happy and content in the future. As a result, I visit with them as I wander through the plant on a random but regular basis during CBWA. How's it going? Everything okay? Anything I can help with? In that way, you can stay in touch and get a pulse reading of your most important asset—your fellow employees. Perhaps this assessment sums it up:

> "It may sound a little corny, but I look forward to getting up in the morning and coming in to work. We work hard and sometimes long hours. But I really, really like it here. I think it's great. You can't be in a better place. You really can't."
>
> *Vera Ornellas (Production)*

All too often we take our fellow employees for granted. And that's shortsighted. It always strikes me as hypocritical, lavishing attention and care only upon the new hires and often ignoring the old-timers. Their needs are no different. They want to be appreciated, to be reaffirmed as part of the family. Besides, the mature pros are often sought after by the competition. So protect your most important asset. But remember, your interest in them, your caring—it has got to be real. Otherwise they'll smell the hypocrisy. And you're dead.

CORPORATE AMERICA AND HIRING

Now let's contrast the foregoing with Big Corporate. In our hearts, we know most major corporations truly don't care about their employees. Yes, the pontifications are there: "People are our most precious asset." The chic vision statements are in place. But, sadly, we know better. Those phrases are deployed for corporate image-building programs, primarily to the investment community or major customers.

Most major companies, perhaps unwittingly, seek out and develop clones—new members to recreate the existing corporate culture of status, hierarchy, perks, and purported intellectual superiority at the top.

Look at their "help wanted" ads. The words are sterile, rigid, sanitized, and impersonal. This language flows right out of the job specifications. And for good reason. "That's the way we are at XYZ Corporation. That's the way we work, and don't you forget it." Here's one telling example: "The final metric is the effective delivery of new products."

Nowhere in any major corporation have I ever seen a job spec that sets forth the kind of human being we want to hire. Isn't that the most important criterion of all? Isn't that the bedrock of our company—its beliefs, its values? And isn't it our fellow employees (including management) who have to live those values every day— in all our dealings inside and outside the corporation? If that's the case, how come we don't include our values as criteria in the employment process? How come, in truth, we never even discuss them?

Now let's look at interview techniques in big companies. Remember those interviews in a small, impersonal cubicle? Bet you never were interviewed after work, as a convenience to you. "Our office hours are 9:00 A.M. to 5:00 P.M. *period*." Did you ever get the feeling the whole procedure was rote, by the book, unfeeling? "Next, please. Tell me a little bit about yourself."

Sometimes it seems the interviewer is trying to trip you up, to find a reason to disqualify you, rather than to discover your strengths. Have you ever left an interview feeling down— frustrated—because you never got a chance to tell the interviewer about the real you, your talents and accomplishments? The simple facts on the résumé or application blank aren't the complete picture of you. "I never got a chance to point out how I organized and ran the entire children's soccer league in our town. Yet the interviewer dismissed me for lack of any experience in managing."

Think back for a minute. Throughout your entire career, in any new job interview, have you ever been offered a choice either of job or hours? I'm not talking flex hours here. I'm talking about being given the latitude to design significant elements of your new job. Maybe you can even work at home a day or two a week. Think about it for a minute. How would you feel? What would your reactions be? Your opinion of the company? Mine, too!

This concept of menu selection in your job is, in fact, not so revolutionary. The U.S. Army has been doing it for over fifteen years in their voluntary Army recruiting ads. "Pick your job in the Army now—when you graduate, we'll guarantee it." And it works. Enlistments increase year after year.

Some critics will say: "Won't work here. Everyone would want to be a____." But that's just another excuse to continue "the system." People are wonderfully diverse, with a wide range of interests. Not everyone wants to be a____. That's what we find again and again at NATD.

Now let's analyze how corporations proceed, once the new employee is on board. It has always amazed me that so few large companies employ the buddy system for new hires. Know what I mean? A current employee is assigned a new hire for those first crucial months of employment to make him feel at home and ease him over the inevitable bumps that every newcomer experiences.

In addition, very few large corporations have even informal reviews early in that critical first year of the new hire's career. Yet we've found it to be of great value. First you calm the new employee's natural concerns. Second, if needed, you can gently but clearly point out what he can do better in his job and provide the help to do it. Finally, and most important, here's yet another opportunity to informally discuss and reinforce your company's basic values and beliefs.

Let's stop for a minute and address a key point. The presidents of most major corporations are far too busy to interview all potential new employees. It would be physically impossible for the CEO to interview every potential coworker. Yet we're all abundantly aware of the impact of the CEO. Think of the far-reaching implications if the CEO took a sincere and active interest in the hiring process. What if he periodically interviewed at key universities and schools? What if he regularly contributed in indoctrination sessions for new employees? (Jack Welch, CEO of General Electric, for example, regularly participates at his company's training facility outside New York City, as described in G.E.'s 1991 annual report.)

If you truly mean what you say—that your people are important—then show your fellow executives, and most important, show other fellow employees that you mean it. If you sincerely want great employees in your department, your division, or your company, then you've got to get involved—personally involved—and now.

What can we learn here? How can you apply this information to your own job, whether you're a manager, CEO, or owner?

**THE *ESSENCE* OF A NEW PARTNERSHIP—
HIRING THE EAGLES**

1. To hire and keep good people is your single most important responsibility.

2. The definition of good people goes far beyond mere job competence. The basic values of your fellow employees are the real key to success—theirs and yours.

HOW *YOU* CAN BUILD A NEW PARTNERSHIP BASED ON HIRING THE EAGLES

1. You *must* get and stay involved in the entire hiring process, both with new hires and long-time fellow employees.

2. Be sure your job specs (if you insist they're necessary at all) include a clear definition of the human values you believe in.

3. Be relentless in hiring *only* those people who embody these values. Don't compromise even once; you'll always pay for it in the end.

4. Make the entire employment process user-friendly.

   - Use simple and straightforward words in both the job specs and your employment advertising.

   - Interview prospective employees to determine their real values—not just job skills.

   - Don't assume that only college graduates can master certain jobs.

   - Interview at the convenience of the applicant.

   - Offer your potential new employees the choice of job and shift, if appropriate.

   - Provide new coworkers with a buddy.

   - Have frequent and informal evaluations of your new coworkers.

   - Recognize and reaffirm the importance of long-time employees.

5. Start tomorrow. Don't wait—even one day.

CHAPTER EIGHT

Let Me Grow, Let Me Create

How to Release Employee Creativity

"Since Tom Melohn took over, we've developed all kinds of machines to automate production on our own without having to go through engineering. We don't have to ask permission like it used to be. Then you had to go to the engineers and ask because they were higher up than us. We wouldn't have dared to start something without asking them. In this work we're on our own. It's up to us because we have the freedom to do it."

Karl Adam (machinist)

Creativity's an intriguing word, isn't it? When we think of creativity we usually think of poets, writers, artists, painters, or composers. To me, anyone can be creative. A die maker is creative. He takes a big chunk of steel and shapes it into a die with a margin of error of less than one fourth the thickness of a human hair. A skilled punch press operator uses that die to consistently manufacture a precision part with no rejects. That's creativity. An engineer takes a part blueprint and custom-designs the complicated die construction plan. That's creativity. When Karl Adam dreams up automated equipment, designs it in his head, and builds it from scrap material—without any blueprints—that's creativity. Sales people, office workers, machine operators—all of us can be creative in some way.

With that firm belief well in mind, we very deliberately tried to establish a climate at NATD that would allow creativity to grow and flourish within the entire work force.

In my mind, the concept of creativity is an outgrowth of a fundamental premise. You see, I believe in the innate goodness of man.

Don't you sometimes wonder as you watch little children? They're so genuine, so happy, so ready to smile—without guile, open with their thoughts, feelings, and ideas. What a joy it is to come home at night after work and be met by a gaggle of your kids, hugging you and squealing joyously, "Daddy's home, Daddy's home. I love you, Daddy."

How sad it is, later in their lives, to see these same young people be rudely deprived of the wonderful human instincts of openness, of candor, of free expression. Conform. Obey the system. Act the party line. Hide your true feelings, your real thoughts, your ideas—*or else.*

Yet I feel that everyone's inherently good instincts are still there. These feelings and latent ideas are yearning to get out, to be lived every day, to find expression—both at work and in people's personal lives. What we tried to do at NATD was to provide a climate where it was okay to be yourself. It was all right to express your feelings, your ideas—your true self. But this change in "climate" had to start with me.

So I began—and gratefully. I, too, had lived a life of quiet desperation for almost twenty-five years in Big Corporate. At NATD, I just decided to be myself. Yes, we had a business to run, goals and objectives to meet. If we all wanted to eat, we had to make a profit. But that didn't mean we couldn't be ourselves. Individuality and profitability are not antithetical concepts. At NATD, we found that the personal freedom to do your best in fact enhanced our profits—enormously.

Although at the outset it was inadvertent, Melohn's daily garb symbolized a freedom of sorts. Early on my coworkers asked me whether I wanted them to wear uniforms. My answer was clear: "Dress the way you want. Please, no open-toed shoes or tennis shoes in case you drop something, and the women should be sure to wear their hair up for safety. Other than that, do your thing." And they did. After every San Francisco 49ers win, Frank Blasques, in Production, would come in on Monday adorned with his 49er accoutrements. Others wore loud Aloha shirts. Art Goyenche, also in Production, had a T-shirt that looked like a tuxedo jacket. Long before even a few corporations ever experimented with one casual day each week, our associates in the office dressed informally, every day. "Be yourself"—and the good people at NATD were. They were hesitant at the outset, tentative, careful. Yet over time—and it did take time—the group started to open up. They opened their hearts; they used their minds.

YOU GOTTA BELIEVE

Do you remember the children's story "The Little Engine That Could?" *I think I can, I think I can, I think I can*. The little engine thought it could. And sure enough, it did. The little engine pulled the big freight train over the tall mountain. Hopefully this analogy is relevant in the quest for creativity among your coworkers. It certainly is at NATD.

Simply stated, people *must* believe that they are capable of solving a problem, of finding a new and better way. Or they won't. They can't if they don't believe in themselves, in their own capabilities. (No fair asking for new ideas in areas outside a coworker's competence. You don't want to build up a production worker's faith in herself only to suggest that she find a cure for cancer.)

Our coworkers can believe in themselves more if someone they respect is a fellow believer in them. That's what we tried to do at NATD, repeatedly reinforcing our associates' self-esteem, their competence, their capability.

When we first bought the company, no one ever asked the employees for their suggestions. We quickly tapped into that resource. Every month the foremen and I would analyze the low-profit production runs. One day Karl Adam in the machine shop tentatively volunteered to try to automate a manufacturing step in his department. I jumped at his offer. "Great! You can do it! Let me know when you've whipped the problem."

Sure enough, several weeks later, he came into my office just beaming. "Got a minute? Come on into the plant." There it was—admittedly a Rube Goldberg contraption. His homemade production unit was chugging away, automatically drilling hole after hole in the parts, unattended. I was both amazed and elated—and told him so. Amazed because his new machine was so simple and inexpensive to build; elated because our production increased dramatically. I urged him to look for other opportunities to automate our production.

Soon thereafter we visited together. Karl had an idea for another innovative machine but was hesitant to proceed because he wasn't sure it would work. My only advice was to try it—it may be a hell of an idea. The upside potential could be significant, the downside risk minimal. I respected the man not only as a human being, I respected his professional prowess. I provided what I could: freedom and encouragement. His idea worked. And off we went—again and again.

One after another, out of his head, constructed with no blueprints as guidance, built from scrap, Karl's homemade automated machines increased NATD's production significantly. On job after job, increases of 200 percent and 300 percent—in one instance, almost 500 percent—were achieved. Obviously, our costs dropped precipitously.

I called my particular favorite "the 747," a machine that resembled the cockpit of a commercial jet airplane. You'd hit a button on one side and Karl's unit would automatically locate and tap fourteen holes in an assembly—all at one time. The machine then flipped the part over and did multiple spot welding—in thirty-six different locations. Karl's invention was like a miniature elevator that turned upside down and rotated on an axis. It was unbelievable. I told him so—again and again—in person—in front of his peers—and in his paycheck—and quickly.

Time and again, our customers' sophisticated and skilled engineers would visit NATD and marvel in amazement at Karl's creative problem-solving. On one occasion, at an industry meeting, I was even accused by a competitor of give-away low pricing. Yet NATD's average pretax profit was about 18 to 20 percent (versus the industry median of 4 percent), as documented by Robert Morris Associates in their *Annual Financial Statement Studies*. Our prices were low because of our efficiency. Our competitor didn't know of our secret weapons: Karl Adam and his two young associates, Joe Rosario and Rich Hostetter.

The nay-sayers here will be quick to point out that Karl was "gifted," that he was a naturally creative person, that not everyone can be like him. Don't tell that to Raphael Rosas, in Production on the second shift at NATD. One night I was CBWA and saw him with huge shears cutting out a piece of thick cardboard. Fascinated, I watched from a discreet distance. The next thing I knew, he was up on an eighteen-foot ladder jamming the cardboard wedge in, near the top of his punch press. Know why? During a long production run, a minuscule leak developed, sporadically dripping a small drop of oil on the steel coil.

At that point, Raphael had three choices. He could stop the automatic press and wipe the drop of oil off the coil each time. But our production would drop dramatically. The second choice would be inviting . . . for some: to shut down the job completely. Let the maintenance department worry about it in the morning. "It's their problem." In that scenario, we would lose the entire shift's output. Raphael took it upon himself to solve the problem; he knew he could do it. And he did, quickly, efficiently, creatively. He created a homemade cardboard drip pan to catch the oil. He also saved the entire night's production and earned a special check. To me, that's creativity.

Note the phrasing in that sentence in the preceding paragraph: Raphael took it upon himself. . . . That's another critical element for creativity to flourish.

IT'S YOUR BALL

Your associates have to know it's their responsibility to solve problems, to find a new and improved way, to be creative. Not everyone can invent a new wonder drug, but each of us can be alert to a better way in our job. After all, each of us knows our job better than anyone else. In our experience, if the employees know that creativity is an integral part of their jobs, they'll rise to the occasion.

Recently a group from Hewlett Packard in Greeley, Colorado, came to NATD in desperation. They had a major problem. In an effort to save money, they'd bought cheap, from the lowest offshore bidder. They got what they paid for—dies so poorly built that the resulting ten different manufactured parts were not acceptable. They were all scrap.

Would NATD help them out? Would we rework these dies and make them right? There was one additional problem. The customer had to have acceptable parts as soon as possible. Our coworkers went to work. The only solution was to improvise, to be creative in an effort to collapse time. Since another company had built these dies, Clare Stevens (die maker) and his associates had no idea of the die construction until they took each one apart.

This was a crash project. The customer knew our reputation and left us alone; their entire new product introduction depended upon NATD. Our associates knew it. They accepted the responsibility and creative challenge. And it worked. Years later, Dave Brown, Hewlett Packard's mechanical engineer, and I still happily reminisce about it.

One of my favorite recollections of NATD personifies this premise: It's everyone's job to find a new and better way so that we all can prosper. One Friday afternoon I came by to wish Teresa Bettencourt a good vacation in the week following. Here's how I was greeted: "Tom, aren't we in business to make money? You've got to speed my machine up! We're not making enough profit on this job!"

Can you believe it? An employee asking—no, *demanding*—that she work harder so that the company can make more profit. It's hard to envision anywhere, but it happened at NATD. Yet I'm proud to say it didn't surprise me—not with these people.

Here's what happened. Teresa was running a machine that supposedly ran at the same speed as the adjacent punch press. In fact, Teresa's machine output lagged behind. As a result, our efficiency suffered. The punch press operator had to stop and wait, time and again.

Teresa knew, she just knew something could be done. She was right. I called Fred Ferrari (plant manager) and found that Teresa had already hounded him. He was working on a solution. You can say that Teresa wasn't being creative because she didn't solve the problem. But that's not the point. She assumed—and properly so—that it was her job to find a better way. And she did, by pointing out the bottleneck in the first place.

It is the only time in my life that I've been "chewed out" by a coworker and rewarded her with a special check to say thanks. I loved it.

THERE'S NO SUCH WORD AS *NO*

Do you know the safest word in the English language? It's *no.* Think about it: *No,* that won't work; *no,* don't do that; *no,* don't try that. You can't ever be blamed, you can't ever be held responsible, you can't ever fail if you always say no.

Most of us live our lives impacted by that sterile philosophy, whether in business or our personal lives. Is it any wonder that we muzzle our personal expression, in almost every dimension of our lives? Don't show your real feelings, you could be vulnerable. Don't express a new idea, you could be embarrassed—or, worse yet, wrong. Heaven forbid, you might even fail.

At NATD, we just eliminated the word *no* in the area of creativity. We had to. In my judgment, it was mandatory if we ever wanted our fellow employees to speak up, to find a better way, to be creative, to win. There is no quicker way to squelch creative thinking than criticism or doubt early on, particularly from the boss: That won't work, that's a stupid idea, etc. "Forget it. Why should I stick my neck out only to have it chopped off or, worse yet, be met with a put-down in front of my coworkers? It will be a very long time before I ever open my mouth again when they ask for a suggestion."

At the outset we didn't have much money. Since we couldn't afford new and more efficient capital equipment, we had to compete by "out-thinking" our competitors. And we did—by human ingenuity. The other immutable fact of life is that you can't possibly do it all yourself. All our employees *had* to participate in discovering ways to work more effectively—in a new partnership. My job was to provide a climate conducive to creativity. Taking away the word *no* was a key step in that process.

Perhaps Dave Lopes at NATD best personifies the attitude that there's no such word as *no*. Dave started at NATD while still in high school, at age sixteen, sweeping floors every afternoon. He had no technical training or experience in machinery repair. Yet Dave badgered the former owners to let him fix the equipment breakdowns. He just wouldn't take no for an answer.

Finally, our predecessors relented—just once. It was quickly apparent that Dave was gifted, very gifted, almost intuitive with machinery. Shortly after we purchased NATD, we asked Dave to head up all maintenance—plants and equipment. And am I glad we did because Dave helped NATD earn our first million-dollar order.

NATD had two competitors for this contract. One adversary was a multidivision conglomerate from Southern California, replete with a corporate jet that often whisked our prospect's engineers and buyers up to Reno for dinner and a show. The other competitor was the current producer, who was approximately six times our size and a legend on the West Coast.

The job was to manufacture an assembly for Data Products. Ken Mudge was the buyer. The part had twelve rivets; each had to fit perfectly for the unit to function properly. That's where the current supplier was having major quality problems.

Traditional thinking called for the rivets to be inserted individually. It was such a critical operation that everyone agreed there was no other way.

Except Dave Lopes. There was no such word as *no* for him.

Dave designed and built a machine at NATD that solved two problems. It installed all twelve rivets in one operation instead of individually. Even more important, each one was seated perfectly every time. Eventually our machine operators became so proficient that Dave had to speed the machine up. Listen to Dave's description:

> "We made it kinda like a game. The operator's loading rivets in this second cartridge while the machine's running by itself. The operator's trying to get the rivets in before the machine cycle stops. Eventually I had to speed the machine up because the people kept beating it."

It was "kinda like a game." What a wonderful self-effacing description, so typical of Dave, to see creativity as a game. It's equally typical of our coworkers to see it as a contest, to see if they could beat the machine—without any rejects.

NATD beat the published target price by almost 20 percent and never shipped one reject—ever. Our first million-dollar order—because one man didn't know the word *no*.

COURAGE

It takes courage to be creative—to be different, to go your own way. Think about it. Figuratively and literally, you have to stand up in front of your peers, your boss, and most important, yourself, and be judged. You could look foolish, naive, stupid or worse yet . . . fail—in front of everyone.

So why do it? Why do people—everyday people like you and me—why do we do it? In my opinion, it's fairly straightforward. We do it for ourselves. We are proud of our accomplishments. And we value the recognition from our peers, from the boss.

Here's just one example at NATD. Not long ago we had a major problem. One punch press had jammed; production had completely stopped on this part. Yet our customer expected his regular shipment the next day. The pressure was on.

Everyone tried to help—the punch press foreman, the head die maker, the engineers, even the plant manager—but to no avail. Then Joe Rosario from the machine shop happened to walk through the area and stopped to see what all the commotion was about. After

listening quietly for a few minutes, Joe spoke up: "What if we . . ."
That was it. There was the solution. "Why didn't we think of that?"
Joe's idea worked; the problem was solved. But that's not the point.
It took courage for Joe to speak up. This was not Joe's department.
This was not his responsibility. No one else had been successful. Joe
could have looked foolish in front of everyone with his suggestion;
he could have failed. What did he know about the operation of a
punch press? Yet he spoke up. We thanked Joe for that in person, in
front of his peers, and in his paycheck. Everyone knew why; I told
them at the next all-plant meeting.

IT'S OKAY TO MAKE A MISTAKE

Would you be more willing to try something new if you knew you
couldn't fail? Of course. In truth, we're not really afraid of making a
mistake, are we? It's the subsequent embarrassment that inhibits us.
If you take away fear of failure (of embarrassment), then it should be
easier for people to be creative. That's just what we did at NATD.

If you recognize the fact that everyone makes a mistake sometime, then why not take advantage of it? When an employee makes a
mistake, most bosses will simply reprimand the worker and consider
the incident closed. But it isn't. If criticism is the standard response,
then people will simply hide their goof-ups. Wouldn't you? Nobody
likes to be called on the carpet. The consequences are predictable.
First comes hiding the mistake, then the contrived cover-up, and
finally, deliberate lying. Ultimately that environment will permeate
and smother creativity throughout the entire organization.

There's another factor at work here. Have you ever made a
mistake? What were your feelings? You felt sick about it, right? If
that's the case, then what good did it do for your boss to criticize
you—to simply chew you out? You had already chewed out yourself more harshly than he. Our employees are no different.

We go another way at NATD. The house rule is simple. Whenever a mistake occurs, we ask these questions. Who did it, how did
it happen, and what can we learn from it? Then let's go forward. No
big deal. Over time, our coworkers see this pattern applied again

and again—at all levels. Melohn deliberately sets the example. It was easy—I make lots of mistakes. Every one I make, I broadcast for all to see and hear. It is okay to drop the ball. It is okay.

When we opened Plant #20, I made a major error. At that time, the industrial real estate market was tight. There were very few buildings available, particularly with our requirement of major electric power. We had to expand—and quickly. We were bursting at the seams in our other facilities. The pressure was on.

Then we found the perfect spot: power, size, location, occupancy date. Everything meshed. Remember when you rented or bought your first apartment or home? Our emotions here were almost identical. We had to have that building. Everyone from NATD who toured the building agreed that it was perfect. Let's go! Charge! Close the deal—quick! And we did. I can still remember my euphoria when the realtor told me by phone on Saturday night, "It's yours." I immediately called the plant manager to share the good news. He was equally elated. "We'll begin the move right away." It was really exciting—until we actually moved in.

It was cold in San Francisco that first winter—unseasonably cold. No problem. Just turn on the furnace. What do you mean there's no furnace? That's crazy! I don't understand. You guessed it. In my happy haste to close the deal, I never even thought to check the heating and air-conditioning facilities. There were none. I felt so stupid. I really berated myself. But our fellow employees made light of it. "We'll work around it. Don't be upset. We didn't think of it, either." And that made me feel better. (You see, this philosophy works both ways.) The second and more important reason I broadcast my mistake was to prove to our associates that everyone screws up—and that it's okay.

Some cynics will smirk here. Of course it's okay. You're the boss. Who's going to criticize you? But they miss the point. Our group knows everyone is treated in the same way at NATD. (Incidentally, we brought in portable heater-blowers to warm up the plant.)

Even the pros occasionally make mistakes. Years ago, Eric Karlsson in Production was adjusting a die in a large punch press. He was almost finished when he was interrupted with a question from a coworker. Afterward, he turned around and started the punch press. With the first downward stroke, there was a sickening crash. Have you ever seen a $5,000 die broken in pieces? Eric had forgotten that when he stopped to help a coworker, he'd left a three-foot-long wrench on the die.

I heard about it the next morning. When Eric came to work late that afternoon for the night shift, I sought him out, put my hand on his shoulder and said, "Welcome to the club. Learn from it. Let's go forward."

Incidents like these provide clear evidence to the group that it is okay to make mistakes, to screw up, to fail. As a result, our associates are more apt to reach out, to make suggestions, to try new things. Why not? What is the downside? We took away fear of failure.

Here's what Dave Lopes observed:

> "People know that you shouldn't make mistakes, but if you do, there's no need to worry because everyone can work together to solve the problem. It's a really relaxing kind of atmosphere. People aren't as afraid to make good decisions or to make a mistake."

One admonition here. Be patient. Don't forget: You are asking people to strip away layer upon layer of "protective coloring" and be innovative. You are asking them to peel off years of conformity, of playing it safe to survive. Remember how vulnerable you felt when you first voiced an opinion different from that of the group? You can be hurt—badly—in this position, both emotionally and economically. It's a scary thing. So give your associates time. They'll come around. And then the creative sparks will fly.

YOU CAN DO IT. I KNOW YOU CAN

Ever been down? Really discouraged? Whether in your business or personal life, it's happened to all of us. You've given it your best, you've tried everything, but you haven't been able to accomplish what you wanted.

If you're lucky—very lucky—you have a friend, spouse, or associate who truly believes in you and your worth, your capabilities. She's relentless, single-minded and devoted to one belief—in you and your capabilities. When all else seems black, you can turn to this wellspring of faith and draw from its reservoir. Then you're no longer alone. You're rejuvenated, recharged, and ready to attack the situation anew. Usually you'll win—with that special support. This is quite different from having just a cheerleader. This resource is a deep inner belief in you, not just a series of verbal accolades.

One day Clare Stevens came in my office. He was really low. For days he and his group had been stymied. A customer had ordered a new die months ago. The delivery date was rapidly approaching. The die makers had tried everything—every trick in the science of die construction. They just couldn't lick the problem.

All I could offer was the truth. I reaffirmed my faith in him as a human being and my high respect for his professional accomplishments. We reminisced for hours about the early days together at NATD, how we and they, the die makers, had grown in knowledge and sophistication, how the die makers' current reputation led major customers to assign us their toughest jobs. We laughed at some of our prior escapades together in business. To call this simply bonding would be incorrect. Rather it was a restatement of my belief in and respect for his skills—personally and professionally. Don't be misled here. I did nothing but hold up a mirror. Implicitly, Clare looked within himself—at his accomplishments, at his self-worth. He came away refreshed and renewed. He had the courage and commitment to tackle the problem one more time.

Clare and his group solved the problem. I knew they would. I was so proud for him.

You can provide the same stimulus to your fellow employees— if you truly believe in them as human beings and as professionals. And get the same results. You can also do the same for yourself. There are certainly enough others around, ready to tear down your self-worth, to belittle your accomplishments, even to denude you of your capabilities. Forget them—forget their barbs, sneers, and put-downs. Believe in yourself. No one else's opinion really counts anyway. Believe in yourself and just go do it. The results will amaze even you.

COMMITMENT

Have you ever watched the first time a young child tried something difficult? One attempt, one failure, and what do we hear: "I can't do it, Mommy. You do it." Because she cares, Mommy will patiently wait and encourage the youngster to try again, to do it on his own. All of us are painfully aware of the long-term consequences if we do step in and do it for others. Unfortunately, a resulting lack of commitment and self-confidence will persist throughout that person's life.

Certainly we're in agreement. Commitment is integral to creativity. You have to stay the course, persevere, hang tough. Call it what you will. But it's vital. Nothing good ever comes easy. Not for one minute am I going to even suggest that the NATD experience birthed the trait of commitment within the group. That attribute is already well developed in the makeup of good people who care. What occurs at NATD with happy regularity is instance after instance of commitment, and its importance to creativity. There's no way to prove this connection, but I think our coworkers' repeated commitment to find a better way at NATD stems from three things: They want to win; they want the multiple recognition; and finally, they want to help—each other—and thereby the company itself.

Why else would die maker Ed Rodrigues crawl out of a sickbed and come to work at NATD for only three hours? A new die had to be built and ready for IBM's approval prior to production startup. It was 99 percent done, perfect, and right on schedule. Then Ed got sick, really sick—flu with a 101° temperature. It hung on, day after day, but he kept in touch periodically by phone. There was no problem—the group could finish it up.

The day of his die tryout dawned. Who showed up? Of course—Ed Rodrigues, still quite sick. But he insisted on staying. It was his baby. He was proud of his creation and rightly so. Once his die tryout was successfully completed, Ed lurched home and back into bed. Commitment? You bet.

To echo the same old refrain, NATD has no monopoly on the Ed Rodrigueses of the world. They are at your company, probably laboring unsung, unappreciated, and—sadly—undiscovered.

Go find them. They're there. They are priceless.

CORPORATE AMERICA AND CREATIVITY

Perhaps the best way to contrast the climate of creativity at NATD versus that of big corporations is the employee suggestion box. At NATD, there are none. There's no need for them. Our fellow employees are in charge, and their innovations are regularly blended into their daily work schedules. No review committees, no time lag. If it makes sense to the group, they just go do it.

In contrast, let's analyze how employee suggestions are processed at Big Corporate. First, you must dust the box off. Remember, it hasn't been used in years. Here's a typical "day in the life" of a suggestion. After sitting uncollected for weeks (months?), the ideas are gathered up and logged in the "new idea register." The supervisor of new ideas or his two associate supervisors (pay grade 9-C-1-B) will organize the suggestion by either function or department. They will be forwarded to "the appropriate authority"—through proper channels, of course. There the idea will be cursorily perused for its value. The time frame thus far: perhaps thirty days. If deemed worthy of review, the suggestion will be forwarded—through proper channels, of course—to the very important new idea review committee. They meet quarterly—often off-site—not to be distracted by the banalities of the work-a-day world.

Again, if deemed worthy, the idea will be shunted to a joint technical task group to study the suggestion in detail. Timetable to date: one hundred twenty days. After exhaustive analysis, the idea could be deemed worthy of bench trials—a mini–test run to see if the idea in action actually works. This step should take no longer than sixty to ninety days—if expedited.

In that happy case where success is deemed within the realm of possibility, a crisp synopsis (forty-five pages) of each step is forwarded to the new idea review committee. At their next quarterly . . . Oh, the hell with it. You get the idea. And the employee, who's heard nothing throughout this entire breathless saga—what do you imagine her thoughts and feelings are? How likely do you think she will be to submit another new idea?

Some members of the "new" corporation scoff at the archaic

procedure outlined above. They proudly cite multiple instances of self-directed work teams and employee empowerment—and with good reason. Unfortunately, these are bright but isolated lights in a landscape of industrial dinosaurs.

At NATD it was an absolute necessity to encourage the creativity of every fellow employee. Competitive pressures and frequent technological innovation demanded it.

THE *ESSENCE* OF A NEW PARTNERSHIP— CREATIVITY

1. People are inherently good. Their true feelings, beliefs, and ideas have been sublimated in order to survive, in both their business and personal lives.

2. Everyone is creative—in their own way, in their area of expertise, and at every job level.

3. There is no correlation between either education or job title and creative potential.

4. There is no way that you alone can effectively innovate for your entire department, division, or company.

    • Enlist the brains of your associates. They are woefully untapped.

5. Creativity isn't limited to rare flashes of genius. Creativity in business is often marked by small wins, little improvements, and incremental breakthroughs.

    • These innovations result in quantum leaps in productivity (NATD's productivity increased 480 percent in twelve years).

HOW *YOU* CAN BUILD A NEW PARTNERSHIP BASED ON CREATIVITY

1. Be absolutely ruthless in stripping away the innumerable and deep-seated barriers to creativity—real or perceived, physical or psychological.

2. Once you have only good people who care as fellow employees, let them be themselves. Foster it this every way you can; start with yourself.

3. Give your coworkers freedom to create and thereby find some meaning and added value in their daily work.

4. Think through how to infuse your work environment with these elements so necessary to creativity:

    - You gotta believe
    - It's your ball
    - There's no such word as *no*
    - Courage
    - It's okay to make a mistake
    - You can do it. I know you can.
    - Commitment

5. Sit down with your associates. Use plain talk and review each element outlined above. Listen for the impediments. Eliminate them promptly.

6. Ask the group to tell you how best to go forward together to increase creative problem-solving, in every area, at every level. Then do it.

7. Once your fellow employees are truly running their own show, dispense with management control of creativity through pert charts, review committees, etc. Let them do it—their way.

8. Toss out all employee suggestion boxes.

9. Get started now—right now.

CHAPTER NINE

Thank You

"The Super Person award? At NATD all the people are super people, not just one person. But every month they decide that this person has done a little bit extra this month. So they reward you with a fifty dollar check and your name goes on a plaque on the wall.

"You feel great. You really go home and say, 'Hey, I must be pretty good. I got to be Super Person this time.' You would think that there would be some people who would say, 'How come she got it and I didn't?' But no. Everybody is happy when somebody gets it."

Teresa Bettencourt (Production)

Brother, can you spare fifty bucks?

Would you pay six hundred dollars a year (twelve months times fifty dollars) to have people feel great about their work? Obviously, there's more to it than money, but why not try it? Too busy? Too embarrassed? Too childish-sounding? That's sad. It's your loss . . . and theirs.

Seems silly, doesn't it? Here are a bunch of grown-ups trying so hard and feeling so good for fifty dollars and their name on a plaque on the lunch-room cinder-block wall. What's going on here?

It all comes down to a simple phrase: "Thank you." In reality, that's all we are saying. Thank you for a super job. Thank you for caring, for reaching out, for building our spirit of family. There are so many positive emotions at work here—all interrelated, all wonderful to see and experience.

SUPER PERSON MEETINGS

Super Person of the Month is an award given to a coworker in Production or in the office, to recognize a special achievement. Maybe the person figured out how to do something more efficiently. Maybe he or she devised a way to improve quality. Whatever the person did, the award is for something extra—something that went beyond his or her basic job requirements.

The supervisors and foremen make Super Person nominations verbally at our weekly production meeting. At the close of the month, the same group chooses one person. Once in a great while, I'll suggest someone after a CBWA visit—with the foremen's approval. There are no limitations or constraints. The same person can win forty-eight consecutive times. The award is based solely on merit. If you ever even suggest another motivation, the validity and impact of the award are lost. "We haven't had a winner who's a minority," "We haven't given one to someone on the night shift," "We haven't chosen a woman." Forget it. It's based on merit and merit alone. No corporate charades.

We have the recipient's name engraved on a big walnut plaque with a space for each month's winner. That plaque is prominently and permanently displayed on the lunch-room wall for all to see. Incidentally, all our awards from our customers are also displayed here for the same reasons.

Each month our Super Person meeting is held in the lunch room at 1:30 P.M. on a Thursday with all coworkers attending. The night shift comes in early to attend—and they're paid for this. The format is simple. I always start the meeting with the announcement of this month's Super Person. We usually make it a guessing game with the group with hints like "It's a woman; she's a two-time winner; she works on the day shift; she works in the office." By the second or third hint, usually everyone guesses correctly.

Our happy recipient comes up in front of everyone and receives his or her check for fifty dollars and the Super Person plaque. It is a ritual for winners to hang "their" plaques up on the wall. This is a big deal, and I deliberately try to make it such. Then the winner has to endure standing by me as I relate his or her accomplishment. Usually I go into some detail explaining what the Super Person did. I want the group to see and hear what it takes to win. More often than not, the winner's idea is simple. I want everyone to see that and think, "I can do that in my job. The winner didn't invent a moon rocket. I can be a winner, too."

Oftentimes a coworker will win the Super Person award just for doing her job. Many times these occurrences enable us to visibly and honestly reinforce the values and climate we endorse. Here are some examples from over the years.

I once awarded Super Person of the Month just for a smile. Yes, a smile! Here's what happened. As usual, I was CBWA. I happened to look across the plant floor and saw die maker Ken MacMillan walking toward a brand new coworker. I stopped to watch this moment of truth. Would he acknowledge her as a new NATD family member, ignore her, or avoid the scene? In a flash it was over, but her face told me all I needed to know. She smiled—no, her face lit up as they passed. He had obviously taken the initiative and said hello and smiled. Irrelevant? Not to me. Family is critical to our success. It's a form of teamwork. I want to foster it wherever possible. A longtime employee, Ken had treated a new hire like family. When I related this story at the Super Person meeting and gave Ken his check, our colleagues got the message loud and clear.

On another occasion I stumbled upon a priceless scene that resulted in the Super Person award. One evening while CBWA, I looked up and saw "Madame Curie." This coworker was checking a part she had just made. Holding it up to the light for visual inspection, she looked just like my perception of Madame Curie in her laboratory. Her intensity and care were readily apparent. It was great to watch. And then, with a start, I realized this was Hilda Ruiz, on her first night at work in Production at NATD. I was stunned— her first night, and she cared that much. When she was named Super Person—in front of the entire group—it was natural to once again stress the critical importance of no rejects, no rejects.

Super Person meetings always continue with the award of silver dollars to celebrate employment anniversaries that have occurred during the prior month. One year's tenure earns one silver dollar, ten years' earns ten silver dollars, etc.

A deliberate reinforcement of tenure, of family, of thank you underlies this event. I'm proud that our coworkers choose to stay at NATD. That's one of the report cards of my performance—at least as I see it. If our average tenure is growing, NATD must be a good place to work. When we celebrate a fifteen- or twenty-year anniversary, we all feel pride mingled with awe. After all, the company is only twenty-one years old. Besides, it's fun to clank out twenty silver dollars from a big cloth bag marked FEDERAL RESERVE.

Then we recognize any special awards, which are given to supervisors and foremen who have developed some innovation in production. This is their own award session, their opportunity to receive thank-you's. They receive a check but no plaque, since we don't want to detract from the Super Person award.

I close the Super Person meeting with a candid assessment of our business outlook: sales, new orders, backlog, and any special information—all in plain talk. We look at where we've been, where we are and where we're going. Any special news is then shared, such as "Apple Computer people will be in a week from Monday" or "Here's a special letter from a customer."

You may be wondering: If the supervisors and foremen pick the winner of the Super Person award, doesn't it simply turn into a popularity contest? At NATD, the answer is no. At the outset, we clearly stated that the award was based only on merit. I made sure of it, when people were nominated and chosen as winners. No one ever tried to play favorites with the award nomination.

What's to keep NATD's foremen and supervisors from nominating only their own people to enhance their influence and political standing? One factor: At NATD, political turf is irrelevant. We don't hire people who think in those terms. Furthermore, I would never allow self-serving nominations. Back in the early days, I remember thinking it a breakthrough when Levi Bloomquist in Production recommended someone in another foreman's department. That's when I knew that the Super Person concept would truly work.

Do the Super Person awards really improve the performance of the people? Frank Blasques in Production provides the answer:

"The Super Person awards give people the initiative to go ahead and try to improve their work area, their product, and the quality."

And from Fred Weiser in Maintenance:

"What's it like to win the Super Person award? Great. You get kind of embarrassed at first when you have to get up in front of everybody. Tom tells what you did. Your idea may have seemed stupid at the time but it worked.

"You're being noticed for what you're doing for the company. You feel proud that you've accomplished something. You got it done right. And the people, they notice that."

THANK YOU . . . IN A UNION SHOP?

Oftentimes when chatting with visitors from big corporations, I hear this lament: "You can do all these things; you're nonunion. This 'soft stuff' would never work in a union shop." My answer is always the same: "Go ask Nummi"—the joint venture between General Motors and Toyota in Fremont, California.

Labor union unrest at that former General Motors automobile assembly plant was legendary. For years, wildcat strikes were interspersed with high absenteeism, poor quality, low productivity, and the longest list of union grievances of any G.M. plant. In utter frustration, G.M. finally closed the entire factory.

Several years later, Toyota convinced G.M. to reopen the facility as a fifty-fifty joint venture—with Toyota in charge. Three thousand of the *same* militant United Auto Workers employees were rehired. Here are the results: the highest productivity, the lowest reject rate, the lowest absenteeism rate, the fewest union grievances—of any domestic G.M. assembly plant.

How did Nummi do it? By recognizing the talent and contributions of fellow employees who also happened to be union members. As one of our major customers, you can be sure I was often in their sprawling plant and offices. The changes were easy to see: All the big offices now were conference rooms, preferred parking abolished, and the executive dining room closed.

These physical changes were only a backdrop to more meaningful innovations. Each fellow employee was now an "associate," in title and in fact. Nummi looked upon the work force as a real asset—as a source of innovation and profit improvement. Most important, at least to me: Nummi consistently recognized employee contributions—publicly, and in their paychecks. Simply stated, Nummi said "Thank you."

I'M HELPLESS. MY BOSS DOESN'T BELIEVE IN THIS "THANK YOU" STUFF

Often these same disbelieving corporate visitors will proclaim their personal agreement with our belief in thanking fellow employees. But because their boss is "from the old school," these fellow believers feel that they can't take any such actions at their company.

Our response is simple. Just go do it—now. Ninety-nine percent of our recommended action steps involve emotions, not money. And emotions are certainly within your independent purview as a manager. You don't need the approval of anyone else to proceed in this critical area.

OUR COMPANY'S JUST TOO BIG TO SAY THANK YOU

Is your company's size an excuse for inaction? Be careful; that's a trap. The organization is already in place to execute these new (?) concepts of management, regardless of size. Can we agree that in most corporations, the span of direct reports is about ten or twenty to one? In other words, each supervisor has ten or twenty workers reporting to her. If that's the case, how come we can do it at

NATD with ninety-one "direct reports" versus ten or twenty in Big Corporate? You can start in the morning in your department, division, or company with your immediate coworkers. In turn, your associates can evoke identical emotions, currencies—call it want you will—with their fellow employees. In turn, those people can live these values with their coworkers. And on down the management ladder.

YOU DON'T HAVE TO SAY "THANK YOU" TO SAY THANK YOU

Have you ever received a gift, a token, a gesture—for no reason other than thanks? What were your feelings, toward yourself and toward the giver? The same thing holds true in business with the same impact, with the same results. Sure. You're grateful, grateful that you were noticed. And appreciative of the giver, now, and in the future. The gift may even spark a sense of unity, of companionship. It's not any one big event. It's a bunch of little things, each from the heart.

Once in a while, on no special occasion, I bring each of the women in the office a bunch of roses to say thanks, to show that I appreciate their work, their prowess. I stop at a street-corner stand on the way back to NATD from a customer call. It's no big deal. It's in concert with everything else that we do. And they know it is sincere.

Some experts will howl: "There he goes again, playing favorites." And I do. Often. Our coworkers earn it—and every one of us benefits. One Sunday afternoon, my wife and I were driving through Pebble Beach on the Seventeen Mile Drive. It was gorgeous. Suddenly, a thought popped into my mind: Buy Frank Blasques a golf shirt with a Pebble Beach logo. He is a golf nut. He plays every weekend in San Leandro, California, and regularly shoots an eighty-four. I knew it because almost every Friday we visited together for a few minutes on the plant floor (remember, CBWA). Together we'd guesstimate his score for the next Sunday. Then we'd touch base early the following week to see how he did. It became a tradition between us, something to kid about—a bonding, if you will. I cared about him. I was interested in him as a person.

You should have seen and felt his appreciation when he opened the gift box. We both knew what I was saying; it didn't have to be spoken. He was family.

HOW MANY PEOPLE— FOR DINNER?

Try this sometime. You'll have a ball and so will your associates, with lasting results—if the motivation's sincere. Go out yourself and buy dinner for the entire night shift. They are the forgotten work force of your company. Brush aside all the straw-man arguments against it—logistics, cost, liability, equality (what about the day shift?). Just go do it.

It all started innocently enough. We mentioned earlier that our fellow employees at NATD look like the U.N. Purely by chance, the night shift is populated primarily by people of Filipino extraction. When we meet, you'll readily see the results of one of my hobbies—food. While CBWA at night, I'd often plop down to visit in the lunch room during dinner with the night shift. Sometimes I'd beg a taste of their special Filipino food. It's delicious. One night I got a great idea. Order in Filipino food for the entire night shift as a surprise. A nearby Filipino restaurant was amazed but amenable.

Our timing was crucial. I had to pick up the food and get it set up piping hot in the lunch room, in absolute secrecy. At eight-thirty the group piled in, ready to eat their own dinner. Lo and behold, there was a complete Filipino buffet for everyone. After the initial shock disappeared, so did the food. The group loved it, literally and figuratively. I just wanted to sincerely say thank you to a forgotten segment of our work force.

You know what happened then, don't you? You're right. The Italians wanted equal time; so did the Germans, etc. It was all in fun. But why not do it? Perhaps six months later, I showed up with stacks of pizza for the day shift.

Please don't misunderstand. We don't run around all day effusively thanking each other. NATD's sustenance is profit, and lots of it. That's the focal point of our efforts. Yet there is no reason that profitability cannot coexist with appreciation. So we find lots of ways—spoken and unspoken—to say thank you.

CORPORATE AMERICA AND THANK YOU

Remember the last time your boss praised you? No, not the superficial "Good job, Smith." What I'm talking about here is sincere praise, from the heart, for a job well done. Imagine your reaction. You would be grateful for the recognition, for a sincere thank-you. And you would be determined to earn this recognition again.

In my judgment, this attitude of aloofness toward workers in corporations is pervasive. It stems from a mind-set of superiority that most often starts with the CEO and permeates the entire executive group. "We're better than you; your contributions are negligible; you can easily be replaced. Therefore, there's no need even to acknowledge your presence."

In my travels, sometimes I'll stumble upon an Employee of the Month plaque prominently displayed in an office or lobby. It's so exciting to see—a company that cares! Alas, all too often the last recognition date was December 1960. And what message does that send to all the employees?

In all fairness, some enlightened corporations have instituted gainsharing programs with their associates. I think that's great. Unfortunately, these plans are painfully impersonal and quite rare as you look across the corporate landscape.

A few thoughtful executives still at least send individual letters of congratulations to mark a coworker's employment anniversary. Ken Olson, founder and former CEO of Digital Equipment Corporation, was one such enlightened leader. The list of other CEOs who reach out in this personal way is predictably short.

There's little reason to fault corporations for not adding a human touch in their daily dealings with their employees. The idea of being considerate, thoughtful, and appreciative with their associates probably has never crossed their minds. Sooner or later, people at the top will see the real human needs of their fellow employees and fill them. Then companies will realize the mutual benefits that can accrue.

Certainly these human needs are growing. Aren't you getting very tired of things the way they are, the way they're headed? People seem so rude, don't they? Pushing, shoving—literally and figuratively, trying to get an edge, an extra inch. For what? We see it everywhere. During your commute, invariably someone will cut in line. Some people are rude, selfish, uncaring. "Me first." At lunch, the same thing. Walking down the street, we're bumped, jostled, everybody in a rush, going nowhere, rude and safely anonymous. They're brusque, insensitive, and "looking out only for numero uno," at your expense.

The same climate exists where you work despite the feigned politeness, the automatic frozen smile, the gracious platitudes. What a hollow climate in which to work—and live.

We're so alone today, all of us. We don't even know our neighbor across the hall or down the street. The brief mutual nod of acknowledgment is no substitute for a lasting friendship. There's really no one to turn to—to count on—anymore.

It's so great, finally, to get home after work. You open the door into your own private cocoon—hopefully shared with someone who cares. You close that same door behind you, shutting out all the anger, fear, tension, hassle, and rudeness to be endured each day. You're finally safe. You can be yourself, even if only for a few hours. You share the same values as your partner; mutual respect, simple courtesy, honesty, trust, and caring. These are the linchpins of your relationship.

We create this same environment at NATD. This is our family during working hours, a home where we are among friends who care, who look out for us, for each other. It was Dr. M. Scott Peck who said (in *World Waiting to Be Born*, Bantam Books, 1993), "The glue of civilization is good manners." I think it's true. The small courtesies extended and received throughout our daily lives provide the "lubricant" to ease our way in a turbulent world. A simple thank-you goes a very long way today—perhaps because it's increasingly rare.

In my judgment, corporations can once again fill this growing need for a sense of community. I use the word *again* very deliberately. Think back to our parents' era; think of the role and impact of the corporation in their lives. Remember? Our parents felt a real part of their company. There was a sense of belonging, of benevolence, almost of protection.

There's little question that the brutal dislocations and layoffs have shattered an implicit employment contract. But the need— no, the longing—is still there.

A few corporations will find a way once again to rebuild this bond with their employees. They will learn that sincere appreciation for a job well done, for an act of kindness toward a fellow employee, goes a long way in rekindling loyalty and commitment. The mutual benefits will be enormous.

THE *ESSENCE* OF A NEW PARTNERSHIP— SAYING THANK YOU

1. People desperately want sincere recognition in this increasingly sanitized, homogenized, and impersonal world.

2. People don't work just for money. They seek sincere praise for their accomplishments big or small; praise from their peers, their boss, in their paycheck—and quick.

3. Pay is a form of "Thank you." Equal jobs are not performed equally. Use extra pay as a reward, not an incentive.

4. This broader concept of "Thank you" is the glue of civilization. Encourage it, foster it, as an automatic, instinctive response, not as a device.

5. You don't need anyone's approval to say "Thank you"— sincerely.

6. In a large organization, use the existing chain of command to implement this New Partnership. The CEO of a major company can't easily compliment the guy on the shipping dock, but the person's supervisor certainly can.

HOW *YOU* CAN BUILD A NEW PARTNERSHIP BASED ON SAYING THANK YOU

1. Get your group together and seek out their thoughts and ideas to foster employee recognition.

   • Listen—hard—to their ideas.

   • Go with their suggestions only if you truly believe in the concept and the execution.

   • Limit each Super Person award group to one hundred employees.

2. Develop different award systems for foremen and first-line supervisors.

   • Be sure these awards are based *only* on merit.

   • No politics allowed.

   • To be sure, get involved—personally.

3. Celebrate your fellow employees' anniversary of hire.

   • Make it an event for everyone to see and to share.

   • Rebuild a sense of family, a sense of longevity with the company.

   • Do something symbolic to dramatize this event.

4. Look for lots of small, sincere ways to say "Thank you": not as a device, not as a motivational tool, but as an integral part of everyday living, at work and in life.

5. Every single time you get a sincere compliment from a customer, tell your coworkers. Better yet, ask the customer to tell everyone in person.

6. Do it—now. Don't wait.

CHAPTER TEN

Less Is More

A Lesson from Architecture . . . for Business?

S everal years ago I picked up a book in an airport. One chapter described the Bauhaus school of architecture during the Weimar Republic in 1923. The phrase that expressed this architectural style was striking: "Less is more." It's also a pithy description of our management style at NATD. "Less is more" describes every facet of our operation.

Sustained growth in sales and profit at NATD is dependent upon the concept of critical mass—*except in reverse*. Small is lean; small is efficient; small is fast; small is profitable; small is fun. Here's what I mean.

SMALL IS LEAN

As we grew dramatically in sales and profits, it was surprising even to me how little our operation changed, either in organizational structure or emergence of staff jobs. Perhaps the primary reason for this is that we are always on guard against the vestiges of bureaucracy.

During our tenure at NATD, there were never more than three layers of management between our coworkers and me. In reality, there were none. Remember, "We are all bosses." Fewer management layers tend to minimize bureaucracy. And we were obsessed with keeping it simple.

Over the years, NATD's new hires always increased at a lower percentage than our sales gains. As a result, our dollar sales per employee skyrocketed. Generally they were about four times higher than the industry average (according to *RMA Annual Financial Statement Studies*; see reports for 1980–90).

We soon discovered the reason. When we let our coworkers organize their own work and do it in their own way, we were surprised to see what they could accomplish. Good people who care truly enjoy doing more. They like to stay busy; they like to accomplish things. This is a whole different mind-set from "You had ten people in this department before; now you have to make do with three."

Certainly Janie Johnson, who works in the office, exemplifies our premise. Here are her job assignments starting as a new hire and evolving over a two-year period:

- receptionist

- receptionist and typist

- receptionist, typist, and travel

- receptionist, typist, travel, and general office

Day after day, Janie was unfailingly nice, helpful, and efficient. She wanted to contribute. She was proud of doing a good job. She liked to stay active. She knew her work was important to the company. We told Janie that, again and again.

Overhead doesn't generate profit. As a result, I was adamant never to hire staff people. We had no assistants, administrators, analysts, or expediters. Each of us at NATD is responsible for our own staff work. I've heard again and again the rationale: "Your staff functions to 'free you up' to manage." Sorry, that's not true. If the task's important, do it yourself. If it isn't, don't do it at all.

Here's just one example.

Since there were no staff departments at NATD, I faithfully and laboriously wrote (by hand) our annual business plan. You know the exercise—the standard five-year, three-year, and one-year versions. Not unlike my experience in big corporations, I repeatedly saw how *ineffective* they were. (That hurt—these were *my* pearls of wisdom.) Our competitive world often changed before the ink was dry. All too often, some major and unexpected development would completely change most of our primary operating premises. So I just stopped this futile annual exercise. We knew our basic objectives, our long-term strategy; those didn't change. We just "cut and fit" and went forward. Here some management experts will rejoice and call this "being flexible." In my simplistic mind, you do what you have to do. And it worked, year after year. There simply is little need for staff, who continuously massage the numbers and update the strategy just to keep their jobs.

There are those who argue on behalf of the "assistant to" system. It is their thesis that "assistant to" jobs provide a wonderful background for future advancement. I don't agree. You learn much faster by doing than watching.

With small and fluid "work cells," there is no need for expediters. Just-in-time (JIT) delivery fosters Just-in-time production. You know where you are on every shift. The group in production acts as self-expediters if there is ever a last-minute need. Administrators are an anathema. Administer what? If you're doing your job, you're administering already. So why bloat the payroll and slow down decision-making?

SMALL IS EFFICIENT

My personal transformation from a corporate senior vice president to a scrambling entrepreneur was a real revelation. It soon became abundantly apparent that NATD operated surprisingly well without the necessary corporate trappings. First of all, I didn't have a secretary, private or shared. No one did. The job simply wasn't a necessity for our survival. I sure didn't care about the accompanying loss of status. Besides, we couldn't afford it. When it's your own money, it's wonderful to watch how quickly your priorities switch.

Having no secretaries led to another change that had a significant impact—no memos, no reports, few letters . . . and no bulging files. I discovered our company functioned quite well without reams of paper. The "to, from, cc" just weren't needed. All the new people we hired were good people who cared. They knew what to do—and just went ahead and did it. There was no need for written direction or confirmation of verbal agreements for future actions. There simply was no reason for a paper trail. These people were pros.

Try to imagine your company without any memos or monthly departmental summaries. Imagine your business day without the meaningless floods of paper that, in reality, do little to move your operation forward. Imagine eliminating all future memos and reports. You'd get along, perhaps even prosper more. We're all aware of that old ruse: Stop distribution of a regular report. Wait and see if anyone misses it. Try the same thing here. No written memos allowed, no reports. You'll be amazed at the results. The amount of freed-up time for everyone will be significant, time that can be profitably spent on the work that really matters in your business.

There is a happy but unintentional fallout here. No more tedious (and endless) written analyses of meaningless business history; no more monthly and/or quarterly reviews of plan versus actual performance. Would you believe . . . almost no meetings!!! Every month at NATD, you quickly know your sales and earnings. The rest is superfluous.

Speaking of meetings, they are scarce at NATD, because of our small size. If you start with good people who care, and treat them the way you want to be treated, there's little need for meetings. Everyone knows the objective; they just go and do their thing to accomplish it. Sure, we wander over to Jim, Allan, or Joan. Yes, we meet—but it is stand-up and immediate. It is on a specific issue and solution-oriented. That's all we need, then we go on about our regular job.

There are only three regularly scheduled meetings at NATD: our weekly hot sheet meeting, our monthly job costing analyses, and the Super Person of the Month award. Each serves a specific and actionable purpose.

The hot sheet meeting includes key coworkers from each department. The status of every "hot" production job is reviewed to uncover any bottlenecks and to coordinate all our efforts to ship on time and with no rejects. Duration? Perhaps two and a half hours.

Our monthly job costing analyses session is attended by the same group. Here we review jobs that are not generating acceptable profit margins. The group analyzes the entire production process, looking for some clue that will highlight the core problem with the job. Then our coworkers take on mostly self-imposed assignments to fix the problem. Duration: two hours.

SMALL IS FAST

As we discussed earlier, there is no policy manual at NATD. In my opinion, good people who care inherently know the difference between right and wrong. They certainly don't need a rule book to prescribe their actions at work. Without the policy manual, there is no ponderous set of rules to impede us; there are no written inhibitions to try new ways; there is freedom to innovate in any arena—and fast.

We do have an organization chart at NATD—but it is one in name only. Our associates' manufacturing operation is so wonderfully simple and fluid that rigid organizational lines of responsibility just don't work. Sure, we have a plant manager and appropriate foremen, but that is about it. With work groups involving people from all over the company continually forming, dissolving, and reforming, the blurring of organizational boundaries is a happy fact of life. As a result, the traditional departmental walls came "tumblin' down." We can move fast.

Here's one example.

About nine o'clock one evening, Nummi (a major automotive manufacturer) called us in a complete panic. Their day-shift inventory-control department had forgotten to order for that evening's delivery from NATD. They'd be out of our parts in three hours and the entire production line would stop—at a cost of $600,000 per hour.

After Tom Parrnelli in Quality Control hung up, he got his

coworkers together. The press-room people stopped their scheduled work, set up a new line—all on their own—and manufactured enough automotive parts to tide our customer over. The group in assembly dropped their regular duties and packed up these components. Tom delivered the needed parts in his own camper—just two hours later, at 11:00 P.M., and without any paperwork. Our coworkers were able to turn on a dime to meet Nummi's sudden need. Small *is* fast.

SMALL IS PROFITABLE

Remember Joe Louis, the legendary World Heavyweight Boxing Champion? Remember his famous quote after the Billy Conn fight? "He can run, but he can't hide." Same thing's true in a small department, profit center, or company. It's simply easier to find out potential profit improvements in a small operation, in both office and plant. They can't hide.

One day engineer Larry Vosner found a major source of profit improvement at NATD that had been hiding for years. All our punch presses operated at one hundred to two hundred strokes per minute. That's the way we always had done it. No one ever thought to challenge this procedure—except Larry. One day a group of us were visiting during the coffee break. Innocently, I asked Larry what he would do differently if he owned the company. His response was immediate: "Run the punch presses at their rated capacity." I was shocked. I had assumed (and isn't that a dangerous attitude?) that that's what we were doing. Later that day we asked the hot sheet group the same question. At first we were met with a vigorous defense of our long-standing tradition. Everyone seemed a little embarrassed not to have thought of this better way. Slowly the direction of the session changed from defending the status quo to "Well, maybe." I suggested that Larry pick a couple of associates to analyze this opportunity for major profit improvement.

Several weeks later we reconvened. The mood of our coworkers was somber. Their recommendation was simple and straightforward. About 90 percent of our punch presses could run at least twice as fast as before but . . . they would have to run unattended! The entire operation would be automated. There would be no one to watch for unexpected problems. If the coil feeding into the press shifted one or two thousandths of an inch (less than the thickness of one human hair), thousands of manufactured parts would then be scrap. If the coil inadvertently jammed in the press, the ensuing raw material buildup would smash the die. NATD (along with our customer) could be out of production for weeks. I decided to table that decision. It was too scary even to contemplate.

About four months later, I returned from a business trip to Japan. For three weeks I toured our customers' plants and those of their major suppliers of stampings and subassemblies. In every factory I visited, it was the same. Almost every punch press was running at high speed . . . unattended. Larry Vosner was right. I was wrong—too cautious, as usual.

Slowly, carefully, admittedly with great hesitation, NATD stepped up the operating speed of our punch presses. Over time we shifted most of our coworkers out of the punch press area and into other production/assembly jobs. At the outset, there were some harrowing moments: A die would crash, a feeder would jam. But our group would all scramble to make things right—and fast. We had to . . . and everyone knew it. It's still an eerie sight to walk out into the production area and see rows of punch presses running unattended hour after hour. Yet it's comforting to see the significant increase in our profits.

This breakthrough in profitability at NATD took place because we were small. There were few management layers and they existed only on paper. We all thought like bosses and could pull together a team whose members all knew each other to seize an opportunity . . . quickly.

The same degree of flexibility can exist in large companies. Corporate giants such as General Electric are successfully dismantling their hierarchies, layer by layer. The objective is to create small, entrepreneurial business units that can turn on a dime. They're still not as nimble as some of their fleet-footed competitors, but they're also not as lumbering as they used to be. They've learned the hard way that less is more and small is definitely better.

SMALL IS FUN

Here we go again with the mushy stuff. Maybe so, but both our bank and the IRS seem to approve—again and again. If having fun is so important in our personal lives, why not in business?

Because of our small size, we were able to get to know each other. This in turn provided us with three benefits in business. The first benefit is increased productivity. Second, our group members could more readily forge a new partnership, knowing each other as human beings. Third, we could better ascertain the future career path of each of our coworkers in a more relaxed and genuine setting.

That was always enjoyable for me. It's exciting to recognize the talent, accomplishment, and potential of a fellow employee. Your choice of whom to promote will impact that person's future career and the attendant well-being of his or her family for years to come. Because our company was small, I could learn first hand the strengths and weaknesses of each associate. And thank goodness. Otherwise we would have fired Eric Karlsson, the same man—of earthquake fame—whom we raved about at the beginning of this book.

Eric was a great worker: conscientious, dedicated, and caring. His coworkers admired him and his gentle approach. You could count on Eric—except for one thing.

Eric was an alcoholic. He never drank on the job; he never came to work with liquor on his breath or with a hangover. But once a year Eric would disappear for an entire week to go on an alcoholic binge. We never knew when it would happen. Neither did he. Something would trigger it and he'd be gone, unannounced. Since there was no phone in his apartment, we couldn't reach him.

Because we knew and cared about him, we were doubly concerned. More than once he returned to work sheepish and repentant, with a black eye and multiple bruises. This man was destroying himself, and we stood by mute and let it happen. He was a candidate for promotion at NATD. Yet he was his own worst enemy. It had to stop.

I talked to Eric again and again, year after year. Nothing changed. Finally I threatened him: "One more unannounced week-long absence and you're fired." As the months passed, I became sanguine. Eric had whipped his problem. He could become head of the night shift.

And then it happened. Eric didn't show up for work. No phone call, just silence. As the days passed, my resolve stiffened. No matter what his potential at NATD, I'd have to fire him. I had to; I had laid down the law.

Later that week, I was CBWA. My pal Pee Wee Silva in Production, waved me over to her work area. After some small talk, Pee Wee asked me a seemingly innocent question: "What would you do if I were out sick for an entire week?" I didn't even hesitate: "I'd be concerned. Why do you ask?" I didn't even see it coming. "Tom, Eric's sick. Why are you punishing him with the ultimatum of dismissal? Help him."

I was stunned. She was right. I couldn't have been more wrong. To threaten a sick man was unconscionable. Upon Eric's return, I told him of our respect—from his peers, from his boss, and from me. We had a candid discussion about his opportunity for a promotion at NATD and how his actions were jeopardizing it. I asked him to attend the weekly meetings of Alcoholics Anonymous. He agreed.

The rest of this story is wonderfully predictable. Eric whipped his problem with alcohol and earned a significant promotion. The moral of this story is simple. I am convinced that NATD would have lost a super employee with high potential if we hadn't been small in size. I never would have had the opportunity to know him, to see his work, to observe the loyalty he engendered in his coworkers. It may sound strange to relate this story as an example of "Small is fun." I guess you'd have to have been there to see the joyous response of our coworkers when Eric's promotion was announced.

HOW SMALL IS SMALL?

Someone in the audience at my talks often asks, "What's the optimum number of employees to staff a company?" My answer is simple: "How many names of your coworkers can you remember?

Can you recall something about the personal life of each associate? Whatever the total is, that's the right number of fellow employees." In my experience, this criterion will result in an optimum profit center of about two hundred people.

Invariably, the next question always follows the one posed above: "What do I do if my unit exceeds the total of about two hundred people?" Again, my answer is simple: Break up the large units into small units, never to exceed two hundred coworkers. Reorganizing into small units can be accomplished a number of ways. The criteria are endless: by customer, by market segment, by product class, by production cycle. There's one Canadian company, Magna International, whose sales are in the billions of dollars. Whenever an operating group there exceeds one hundred employees, it's spun off into a separate profit center.

Small operating units are great. You can get to know your coworkers as human beings. You can forge a New Partnership much more simply. You can identify and focus on your problems more quickly. You can move faster because there's a much shorter line of communication. You can turn on a dime . . . and win big.

CORPORATE AMERICA AND SIZE

Don't get me wrong. The concept of critical mass in business is valid. The flaw is in its execution. Break up those sprawling operating divisions into *small* business units that are both more responsive and faster. Johnson & Johnson has long had small semiautonomous operating divisions. Hewlett Packard is another excellent example. Unfortunately, these are the exceptions.

In most big corporations, large is slow. The bigger the corporation, the greater the perceived need for control. Policy manuals are developed; systems are devised; procedures are put into effect. The result is rigidity. "We do things this way at XYZ Corporation." Individual initiative is stymied and conformity becomes a prerequisite for success. The status quo reigns supreme. Everything moves at glacierlike speed.

And meetings—oh, the wondrous culture of meetings, the purpose of which is invariably threefold. First, they provide a forum for the posturers and pontificators. Second, here's a platform for the politicians to weave their duplicitous webs. Finally, meetings are a convenient device to defuse responsibility in case of subsequent failure.

In Doran Levin's book *Irreconcilable Differences* (Little, Brown, 1989), Ross Perot summed up the difference between his company, EDS, and General Motors something like this: At EDS, when we see a snake, we get a stick and kill it. At G.M., they'll appoint a committee to study it and two years later, here comes a recommendation for three different ways to kill the snake.

In all fairness, our newspaper headlines repeatedly attest to the fact that layers of management are being stripped away at one corporate Goliath after another. Interdepartmental work teams are on the rise. Yet we have a very long road to go, and so little time to do it.

Staff is a bad word, both in medicine and in Big Corporate. Both are debilitating and hard to get rid of. Some entire departments and individual staff jobs represent needless overhead and don't make any profit contribution. Often, these staff departments strangle any forward momentum in Big Corporate.

Here's one personal example of the viselike grip of a staff department. In my first life in Big Corporate, our corporate parent Esmark (Swift & Co.) *owned* three thousand automobiles. These cars were used by the various division sales forces and the plethora of executives. The vehicle department was a thriving staff function employing perhaps one hundred people. As head of one profit center, I had the naive temerity to tell corporate headquarters that it was cheaper to lease our unit's auto fleet from an outside firm. The wrath of the damned descended upon me. Yet the savings would have been dramatic. Less is more. (Predictably, my heretical recommendation was quickly squelched.)

Small is more fun; big is not. This premise is so sadly true. Anonymity personifies big corporations. It's Mr. Smith—not Joe. The inviolate pecking order clearly delineates whom you can address, and how. No way can the janitor be presumptuous enough even to speak to a vice president—let alone be perceived as having an idea with merit.

Heightened by the recent recession, and coupled with the surge of layoffs, the daily tension is all too real in big companies today. Fear, foreboding, and pressure abound. And that isn't a pleasant place to be. Fun? You must be crazy.

Small is generally more profitable; big is less so. Here I'm not talking about just small versus large corporations but rather the size of individual business units. Time and again we've seen success come to the small flexible unit housed inside massive organizations, in both the military and business. The legendary Skunk Works at Lockheed is one example. It would seem that today more giant corporations are starting to recognize the multiple advantages of small business units inside their massive corporate shell. Why else would IBM have chartered a small independent group of employees to pioneer their entry into the personal computer market?

THE *ESSENCE* OF A NEW PARTNERSHIP— LESS IS MORE

1. Small is beautiful—faster, leaner, of superb quality, more efficient, more profitable, more fun.

HOW *YOU* CAN BUILD A NEW PARTNERSHIP BASED ON LESS IS MORE

1. Break up big organizational entities into small ones.

    - Limit each profit center to 200 coworkers.

    - Ask your associates for their recommendations.

    - If you're far enough along in total repositioning, let your coworkers draft the reorganization.

2. Get rid of the policy manual and organization chart.

    - Break the old mind-sets.

    - Be sure the unwritten symbols are eliminated, too: all the trappings of rank and power, all the rote and ritual habits of the past—at *all* levels.

    - Live your real values—every day.

3. Eliminate all staff jobs. This will minimize bureaucracy.

4. Eliminate most meetings, memos, and secretaries. Tell your coworkers why. They'll understand—immediately.

5. Stop the annual ritual of the business plan.

    - Be sure your basic long-term objectives and strategy are on target.

    - As circumstances change, do what you have to do promptly in order to reach your long-term goals.

6. Challenge yourself and your associates. Grow small. Subcontract out everything that's extraneous to your basic business—everything. Ask the group what is extraneous; they'll tell you.

7. Have fun with your colleagues. They are great human beings.

8. Start now—right now.

CHAPTER ELEVEN

"I'm in Control Here"*

The Pursuit of Power Is a
Dangerous Disease—Destroy It

"I don't understand. He was one of us—a damn good software programmer. Then he got promoted to manager . . . and changed. We used to sit around talking about how stupid some of our management policies were, the endless meetings, never any decisions, treating us like kids, like dummies . . . the power trips, the politics. Now he's different—just like that. Now he's management. But he knows better. Why? Why is he acting this way? I wish we could sit down together and talk—like we used to. But I can't. It's different now. What can I do?"

A software engineer at a major telecommunications company

I t's all too true. This is an excerpt of my dinner conversation last night. What could I tell this man, who is perhaps thirty-five years old? How could I explain his new boss's sudden change in attitude, which is replicated thousands of times a year, year after year, in major corporations all across this country?

The real tragedy is that this is not an isolated instance. Often after I give a talk, someone from the audience will come up and ask

---

* Alexander Haig, Jr., quoted in his *Caveat*, Macmillan, 1984, p. 160.

me for advice on the identical question posed by my dinner companion. "Why do most people change when they become managers?" To me, the answer seems fairly straightforward. People try to copy success, in all its forms. Millions of us emulate movie stars, rock idols, and athletic heroes. We're searching for acceptance . . . an identity . . . a role model . . . success . . . power . . .

It's no different in business. There's probably some psychological name for it. I call it "the promotion syndrome." If you act in a certain way, you'll be accepted. Your boss looks and acts this way. He was promoted. His boss looks and acts in the same way. She was promoted. "I'm going to look and act like them. Then I'll get promoted. I'll be a success. It doesn't take a genius to figure that out."

Power can be a heady aphrodisiac, leading to self-infatuation. "If I'm chosen to be boss, almost by definition I must be special—better than the others." Gradually I start acting as though I believe that.

> "I'm a manager now. I'm supposed to have all the answers, so I must have them—or at least act like I do. My employees, they don't know anything."

> "I'm a manager now. I'm supposed to be a leader. Therefore I must know where we're going—or at least act like I do. How can my employees lead? They work for me."

> "I'm a manager now. I spend most of my time trying to anticipate my boss's needs, foibles, and whims. He'll get me my next promotion. I'm going to take care of him. Take care of the employees? What for? They can't help me to get promoted."

Ah—there's the rub. In today's brutally competitive climate, your fellow employees can, in fact, have a very direct impact on your performance. More and more today, it's their record that counts toward your next promotion—or, perhaps more realistically, toward just keeping your job. Your coworkers' performance is probably your primary hope for survival, let alone a promotion.

There is absolutely no doubt in my mind that our fellow employees are responsible for our sustained success at NATD. They are the ones who achieve 0.1 percent customer rejects. They are the ones who have attained a 480 percent gain in productivity over twelve years. They are the ones who earn numerous Vendor of the Year awards from our major customers.

But our associates could not attain these records at NATD without a dramatic new definition of power and its redistribution to each person. At NATD, *everyone* already has power; therefore no one seeks it.

When our fellow employees all share power, there must be two elements in place for it to succeed: responsibility and competence. Both must work together in tandem. Responsibility and authority without competence result in bad decisions over the short term, and chaos over the long haul. Competence without responsibility leaves individual abilities untapped—and corporate growth stagnant.

But put the two together, and you've got an unbeatable combination. Everyone in the company has the power to do his or her job exceedingly well. Isn't that what you want?

POWER TO THE PEOPLE

When asked "Do you feel you have a lot of power in your job?" Fred Weiser in Maintenance responded this way:

> "Yes, because I like my job. You don't have to be told anything because you know what your job is and you are willing to do it. It's not like you have to have somebody over you: 'You have to do this and you have to do that.' It doesn't work that way here because everybody is willing to do their job because they know what their job is and they do it on their own."

Our associates are also willing to assume the responsibility of power at NATD. All too often, worker empowerment fails because the employees won't take the responsibility for the results of their work. Unfortunately, not everyone will assume that burden.

You can be sure this attitude and atmosphere took a lot of time, effort, and patience to engender at NATD. First, you must have good people who care. Once you've got your kind of coworkers in place, you'll discover a fascinating personal trait of these people. They are not interested at all in the traditional forms of power. These are "giving" human beings—ready to help one another. They enjoy working with others. They value teamwork; they are task-oriented. They have a sense of self-worth. They want power over their job, not over other people. These traits are the antithesis of power seekers.

Of course, we are careful to be sure that this new definition of power is lived by everyone. It makes little sense for the Head Sweeper to abdicate power, only to find that others usurp it for their own purposes. So often today we hear the lament that middle-level bureaucracy is the bottleneck to innovation in business. There are so many people proving they have power that nothing gets done. That's one of the reasons we set the goal of sharing power among coworkers. Everyone has to have the same mind-set. At NATD, the group is in agreement. That's why this new partnership works. No one acts like a boss—because we all are bosses.

This Head Sweeper flipped the organization chart upside down and tossed it out the door. That action avoids any lingering propensity for power trips by the group. Without an organization chart, it's the same as being at Club Med. There's no point of reference. A swimsuit and beads eliminate all the traditional symbols of power and status: You're judged simply as a person and as a professional, which is as it should be. The same holds true at NATD.

By obviating the organization chart, we also defuse any potential battles for turf. The ageless chant "*my* people, *my* department, *my* company" simply disappears. There can be no sniping between departments because, in reality, all departments simply blended together.

Tony Cabral in Quality Control summed it up this way:

> "We all work together here. We're not aware of who works for who. We just want to do the job right."

COMPETENCE

One thing became clear to me once we started down the road to shared power: The more skilled our coworkers were, the more effective they would be. As noted earlier, responsibility without competence gets you nowhere but in trouble. So I began to look for ways to help the group at NATD increase their technical competence.

In the early days at NATD, our competitors used price-cutting as their only marketing tool. They had inadvertently become commodity sellers. No company had a meaningful point of difference— a benefit—for the customer. The competition's concern for quality was almost nonexistent. Endless price-cutting to get the order had eroded any desire to achieve top quality. Everyone was competing for the low end of the quality market.

There was, however, an inviting growth opportunity in the high-quality end of our marketplace for two reasons. First, our competitors' work force had limited technical skills. Besides, their workers were generally dispirited—they were just going through the motions. They just didn't care. Top-down rigid hierarchical management had sapped any desire to contribute, to excel.

The major computer manufacturers were designing fewer and fewer mechanical parts—yet each part was increasingly complex and very difficult to produce. High quality was mandatory. There was our wedge—our opportunity for profitable growth. There was our target market!

But where to begin? It was readily apparent at NATD. The more our coworkers learned their trade or profession, the higher our skill levels would be. As a result, we could then successfully bid on these really difficult jobs from our customers. We would also be able to manufacture them successfully—in very large quantities—and with a 0.1 percent customer reject rate—because our coworkers cared, really cared about their work. We could charge more.

That's it! Our point of difference then would be our associates! They would become a highly trained and skilled work force. In addition, they already cared: about quality, about service, about the customers, about doing their best. Simply stated, we would fill our customers' needs—and in a way that our competition could not match. Only NATD would have our special work force.

The concept was great. At the outset, it's execution was laborious. Again and again I'd urge our fellow employees to go to Chabot Community College nearby, which offered a two-year course in machine-tool technology. We volunteered to pay the tuition of any employee who graduated. Yet no one would go.

Time after time, the excuses were plentiful. "I've got to fix my car tonight." "The Mrs. wants to go shopping." "There's a good movie on TV." Yet I couldn't give up. If we didn't improve our skill levels in production, we'd slowly stagnate—all of us together. I had to help them help me, and each other.

As usual, the answer was simple. If our associates wouldn't go to college, we'd bring the college to NATD. Every Wednesday afternoon at the end of the day shift, Bob Brown, a professor at the college, would teach our coworkers how to improve their skills. They made real production parts on our equipment in the plant. Classes were purely voluntary. Anyone could attend. No attendance records were kept nor were any test grades ever divulged. The arrangement was simple: NATD paid the instructor but not the students. NATD provides the training; you provide your attendance and interest.

Slowly, ever so slowly, fellow employees signed up. Soon the class was filled. Sure enough, at graduation, a new crop of students signed up. And the result? You guessed it: Our skill level also increased. There was a slow realization that we sincerely wanted to help our fellow employees grow professionally. In turn, their increased skill level helped all of us. A budding sense of cohesiveness resulted—an ever so slight feeling of attainment and appreciation. "He wants to help us help ourselves."

As a result, we soon accelerated the tradition of "NATD University" whose "campus" was right in the plant. As our technical skills increased, the foremen and leadmen trained their coworkers. For specialized needs, we sought out the best teachers in the local area and paid them to hold regularly scheduled classes on our "campus," usually in late afternoon, after the day shift ended. The conference room was often turned into a classroom.

On one occasion, Rich Hostetter in the machine shop and several other coworkers requested a course in geometric tolerancing. (Don't even ask what that is—above all, me.) "Sounds fine by me. Just go do it."

"Who, us?"

"Sure, why not? You know more about it than I do." So they did. After contacting the local community college, this group interviewed several professors, analyzed the proposed course content, chose the winning teacher, negotiated his pay, set up the course schedule, and away they went. The results were soon apparent.

That was not a one-time event. After several die makers spent a week in Los Angeles in a highly technical seminar, they returned and set up classes in-house to teach their associates. To further extend our technical competence and competitive advantage, we often purchased state-of-the-art manufacturing equipment—highly sophisticated and automated die-making machines, computer-operated feed lines, technologically advanced punch presses, etc. In every instance, we spent both time and money to educate our coworkers. They responded by learning, by growing professionally—and were paid commensurately.

And I'll be darned. It worked. The increased skill level of everyone, attained through continuing education, was the key element in this deliberate strategy of market segmentation. Alone, at the high end—with top quality, an unmatched work force, and generous profit margins. I like it. And so will you.

ELEMENTS OF POWER

There are four elements of power in organizations: the ability to allocate resources, to make decisions, to gain information, and finally to have the latitude to act. I didn't know all this while at NATD. To me, developing all four elements just seems like the sensible thing to do. I knew our associates at NATD, both personally and professionally. I trusted them. So we did it, and it worked, year after year.

Let's take a moment here to illustrate the application of these four elements of power at NATD.

POWER TO ALLOCATE RESOURCES

I couldn't believe it. That darn crane was seven stories high and cost $4,000 a day to rent. There it stood, outside our newest plant, ready to go. The occasion? Installation of our new punch press with 500 tons of stamping pressure.

The logistics were mind-boggling. The press had been completely built and tested, and then literally cut into three huge pieces, each weighing about twenty-five tons. The delivery service had hauled each segment on an oversized flatbed truck through nine states. The loads were so ponderous that en route, the trucks were prohibited from driving over the weekends. Each state was afraid of possible traffic gridlock.

When the three trucks finally arrived, the giant crane carefully hoisted each section to the top of the roof of our plant. Slowly, ever so slowly, each section was lowered through a new and enlarged opening in our roof (formerly a small skylight).

Down it came, ever so gently. Our group secured the base of the press to four giant shock absorbers—each two feet thick, bolted to the plant floor. Several weeks before, our coworkers had jackhammered up a section of our cement floor and replaced it with new reinforced cement four feet deep!

The biggest forklift in California was rented to lift the other twenty-five-ton segments into place.

A new transformer had to be installed that was the size of a compact car—stood on its bumper. Special wiring was strung from the transformer to the press.

The computer-driven feed line had to be located with the bed of the press and then leveled. Each alignment had to be exact—to within one-fourth the thickness of one human hair.

Who allocated the resources at NATD to initiate, coordinate

and successfully execute this job? Our coworkers—people like David Lopes from Maintenance, Frank Blasques from Production, and Allan Kemline in Engineering. The list goes on and includes co-workers in the front office, in Quality Control, in the die shop. Everyone got involved—except me. I watched in amazement, and with great pride.

POWER TO MAKE DECISIONS

Ever bought a computer? A complicated laborious decision, isn't it? Ever bought an entire system of computers? The ramifications are endless. But we had to upgrade our computers; it was critical to our future at NATD.

Plant manager Fred Ferrari organized a group of coworkers to make the choice. These associates had no expertise in the selection of computers and appropriate operating systems. As a result, they sought the help of experts. Our office reception area should have had a turnstile. Day after day, competing manufacturers traipsed in, laden with their machines, charts, and graphs. Then there was silence. No more meetings, no more presentations. I wondered what was going on.

Realizing their limitations, the group agreed among themselves to hire a consultant. To me, their decision was impressive. They could have faked it; they could have gone on a power trip and spent a lot of money. They had the power to make such a decision. But they didn't—they couldn't. They were fellow employees of North American Tool & Die.

POWER TO GAIN INFORMATION

The computer is a priceless tool in business. You can get all kinds of information. And that can be a problem. Reams of information are worthless unless someone has access to it and then *acts* on the data.

I've mentioned earlier that any coworker at any time can look at the complete production costs of any job at NATD. Our associates have that right. After all, it's their report card. Besides, these same people can improve their performance by analyzing the data. Here's just one example.

Our assignment was to manufacture the entire chassis for Apple Computer. The volume was enormous; so was the potential profit. Month after month, we shipped these chassis without any rejects— and without much profit. Our preproduction estimates, used to develop our price quotation, were not achieved in the plant.

Our coworkers went over our cost data again and again. Each step in the entire operation was dissected as they examined prior production information. In desperation, the gang decided to group all the production units of the chassis into small self-contained modules of workers. In this way, we could minimize the "lost" time involved in moving component pieces between various subassembly areas.

That was more like it. Our profit margins on the job improved. But we didn't realize the primary benefit of the analysis until about six months later. We had inadvertently discovered the enormous benefits of in-line manufacturing—of self-contained production cells. Happily, our profit margins showed a marked improvement.

POWER TO HAVE THE LATITUDE TO ACT

Here's yours truly giving a Super Person award at NATD:

> "You all know who the Tin Man is in *The Wizard of Oz*. Well, who knows who NATD's Tin Man is?" . . .
>
> "Jim Norsworthy—where are you? Come on up here. Here's NATD's Tin Man. Let me tell you why.
>
> "One day I was wandering around the plant and saw Jim oiling each of our machines one by one from a big can, just like the Tin Man.
>
> "Let me tell you why Jim won the Super Person of the Month award. We buy a lot of oil—in fifty-five-gallon

drums—to lubricate our machinery and oil the millions of our manufactured parts.

"Until Jim joined NATD, we just gathered up this used oil and disposed of it—possibly causing hazardous waste and potential harm to the environment.

"Jim had an idea to buy a small recycling unit and refurbish the used oil. He did it and it worked. He not only saved NATD a bunch of money but also helped our environment.

"That's creativity. Here's your fifty-dollar check, Jim. Thank you for a super job."

This may not seem to be an important example of having the latitude to act. The oil recycling unit cost only five hundred dollars. But money is not the issue. Jim Norsworthy was a new hire at NATD. He had only been with us for three or four months when he made this purchase—on his own. He had no authorization. Yet Jim had seen and quickly recognized the way NATD functioned: Just go do it. And he did.

CORPORATE AMERICA AND POWER

Power is the basis of Big Corporate, its primary currency. From the top *down*, the attainment and exercise of power are the very underpinning of many companies. The widespread use of perks as a symbol of power is graphic and tangible for all to see, and they act accordingly. The organization chart is a roadmap of power. It delineates the exact power level of each job, even across departmental walls. You can tell at a glance whether the manager of production planning is higher on the chart and therefore more powerful than the division controller. If there are any lingering doubts, the corporate pay-grade system will pinpoint your place relative to all others in the scheme of power. And you will be expected to act accordingly—muted and subservient or omniscient and superior. Granted, flattened organizations have fewer layers and thus less top-down-type power. Yet in most cases the symbols of hierarchy and power remain.

The language of power in corporations is equally significant. In Japanese business, the subordinate bows first, deeper, and stays bowed longer than the higher-up. Here in America we also have our own nonverbal techniques for recognizing power: who calls the meeting, who's invited (or not), who sits where at the conference table, the selective use of first names, who goes to whose office for a meeting, who's on the "cc list" for your memos—and in what order. All of these acts convey clear messages in the exercise of power in American companies.

What management characteristics have traditionally led to success in most corporations? Here are the adjectives that come to mind: aloof, guarded, politically attuned, conformist, risk-averse, superior, controlling, turf protector, empire builder, power seeker, bureaucratic, paper shuffler. And we wonder why Big Corporate has slowly strangled itself from within—why it's ground to a halt, paralyzed.

Now let's compare these adjectives with the four sources of power: to allocate resources, make decisions, control information, and act independently. Let's examine how each trait manifests itself in many companies.

POWER TO ALLOCATE RESOURCES

To be successful in Big Corporate, many people feel they need to be risk-averse conformists. Ever look at a check written by a big corporation? More often than not, we'll find words like these: "Requires two signatures if over $____"—usually either $1,000 or $5,000. What does that phrase really state to *every* company employee, *every* vendor, and *every* bank? That's right. "We don't trust our people—certainly not the person who signs this check. We don't take any risk on him over $5,000." A risk-averse climate? You decide.

Conformity? In Big Corporate it's a way of life—for survival and success. Remember that Apple Computer TV commercial that aired only once, on Super Bowl Sunday in 1985? There's little need to wonder why it struck a raw nerve all across corporate America. It featured a bunch of faceless gray-suited legions marching mindlessly in a lock-step cadence. They sat down by rote in row after row in an auditorium and were watching a screen where Big Brother was talking. They were completely programmed and mesmerized. A Wonder Woman came running down the aisle, and before anyone could stop her, she threw a huge sledgehammer at the screen and smashed it. That broke the audience out of their stupor.

That TV commercial said it all because that's the way it is.

POWER TO MAKE DECISIONS

Paper shufflers and bureaucrats are legion throughout big corporations (and big government). Decisions wend their way slowly through an impenetrable middle-management jungle. Layer upon layer of checks and balances massage and often emasculate policy decisions.

After a promising start, even the few employee empowerment programs that some corporations initiated are being abruptly halted in the name of the recession. Times are tough, there's less margin for error, therefore all the decisions will—once again—be made at the top.

POWER IS INFORMATION

In order to move up the ladder, many corporate managers become aloof, guarded, power-seeking, and politically attuned. How does this happen?

"Need to know" is a military intelligence term that has found widespread and fashionable application in many corporations. Only those who need to know should have certain information. That precludes most of us from getting it. The arbiters of this charade gather and give power through their choice of recipients of information. If I choose you to be in the know, power accrues to both of us. The players in big corporations use this tool to dispense power. Their political antennae are constantly out, discerning where best to deploy their precious information.

The inner circle who are in the know are aloof, guarding their special knowledge. It gives them power. If everyone knew this information, then the inner circle's power base would be dissipated.

POWER IS THE LATITUDE TO ACT

People who are controlling constrain others' freedom to act. Hierarchy depletes human initiative.

Remember the lament that the late Tennessee Ernie Ford made famous? "I sold my soul to the company store." Those lyrics are relevant even today. When each of us walks in the door the first day of work, we cede power over us to our new corporate employer. We no longer have the latitude to act. Corporate employees must always ask permission by checking with their superior prior to taking action. There can be little individual decision-making, little innovation, and certainly little risk-taking. Layers of management, of committees, of checks and balances, effectively smother independent action.

But it doesn't have to be that way. Remember the secret of power at NATD: Everyone has it already, so there's no need to grab more—or to keep someone else from getting it. Once power is shared, workers focus on leveraging their own empowerment to the fullest. How? By increasing their competence, taking even more responsibility for results, and working together.

THE *ESSENCE* OF A NEW PARTNERSHIP—RESPONSIBILITY

1. Understand how power works at Big Corporate—and avoid the pitfalls.

   • Many employees will emulate their boss, hoping to benefit from the "promotion syndrome."

   • Power means control. It's a need for self-protection and contrived self-esteem.

   • Power can be heady—with resulting delusions of omniscience, superiority, and disdain of subordinates.

   • Organization charts, titles and perks, and specific pay grades serve to identify and reinforce the existing system and structure of power in many corporations.

2. At NATD, power has two elements: responsibility and competence.

   • the desire to accept responsibility for the results of your work

   • the competence to do your job well

3. Power means having power over your job—not over others at NATD.

4. Good people who care don't wield power over others. They like other coworkers and enjoy working together and helping each other.

HOW *YOU* CAN BUILD A NEW PARTNERSHIP BASED ON RESPONSIBILITY

1. Dump all physical signs of power: the perks, the organization chart, the pay grades.

2. Create a new (and sincere) role model for managers— starting with yourself.

3. Forget about power as a control mechanism. If you hire good people who care, you don't need that kind of power.

4. Do it—right now!

CHAPTER TWELVE

Quality: In the Head, in the Heart

"Machines don't achieve zero rejects.
"Systems don't achieve zero rejects.
"People achieve zero rejects—people who care."

Tom Melohn (head sweeper)

I t was sad, yet predictable. The quality experts just didn't understand. It was simply beyond their comprehension, their range of experience, the gamut of their human emotion.

After NATD became newsworthy, the deluge of visitors began. They came from all over the world—Australia, Japan, England, France—and from all across the United States. These were the so-called experts on quality who magically proliferated across the business world during the 1980s. They were eager to learn how NATD achieved 0.1 percent customer rejects. They came armed with calipers and computers, charts and graphs, stopwatches and calculators. More often than not, they came away empty-handed. They saw but they did not see.

Our procedure for these delegations was unchanging. After I met with them for thirty minutes, I turned our guests loose. They were free to wander about the plant, to see whatever they wished, to chat with anyone, to inspect any records. We would generally reconvene one or two hours later to answer any lingering questions.

Almost invariably, our visitors were perplexed, confused, and, yes, even frustrated. They just didn't get it.

We were not equipped with the latest and most sophisticated quality control (QC) equipment. Our procedure manual to ensure quality was standard. The ratio of NATD floor inspectors for quality was woefully insufficient—according to these QC experts' formulas. And the size of our QC department was certainly not commensurate with our sustained quality performance.

That was the nub of their oversight. Their examination criteria did not include the human factor. At NATD, that's all there is.

You can be sure that wasn't always the case. At the outset, our customer reject rate was around 5 percent, about par for our industry. Sure, we had a QC department. Everyone at NATD knew that quality was the responsibility of that group. It certainly was no one else's job. Production workers just made the parts. It was up to the Quality Control Department to inspect and find the good ones. Those were shipped to the customer. Our rejects were either reworked or scrapped.

There were two strong incentives to sharply reduce our reject rate at NATD. Quality was the centerpiece of our strategy for growth. Simply stated, we filled our customers' primary need: no rejects. Yet there was a second motivation to radically improve our quality. And that's called profit.

It didn't take a rocket scientist to figure out that for every percentage point reduction in rejects, there would be a corresponding increase on our income statement, in our profit—point for point. In other words, in our early years, we could literally double our pretax profit if we simply cut our reject rate in half. Even I understood that. The question was: How do you do it?

QUALITY THROUGH PEOPLE

In theory, we had two options to improve our quality: equipment or people. We chose the latter because we didn't have the money to buy all the test measurement systems. In retrospect, I'm overjoyed that we were "poor." We turned to our associates for their help. It seemed to make sense. Each of us would be responsible for the quality of our own work, be it in the office or the plant. Each of us would also be responsible for checking our own performance. Our Quality Control Department would be there to help, not to police us.

Our focus on the quality goal of no rejects showed up in a number of ways. First, we make sure our people completely understand the requirements of a job before we take it on. That means collaborating with our customer's engineers to be sure we understand the blueprint, can verify its accuracy, and know what they are trying to accomplish with the part. We also quote the job in the shop and in the office separately. The engineers talk with the department heads in Production on the shop floor to get their input on how best to make the part.

We get the toolmakers and the engineers together so they can work out the best way to build the part and decide what the bid should be. They work as a team so if there are any problems down the road, they're already cooperating, not finger-pointing.

We discovered a number of truisms during our quest for quality. First, quality is *not* the responsibility of the QC department. If you wait for QC to uncover your rejects, it's too late. It's a little bit like speeding and the traffic cop. When he gives you a ticket, you were already speeding. A better idea is to avoid speeding at all. The same holds true with quality. The best method to ensure great quality is to prevent rejects from ever being produced. And that's where our coworkers come in—at both your company and mine. Be it manufacturing or service, office or plant, sales or service personnel, the underlying principle is the same.

> "Quality doesn't come from TQM, TPC, SEX, or SPC. Quality's got to be here . . . in the head, and here . . . in the heart of every fellow employee . . . or we're dead."
>
> *Tom Melohn (head sweeper)*

All our fellow employees are good people who care. They want to do good work; they want to do their best—every operation, every shift, every day, every night. Tom Parrnelli of Quality Control comments:

> "If we can't get quality parts, then we have nothing. It's not so much an outside pressure, as within ourselves to get quality parts out the door."

Our coworkers had no knowledge of or experience in QC measurement tools. As a result, Joddy Lam and Tony Cabral in QC developed a course to teach our group. It was slow at first. In effect, each fellow employee was being trained to be a "traffic cop"— trained to turn themselves in. Yet once our associates realized the faith and trust we had in them, the learning curve accelerated. They were responsible for their own work.

Each coworker feels the same way. You can't toss our parts into bins; they are too fragile. You can't stack our parts to save space on the plant floor; the weight would distort them. You can't throw cartons of parts on our trucks; that would bend them. This attention to detail permeates NATD. We even bought extrasensitive shock absorbers for our delivery trucks to cushion the ride. But beyond anything else, your coworkers have to care.

Although I espouse turning the organization chart upside down, quality is one key dictum that has to start at the top and be sustained—unerringly. Teresa Bettencourt made some observations about the ongoing attitude about quality at NATD:

> "It's not just that Tom wants a lot of production out, which I'm sure he does. We are in business to make money. But he is very big on having the job done right, more so than 'Go fast!' 'I want the job done right'—This is very important with him. The people here realize that his is the best way to work on things, to do it this way, and, in return, we're treated really good. So I really enjoy working here."

Our only objective for the people on the shop floor is "no rejects." I reinforce that in every way I possibly can. I drive people out of their minds repeating it. Every Super Person meeting stresses quality. Most of the awards are for it. Special awards are accompanied with something like, "Do you realize that Karl tripled production on this? And with no rejects." I never let our group forget the importance of quality.

Actually, it didn't really take a big selling job to convince our fellow employees that quality was the right way to go. It was in happy harmony with one of their basic human values: to do your best.

Vera Ornellas in Production put it this way:

> "Our reject rate? It's very, very low. And we are proud of that. But then again, that's because we care. We don't want to put out anything bad, so we don't."

There's a sensitive point lurking in the quality issue. Often I hear the lament "Look, 'my' people are illiterate, uneducated, sometimes foreign-born. They make a minimum wage. They have no skills. How can they care about quality?" My answer is invariably the same: So what? What does any of that have to do with quality? Are these decent human beings? Do you all share the same basic values? Are they honest? Trustworthy? Do they care? Are they willing to work hard—to learn? If so, hold on to them. They already care about quality. You can see their concern for quality in their own possessions, however modest. Look at the toolkits of these workers. You'll find their tools are clean, well organized, and cared for. Look inside their cars. The cars may be old; they're probably second-hand. But I'll bet money they are neat inside, clean, and well maintained.

In my experience, there is absolutely no correlation between an individual's innate concern for quality and her education level, pay, country of origin, or intelligence. Let me cite several actual examples here within the fold at NATD. In Production, you should see Jeff Taylor-Weber's pride, caring, and accomplishment in setting up dies to run in our punch presses. They have to be perfect—or he won't stop working. From time to time I have to shoo him out of the plant, hours after his shift is over. No, he isn't trying to pad his overtime pay. Invariably, he has punched out (the time clock) at the close of his shift. This is all on his time.

Although I never looked, I'm sure Jeff probably didn't finish high school in his native Indonesia.

Ku Park in Production joined NATD soon after his arrival from Asia. He took English courses at night at the community college and then earned a high school equivalency certificate. In three years he saved enough to buy his own home. The day he became an American citizen, we all celebrated. His innate concern for quality? Let's put it this way. I call him "Eagle Eye." And that is no accident. Often he can spot a reject part without even measuring it. He cares.

Perhaps the most telling story to illustrate the premise that quality people come from all walks of life—from all levels—involves a "little old lady." His name was Bob Milan. He was head of QC at NATD when we bought the company and retired about five years later. Bob was self-taught. He had never completed high school but was very proud of his educational achievements—in trig, calculus, electricity, blueprint reading, dimensional tolerancing, the entire gamut.

But that's not what made Bob great. His coworkers called him a little old lady. In this context, however, it was a term of endearment. Simply stated, Bob cared a lot about quality. It was part of his makeup. Here's the most famous example of Bob's commitment to quality.

The phone rang late one afternoon, about ten minutes after the close of the day shift. It was the head of QC at Xerox, our biggest customer at the time. And he was mad. "Bob, get over here—now. You've got a bunch of rejected parts. My measuring machine says they're out of tolerance. Our production line will soon be completely stopped because of your mistakes." Ever unflappable, Bob went home, had a sandwich, and then drove over to our customer's plant with his spouse, a housewife, not an NATD employee. Yet she painstakingly sorted out each NATD part. Bob, in turn, carefully measured each one to determine the error. There was no NATD error. The customer had measured our parts "upside down."

But the story doesn't end there. Bob and his wife stayed at our customer's plant until after 10:00 P.M. They wanted to help—they wanted to be sure our customer's quality problem was solved.

And they did—together. The next morning Bob reported to work promptly at seven o'clock. The customer called later that day, very apologetic and somewhat in awe of Bob's commitment to quality. At the next Super Person meeting, we invited a surprise guest— Bob's wife. I presented two special checks that day.

QUALITY: THE CUSTOMER PERSPECTIVE

It's critically important constantly to reinforce your beliefs about quality with your associates and with your customers. Words aren't enough; *only* action—consistent action—says it all. Again and again I try to find new ways to reaffirm quality as a cornerstone to our continued success. Every quality report we receive from our customers is read at Super Person meetings and posted on our bulletin boards for everyone to see. It is our report card.

We invite our customers to come over at any time. We ask them to bring over their latest new products. Invariably our coworkers' response is the same. Once the cover is off the new machine, once the group can see its inner workings, they get enthused. "There's the part I make." "There's the assembly I work on." "Now I see how my part fits in." It is priceless—for the customers and for us. The empathy, the teamwork, the sense of belonging leads to even greater awareness of the need for top quality at NATD.

One time we rented a shiny yellow schoolbus. We took some of our group at NATD over to see Hewlett Packard's new production line in Silicon Valley. We had just been awarded a very nice new order. This plant tour was an eye-opener. We saw how and where our manufactured parts would fit into the customer's new machine. Once again, we saw the critical need for quality. Back at NATD, a number of fellow employees commented on the importance of that visit. Each person felt an empathy with the customer; each one felt a responsibility to do his or her best.

Living your values—in this case, quality—is equally important with your customers. Here is a comment of Tom Curtis, an engineer at Apple Computer:

"I think the last time we've seen a failure from NATD was a couple of Christmases ago. It was the result of a change of weather that caused some rust problems. It's hard to find quality problems from NATD. Of all the products that come into our warehouse, I don't know of another supplier that performs better."

Every chance I get, I talk quality with the buyers at our customers'. Until recent years, buyers have been trained to be adversarial. It was their job to get the lowest price. That's how they were measured. My job is to help them understand that their real objective is to buy at the lowest total cost, not at the lowest price. Quality is a primary ingredient in the difference. Remember, at NATD we like to compete on our terms—our strengths—and not on our competitors'. And quality is NATD's critical point of difference.

From time to time I send a letter to each of our customers and prospects. Over time, this list of names has grown into the thousands. I sign each letter individually. All the subjects are newsworthy, but our favorite one is quality. Again and again I remind our customers and prospects of NATD's quality record. Quite often I include an actual performance evaluation of NATD by a major customer. This added realism hopefully heightens our credibility.

One time we got a pair of pristine white gloves in the mail from Hewlett Packard in response to one of my letters about quality. At first, I couldn't figure it out. Then I remembered. They were responding to one of my regular letters. One year, after the close of our fiscal year, I had been pawing through our financial reports, looking for areas of possible improvement. One entry struck my eye. Glove purchases: $5,796.25. Almost six thousand dollars for gloves? What was going on here? The folk in Accounting gave me the answer in no time. Our colleagues had used 4,636 pairs of gloves that year to protect their hands. It seemed like an absurd total. Yet once I understood their use, it all made sense.

Then I got a big idea: Let's use these gloves as a symbol of quality at NATD. The next letter to our customers and prospects had gone something like this:

Dear Joe,

When we manufacture your parts, we care so much that we handle them with "kid gloves." Last year the employees at NATD used 4,636 pairs of gloves while producing your products. Perhaps that's why NATD's customer reject rate is 0.1 percent—all parts, all year, all customers.

We care.

Sincerely,

Tom Melohn
Head Sweeper

Sure enough, a group of engineers at Hewlett Packard promptly responded to my letter with one of their own, signed by five or six of their decision-makers—and they included that pair of gloves. Their letter to NATD read along these lines:

To the employees at NATD:

Here's a pair of gloves numbered 4,637. Please use them only on our production.

Keep up your great job in quality.

Sincerely,

HP engineers

I posted those gloves and that letter for all to see. Today I still have that pair. Obviously, my letter created a lasting impression on Hewlett Packard. That pair of gloves had the same impact on me— and our coworkers. And that is all that matters.

SERVICE QUALITY

It's a normal assumption to think of quality only in connection with production when you work at a manufacturing company. Yet quality is equally important in every other facet of the organization— the front office, field sales, whatever. If a sense of quality permeates your company, because it's staffed with good people who care, it will be evident in everything you do—inherently. At NATD, our associates in the office are great. Quality isn't a buzzword with them; it's their way of life. Quality is an automatic part of everything they do. That's just the way they are.

Our outside accountants used to berate their counterpart at NATD. "Look, it's good enough to balance the general ledger to the nearest thousand dollars. It just isn't worth the extra effort to be perfect." Our accounting person couldn't agree. It's not that she wouldn't. She couldn't. That's not the way she was raised. It just isn't part of her makeup to settle for good enough. The numbers have to be right, to be accurate. So much is dependent upon her calculations; they impact everyone's job. As a result, she is even more conscientious.

The same holds true in our computer operation. Gloria Bega inputs all day, every day, day after day. The monotony of that job would have driven me crazy. Yet Gloria is motivated every day. Why? Simple. She wants to do her best. She is so proud of her consistent accuracy.

Field Sales is the same way. More than once our sales people have delivered parts themselves, in their own cars, in an emergency. We *have* to be on time. It is part of the deal. NATD fought too hard to get our reputation to have it blemished with late delivery. That's all part of quality.

There's little question that top quality pays big dividends, but here's one bonus that surprised even me. Happily, both our workman's compensation and employee health insurance carriers were startled, too. Our colleagues don't get sick. Our coworkers don't often get hurt. No, we don't have a bunch of physical fitness fanatics. They are regular people, and that's the key. They care about themselves. They are quality people and treat themselves in a quality way. One day early on I watched die maker Ed Nordhausen wrestle a heavy die set around on the floor. He did it in a unique way. He stooped down to lift it; he didn't bend over from the waist. When I asked why, Ed's answer was right to the point: "Tom, if I don't stay healthy, my family doesn't eat. I lift that way to protect my back." Our insurance company was happy to pay NATD record refunds on our premiums each year because of our low injury rate.

Their total payments to all the people at NATD for medical-care reimbursement were minimal, year after year.

Have you ever seen a vice president of a worldwide insurance broker in shock? Ever seen a man's facial expression change from derision to amazement? You should have been there. One day we were reviewing our insurance coverage. Peter Kautz, our agent at Alexander & Alexander, commented on the escalating costs of health insurance. He remarked that so many workers today feign illness to collect sick leave. My response was "Not at NATD." Peter seemed doubtful as he looked up the performance of our associates. When Peter saw the performance records, his expression suddenly changed. He looked up, smiled, and said, "They really are quality people." And they are.

CORPORATE AMERICA AND QUALITY

Managers today often just preach quality; they don't live it—every day. To use a current phrase, "They don't walk their talk." We all have twenty or twenty-one shipping days in each month. Here's what so many employees elsewhere hear every month from their boss:

Shipping Day 1	"No rejects. That's an order!"
Shipping Day 6	"No rejects. That's an order!"
Shipping Day 12	"No rejects. That's an order!"
Shipping Day 16	"No rejects. That's an order!"
Shipping Days 19, 20, 21	"Ship it. Ship it. We've got to make budget!"

Fellow employees see this hypocrisy every month. And they know. They know that we in management speak with forked tongue. They don't trust us. They don't respect us. They don't like us. And that, you'll agree, is not a productive work environment.

I'm really worried that the legion of statistical soothsayers will once again divert the attention of big companies. Mesmerized by statistical equations and piles of computer printouts, many companies have adopted other fads in the search for quality: statistical process control (SPC) and total quality management (TQM). These are the panaceas for solving all quality problems.

I have nothing against SPC or TQM. They are productive tools in the arsenal of approaches to quality improvement. Yet, like everything else that promises an instant fix for all your problems, SPC and TQM aren't cures at all.

In twelve years at NATD, we learned that gains in quality—just like productivity—don't occur in quantum leaps. It's a little bit here, a little bit there, one day at a time. Perhaps we could liken quality gains at NATD to Ohio State's football offense under coach Woody Hayes: "Three yards and a cloud of dust; three yards and a cloud of dust." Nothing dramatic, certainly no sensational break-throughs. Quality gains at NATD were the result of grinding it out every day and sticking to the basics. And the real taproot are the people: good people who care.

The "Sigma" devotees also rely on calculators, computers, graphs, and charts. But there's nothing in their equation for the most powerful tool of all for quality: good people who care.

Reengineering promises to create a revolution in corporate America, as long as companies are willing to start with a clean slate. What does that involve? Nothing less than a total redesign of all processes within a company—everything from how global customers are served to how local bills are paid. The desired end result is higher quality and productivity, lower costs, and more satisfied customers.

Sounds too good to be true. And it may be. When reengineering is accomplished by waves of downsizing, short-term quality gains are likely to vanish in the face of long-term burnout and loss of morale.

Another source of quality improvement is the self-directed work team. Here staffing principles encompass cross-functional personnel and team members drawn from different hierarchical levels. Huh? In plain talk, everyone on the team has different skills; some are bosses, some aren't. In my judgment, the intent here is sound, the results impressive.

Yet interminable meetings are often the hallmark of this team approach to increase both productivity and quality. You can bet that meetings and written summaries will slowly undermine team effectiveness. Just let the people go do it. They are pros; they know what they're doing.

Another magic pill in Big Corporate's instant quality-improvement kit is gainsharing. The concept makes sense. If, through the group's efforts, quality improves, then share any resulting financial gain with your coworkers. Where I have problems is in its execution. Let me cite just one example of what I mean.

Not long ago I toured a manufacturing plant in the Cleveland area. Neat, clean, tidy, and extremely well organized. As we passed a plant bulletin board, my tour guide—the vice president for quality—stopped and proudly showed me the written announcement of their gainsharing program for quality improvement. Next to it were several typed sheets outlining the mechanics of the program. I got all excited. Financial rewards for quality improvement, sharing with their fellow employees—within a major corporation. How great. Then I pretended I was an employee in department 17—how about pay-grade six? Let's see now. Okay, my tenure with XYZ Corporation is—try twelve years. Now let's choose a rate of projected quality gain for a three-month period of 2.35 percent (all permutations carried to two decimal points). "I'm lost. Mr. V.P., can you explain this system for me? All I want to know is how much dough I'll actually see in my paycheck."

After several unsuccessful attempts to figure it out, my host blithely announced his solution. "I'll call someone in the financial simulation department of the Quality Division. They can explain it better than I. Come on, we're behind schedule on our plant tour. Let's discuss the program as we walk. Think of the impact of our gainsharing program for quality—on our profit, on our employees, on our future." Sure.

Statistical process control, total quality management, self-directed work teams, reengineering, and gainsharing programs can all contribute to quality improvement. But the real source of lasting gains is quality people—good people who care. People who take pride in producing perfect parts, or providing impeccable service, are motivated to follow their own rigorous quality control standards. And because those standards come from within, from the head and the heart, they won't be compromised.

THE *ESSENCE* OF A NEW PARTNERSHIP— QUALITY

1. Machines don't achieve zero rejects.
   Systems don't achieve zero rejects.
   People achieve zero rejects—people who care.

2. Top quality comes easily to good people who care. It's inherent with them.

3. There is no correlation between quality awareness and pay, education, or national origin with people who innately care about quality.

4. Quality doesn't cost money. It makes you money.

5. Quality must start with you. You must live your values every day.

6. Top quality is the best sales tool of all. Every customer demands it.

   • Leave the low end of the market (low quality and low profit) to your low-priced competitors.

   • Let them practice intermural hara-kiri among themselves.

7. Quality must be a way of life throughout your company— in both manufacturing and service areas.

   • All departments are interrelated; you can't have high quality in one group and not in another.

   • If one fails, all will fail.

HOW *YOU* CAN BUILD A NEW PARTNERSHIP BASED ON QUALITY

1. You—*personally*—have to *live* top quality every day, every step of the way.

2. Get your group together. Give them only one order: "If it's not right, don't do it, no matter who tells you otherwise—including me."

3. If you don't have good people who care in every area, get them—now. Don't procrastinate; quality isn't important to people who don't care.

4. Get your coworkers together and ask for their help.

   • Have each person think through how they can reduce rejects in their own area by just 10 percent.

   • Let them try their suggestions.

   • Repeat this prescription—again and again.

5. Start now—right now.

CHAPTER THIRTEEN

The Customer Is King versus Howdy Partner

"Unless we can learn to work together as customers and vendors, we cannot succeed. We cannot continue to have a them-versus-us philosophy. You have to work together as a team. You have to promote partnership. That's the only way we're going to succeed." *

Tom Curtis, Apple Computer Engineer

When I arrived at NATD, the customer list was haphazard. Whoever came through the front door was a prospect. As a response to this lack of focus, we soon developed three simple criteria for future NATD customers. First, they had to be growing faster than their total market. Second, they had to be decent people to work with. Finally, they had to pay their bills promptly. Let's have a closer look at the first two criteria; the third is self-explanatory.

From prior experience, we knew our sales increases would be directly dependent upon our customers' growth. There was little sense in aligning ourselves with the plodding workhorse industries in our market area. NATD deliberately sought out growth companies such as Apple Computer, Hewlett Packard, and Nummi, whose critical mass provided the potential for their long-term

---

* Quote from *The New Partnership* (training film), Enterprise Media, Cambridge, Mass., 1989.

financial stability. Their rate of successful new-product innovation assured us of two things: rapid growth and multiple opportunities to participate in their expansion.

In reality, this is merely a variation of the proven 20/80 rule: 20 percent of the customers in almost every business will account for over 80 percent of total sales. All we did at NATD was to concentrate in the computer industry and ride the winners.

The second criterion of NATD's potential customer selection was critical: They had to be decent people to work with. Implicitly, we looked for some of the same values we sought in our own coworkers' honesty, trustworthiness, fairness, and mutual respect. I hoped our customers would become part of the NATD family.

CUSTOMERS AND SUPPLIERS AS "FAMILY"

In my judgment, a long-term business relationship is somewhat akin to a marriage. If you don't both have the same underlying values, you're headed for trouble—and perhaps divorce. Obviously, that's disruptive and expensive for all parties.

Somewhat surprisingly, our concept of external family was well received by a few of our customers. Greg Watson, buyer at Hewlett Packard, observed:

> "Tom really wants his people to be the first line of relationship with the customer. You become almost part of the NATD family. You'll feel it's a family and you—as customer—are just part of that family. You'll feel a closeness with them. It's very different."

Isn't it interesting? Outside of business, when someone likes you, you are more apt to like them. The same holds true in business. We liked Greg's employer. They were straight shooters—in all fourteen divisions. They were great to deal with—fair, honest, and open. They liked our work, our way of doing business. And we liked them. As a result, we'd do almost anything for them. Some cynics would say, "Sure, scratch my back and I'll scratch yours." But it was much more than that.

Here's one example of our rapport. One division of Hewlett Packard in Southern California was in trouble. Their new product-engineering team was worried that a critical part was not manufacturable. They came up to NATD for a work session with our group. As it happened, I was out of town. After brainstorming possible design modifications, both groups agreed to reconvene in about ten days. Clare Stevens and his die makers decided to experiment on their own. There was no purchase order, no client authorization. His group just went ahead, built an experimental die, and ran some parts. Their brainstorm worked; the part could be manufactured in volume. We shipped samples to the client.

They were ecstatic. The new-product program could move forward. When Betty Gilbert, an HP buyer, asked about the bill, our response was straightforward. "Forget it. We're in this together." Sounds idealistic, doesn't it? Perhaps. But what a great way to work together in a new partnership. By the way, we later received the purchase order to build this part in mass production—and at a very nice profit.

An aberration? Not really. Our customer list was deliberately short. But those clients we chose, we lived with, and for— particularly those that shared our values. Here's another example that illustrates our beliefs about and NATD's response to a good customer.

Alex Nikeshin, a quality engineer at Nummi, tells this story:

> "We had an incident with an NATD part one day. The unit was to 'spec' but didn't fit easily. I called NATD. That afternoon they were down here at 'line side' in our plant. They came down to see and feel what my complaint was. Within about fifteen minutes we had a long-term counter-measure and schedule to fix it. The reason we could move so fast together was because they brought both their tool-maker and quality control man down here. 'It's an easy fix. Let's do it.' That was the end of that. We implemented the countermeasure right then and there. And we lived happily ever after."

Did you know that NATD provides free babysitting as a service to our customers? I didn't either. But we do. Here's what transpired at Sun Microcomputer.

One night the phone rang at NATD at about seven o'clock—long after our associates in the office had gone home. Sun Microcomputer had a crisis. They had run out of our parts. Production was completely stopped. They admitted: "We just blew it. You gotta help us—right now." Happily, we had some of their parts already packed, ready for future shipment. No problem, right? Yet when we called back with the good news, this was the response: "Bring them right over. We'll be here. And be sure to bring the proper paperwork; we can't deviate from our inbound delivery system." Now what?

Larry Curtis, one of our engineers, was working late that night. He called Laurie Thomasy, one of our coworkers in the office who lived nearby, for advice on how to process our paperwork. It was soon apparent she would have to come over to NATD to do the job right. Since her husband worked nights elsewhere, Laurie was with their eight-month-old twin boys. So Larry drove over to her apartment and babysat while Laurie processed the paperwork at NATD. Later, Larry drove back to the plant, picked up the parts and the all-important paperwork, and delivered the cartons to one very happy customer. You can be sure both Laurie and Larry received many accolades—verbal and financial—and for very good reason.

Our partnerships work in the other direction as well. Relations with our suppliers are just as critical as the ones we have with our customers. If a shipment of steel is pitted, bent, or rusty, we can't make quality parts, no matter how good our dies or our people are. The same thing holds true with plating and the components we buy and attach to assemblies.

Joddy Lam, head of Quality Control at NATD, saw the need for a new partnership with our suppliers. He visited each major vendor and told them how important they were to NATD. Joddy showed them what criteria he would use in measuring their work. Most important, he wanted them to know we would send shipments back if they weren't right. We refuse to compromise.

Every time we have a new part that has to be plated, Joddy goes to the plater and says, "Here's what I'm going to measure. Do you agree with that quality standard?" If they do, they sign off and keep one part as a sample. When the finished parts come back from the plater, Joddy has already jointly established the criteria he uses to check for defects. That's something new for them. They're accustomed to the traditional adversarial approach to a buyer-seller relationship, where both sides blame each other if there's a problem—the old "I'll catch you if I can" approach to quality control. But we simply don't do business that way.

I didn't have anything to do with NATD's partnerships with suppliers. Joddy handled it all. In fact, at the outset I didn't even know he was doing it. Joddy was the first to establish the precedent of QC as a friend and helper to our suppliers, years before it became fashionable. He was so nice, gentle, and deft. And he really did want to help. That made all the difference.

KEEPING CUSTOMER SERVICE IN PERSPECTIVE

Customer service is currently a hot subject. But I think we're getting carried away. All too often, suppliers get swept up in their initial burst of enthusiasm after they first "discover" the customer. "Nothing is too good for my customer." "Whatever it takes." Yet unless there is a true partnership, the relationship quickly becomes one-sided—at the expense of the other party. Then disillusionment and the traditional adversarial relationship set in.

Perhaps the philosophy "the Customer is King" was best summed up by the CEO of one of our current customers: "Just remember, we're your sole source of income."

He made this observation at his company's annual meeting with its key suppliers. Although spoken with a light tone, the meaning was clear. His purchasing people soon turned the implications into action. Their checks were slow in coming. The lowest price was their sole purchase criterion. Their product designs changed repeatedly while in preproduction at NATD. The added costs became a significant expense. Guess who was expected to "absorb" these charges—if we wished to "enjoy" their continued business?

Soon it was "plain talk" time. After a candid discussion with their purchasing personnel, we informed this customer that NATD no longer wished to "enjoy" their continued business. It just wasn't worth the constant hassle . . . and reduced profit. They were bullies. It was obvious their one-sided demands would never end.

So often vendors confuse customer service with giving away the store. In an effort to curry favor with their customers, they fulfill the customers' every whim—now, right now. The results are predictable: an ensuing lack of respect and ever-increasing customer demands. Then an attitude of condescension on the customer's part develops, followed by price-shopping elsewhere. Parity within the partnership is nonexistent.

Please don't let me mislead you. Customer service is a potent competitive weapon. In today's marketplace, it has become an absolute necessity. But service means just that—service. Customer service does not mean continued price concessions. In fact, customer service, if it is truly superb, can negate an unfavorable price disparity with your competition.

Perhaps the purchasing agent at Micropolis Corporation summed up NATD's concept of customer service best during a conversation with me:

> "Do you know what you really sell at NATD? Sleep. You guys sell sleep. When I place my orders with you, I know there won't be any problems. None. I can sleep at night."

In retrospect, it would seem that NATD's concept of "family" was our precursor to the partnering that's become so chic in recent years. Ten years of forging partnerships with some of our major customers have taught us some hard-earned lessons at NATD. Partnering just isn't going to happen—it won't be self-sustaining or flourish with mutual benefit—without a lot of hard work and plain talk.

"AND THE WALLS CAME TUMBLIN' DOWN"

The essence of a successful customer-vendor partnership at NATD is to knock down the walls between our two companies. We foster a feeling of family with some customers, working together in reasonable harmony and moving toward a common goal: mutual profit. Not for one minute do I want to suggest that our notion of family works equally well with *all* our customers. It doesn't. But even with those customers who don't totally embrace this idea, our business life together is dramatically improved. At least we can start a candid dialogue to improve overall communication and coordination.

Here are the three major obstructions to a real partnership with the customer:

- restricted information
- power and authority
- nonfraternization

RESTRICTED INFORMATION

As we discussed earlier, information at NATD is readily available to every fellow employee. It just makes no sense to play games of "need to know" and "confidential." Since we pick our customers, they generally are our kind of people. Therefore we work with them the same way we do with our associates: Tell 'em everything. And we do (except profit). It is our hope that the customer will treat us the same way: openly, honestly, as equals.

Big Corporate hierarchy and protocol have long dictated that vendors deal only with the purchasing department. The buyer in turn is the umbilical cord to other departments in the corporation such as engineering, shipping, delivery. ("We've got to maintain control.")

Once NATD earns the trust of our customers, we short-circuit corporate hierarchy and ritual. We go direct at the customer, to whoever can get the job done. There's a difference, though: Our coworkers do it themselves. Our coworkers in Shipping deal with their customer counterparts directly. They share information openly. The same level of cooperation is commonplace in Engineering, Quality, Accounting—everything. The group gets it done, more quickly and with no hassles, by skipping the senseless corporate hierarchy that restricts information.

Perhaps the most startling and profitable example of this direct counterpart interface occurred with Digital Equipment Corporation (DEC) in Colorado. They asked NATD to be a "guinea pig" vendor to test Just-in-time (JIT) delivery to their plant. At that time JIT was a relatively unknown concept. The logistics were formidable. NATD had to develop a system of daily production of their parts. In addition, we also had to arrange the complicated logistics of our delivery each and every day, over a thousand miles away. There could be no mistakes; otherwise their entire production line would screech to an expensive halt. To preclude any problems, DEC had set up an internal joint task force that could act as a clearinghouse and make decisions readily.

Shortly after the beginning of the program, our Shipping Department was a disaster. Phones were ringing continually; daily invoices and shipping information sheets were scattered throughout the area; boxes, cartons, and parts were stacked everywhere.

The problem? The joint task force convened only once a week. In the interim, there was chaos. We were not exchanging information freely unencumbered by corporate hierarchy. Fortunately, Bea Bloomquist, head of NATD's Shipping Department, knew how to get things done outside official channels when needed. She asked me to get her the name and phone number of her counterpart at DEC. Shortly thereafter, the waters calmed, and order rose out of chaos. I didn't ask how it happened—but then, why should I? That was her job—and her counterpart's. Just let 'em go do it together, without the walls of hierarchy and restricted information flow.

POWER AND AUTHORITY

Implicit here is a critical assumption: no power trips or games of authority by either partner. That's the second wall that has to come tumblin' down if the partnership is to flourish.

If I'm the buyer and you're the seller, who's better? Who's on top? Neither, if you're in a true partnership. But you and I both know that for some people, the status or power implicit in their job is their real "pay." "I'm better than you. What do you know? You're just a supplier."

Here's where choosing your customers can be of great value. If you select your customers carefully to reflect your values and see that their beliefs are akin to yours, the propensity for power trips by your customer should be minimal.

There's an interesting sidelight to this JIT story. Once we had mastered the intricacies and nuances of long-distance JIT, we offered our expertise to other customers. A long time ago we learned the adage "Be a go-giver, not just a go-getter." It's always fun (and profitable) to anticipate your customers' needs and then fill them.

Two incidents illustrate this point, which is so critical to the success of partnering. Allan Kemline, our chief engineer, is a competent and thorough pro. He is also a gentle and unassuming man. On one occasion, we received part drawings for a new computer from Apple Computer. These parts were almost impossible to produce in high volume. Allan politely declined to quote on this work. It meant nothing but headaches. The customer's design engineers called, insistent that NATD manufacture them. In a subsequent joint meeting, Allan carefully pointed out the almost insurmountable production problems with the customer's part designs.

I'm sure you're familiar with the "not invented here" syndrome that permeates many big corporations. "If it isn't our idea, it's a stupid idea." Neither Allan nor the customer engineers played that game during their meeting. Apple's engineers quickly recognized Allan's quiet competence. As a result, the group worked together as equals to develop a mutually acceptable design solution. At the meeting's close, Allan was assigned to redesign the customer's parts.

He did, and they were accepted. Our subsequent production orders were completed uneventfully, happily . . . and with comforting profit margins.

Obviously, the key word in that episode is *equals*. The group worked together as equals. Today, smart customers recognize the untapped technical resource available from competent suppliers, who are their equals in a New Partnership. The results for both parties are heartening.

Let's contrast that episode with NATD's experience with a prospect who became a former customer even before he was a customer. Allan and I were summoned to a meeting at a rapidly growing computer company. There we were informed that NATD had been chosen to be their vendor. I got the feeling that we should genuflect or at least consider ourselves extremely fortunate. Their benevolence was dispensed with an air of studied authority.

Allan reviewed their proposed new part designs and found them to be incomplete. Have you ever talked to a wall? Allan has. The customer engineers listened with barely disguised impatience to his technical observations. They refused to acknowledge that Allan's concerns were valid. When Allan offered to help redesign the part, the engineers responded only with condescending platitudes. We left shaking our heads in disbelief. They listened but did not hear. How could they? In their minds, a lowly supplier could not possibly have any competence or good ideas. We subsequently declined their business. I was interested to note the announcement several years later of their corporate demise.

By the way, once our Engineering Department earned the respect of their counterparts at our key customers, we were able to "sell" our technical expertise. Again and again, Allan and his cohorts would hold engineering design seminars at our customers' offices. These two-hour sessions provided an engineering overview of the art and science of our profession. Customers were urged to bring problem part designs to the meeting for review by our engineers. These programs had two objectives. First, we wanted to reinforce our technical expertise in the minds of our customers. Second, NATD hoped to generate new orders by finding an additional way to serve our customer. And it worked, again and again.

NONFRATERNIZATION

The final impediment to establishing a lasting and true partnership is nonfraternization. Even today, there still is an unwritten tradition of an arm's length relationship with your suppliers. By this I don't mean refusing an invitation to a football game or the age-old ritual of business lunches. Instead I'm referring to the lack of continuing interaction between the two companies on an emotional basis. There are very few corporations today who are actively pursuing supplier involvement on this level.

Emotional involvement is a major factor in our personal lives. A sense of belonging in business is an equally potent force. NATD's success is testimony to the impact of this powerful human need. Yet corporations have traditionally avoided any involvement in this area (internally and externally).

Some very perceptive companies today are filling this void with great success. If you buy the premise of family (or partnering) with your supplier, then by definition emotion is an integral part of the relationship. At NATD we saw its power again and again.

The setting: NATD. The occasion: our monthly Super Person meeting. The speakers: the buying team (buyer, design engineer, quality person) from one of our biggest customers.

> "We're from Apple Computer. Tom welcomed our request to visit with you today. Our message is simple: Thanks for doing such a great job for us day after day. Your quality and delivery record is outstanding. Would each of you please accept this pin with our company's logo? You are truly part of our company."

The group at NATD "melted" emotionally. By those simple and sincere words, by the brilliant gesture of giving their company pin to their NATD family, this customer captured our fellow employees' hearts. From that day forward, those pins were in happy evidence throughout the plant. The buying team had formed a sincere emotional bond with everyone at NATD. Their gratitude extended to the people who really make things happen—those on the plant and office floor. In one simple gesture, these three people "humanized" a multi-billion-dollar corporation in the hearts and minds of each employee at an important vendor.

CORPORATE AMERICA AND CUSTOMERS

Contrast that "living" definition of partnership with that of most big corporations today—if they even give lip service to the concept of partnership. The traditional mating dance between companies and their suppliers goes something like this.

First, your customer will suggest setting target prices; that is *their* best estimate of *your* item's selling price. Of course, it's always lower than your current price. Then the guise of annual contracts will emerge. The customer rationale will go like this. You fix your price at X (their suggestion) for X months. In return, they'll give you firm orders for all their needs. Except that these are not firm orders at all. The ruse can take one of two forms. Either the quantities are only estimates or there are no figures at all.

Now let's step back and review the ledger together—the agreement that's supposedly built on mutual trust. What has our "partner" really offered in this contract between equals? Nothing. And you—the supplier? You're legally committed to a fixed price for at least a year, and at a reduced price—regardless of volume.

Incidentally, beware of the information you share. "Please share with us your profit margins by job. We're partners now; nothing should be held back from each other." Soon there will be nothing to share—no profit, nothing. Your customer/partner will dictate acceptable profit for you on his business. Acceptable profit is most often minuscule.

Such a deal!

When these customers are confronted with this duplicity, they act surprised at your indignation. It would be much simpler if this subterfuge were dropped. Instead of posing as partners, let's return to our adversarial roles and proceed from there. Then, if the vendor is lulled into financial concessions, he has only himself to blame.

This adversarial relationship between supplier and customer benefits neither company in the long run. Replacing it with the spirit of partnership opens the door to lasting mutual benefit and enduring two-way loyalty. Then the sky is the limit on what the supplier and customer can create—together.

THE *ESSENCE* OF A NEW PARTNERSHIP— CUSTOMERS

1. When you work with customers who have similar values to yours, you have a better chance of a successful long-term relationship.

2. A business relationship that's equally successful for both parties is analogous to a good marriage. Both parties must nurture it constantly with equal input, honesty, and lots of hard work, if they want sustained success.

3. Customer service is an absolute necessity today just for corporate survival. Outstanding customer service can be a meaningful competitive point of difference.

4. Outstanding service does not mean abject servitude to every whim of the customer. Service means service—not price concessions.

5. A lasting partnership between vendor and customer should be like a family—with open communication (except about profit), true equality, and sincere emotional involvement.

HOW *YOU* CAN BUILD A NEW PARTNERSHIP WITH YOUR CUSTOMERS

1. Choose your own customers. Emphasize your values as you define specific criteria for selection of customers.

2. Don't accept orders from prospects whose values are different from yours. You'll regret it and will pay in the end.

3. Sit down with your chosen customers at least quarterly, in person and across departmental lines.

   • Ask for their criteria of vendor selection and performance evaluation.

   • With "plain talk," find out how you rate and where you need to improve.

4. Then meet with your associates and go over each of these quarterly evaluations.

   • Any pleas of unfair indictments from the customer should be met with a reminder of one obvious reality—the customer is our sole source of income.

   • Your coworkers know how to fix the areas that need improvement. Let them.

5. Resist pleas from the Sales Department or threats from the customer. Repeated price concessions are not an integral part of great customer service.

6. Create a family feeling, a partnership with your chosen customers.

   • Foster it by making the walls between you and your customer come tumblin' down—the walls of restricted information, power and authority, and non-fraternization.

   • Begin at your own company.

7. Start now. Do it now.

CHAPTER FOURTEEN

That's All There Is

How This Management Strategy Generates Impressive and Sustained Profits

"Profit is the name of the game."

Anonymous

There's little disagreement on the subject of profit. All across the world of business, from academia to captains of industry, profit is deemed essential.

Yet there is conversely little agreement on the role of profit as motivation in our daily business lives. Let's visit together for a few minutes about the impact of profit as a motivating force. First, let's have a look at its impact on our fellow employees at NATD. We can then analyze profit as an impetus for change in our daily operations at NATD. Finally, we'll review the impact of profit on top management in big corporations.

THE JOY OF MANAGEMENT

Money has never been important to me. The material rewards purchased with money don't hold much appeal. I want to do my best; I want to create—to build a good company; I love to win.

Those are my incentives. Yet, in the final analysis, it is the joy of management that provides true meaning to my life in business.

I'll kill for an outstanding P&L—that's my report card—but not at the expense of our fellow employees. They create our profit. It is through their effort that we win big financially. No one in his right mind would want to abuse this wellspring of our success.

Have you ever helped someone? Have you ever shared in their resulting happiness and pride when they achieve something special—something important to both of you? It's a great feeling, isn't it? When you do that in business, that's the joy of management.

Here's the key, the very essence of being an effective manager: By helping others, you help yourself. No, not just in the soft and furry arena of helping your fellow man (and no apologies are ever needed for that), but in the brutal reality of business today. We have succeeded for years at NATD by living that belief in the competitive marketplace.

Each day brings a new challenge, to marshal diverse human resources toward common goals. By helping each other, we all achieve our own personal objectives—be it company growth and profit, job security, increased pay, career advancement, or personal expression. That is the true joy of management. That is my "real profit."

I want you to meet Edwin Malveda who works in the machine shop. When Edwin first joined our company, he was about nineteen or twenty years old—a bit shy, perhaps even introverted. Hesitant and tentative in his work, Edwin was fearful of making a mistake.

Over time and with the tutelage of Joe Rosario and Rich Hostetter, also in the machine shop, Edwin slowly blossomed, both personally and professionally. About the same time, Hewlett Packard came to NATD with a tough machining and assembly assignment. Four successive suppliers had failed because of the exceptionally stringent quality requirements.

We took on the job. The challenge was just too tempting. Edwin's assignment, final assembly, was critical. Looking through a huge magnifying glass, Edwin used a jeweler's file to remove minuscule metal particles from the interior walls of the unit. It was tedious and yet delicate work. Edwin became a star in this task. Day after day, he looked like a doctor doing microsurgery. We had only one reject in three years. On more than one occasion, the senior engineer on the project at Hewlett Packard, Dave Simmons, came down from Spokane, Washington, just to compliment our group—and Edwin in particular. It was a joy to see Edwin receive this recognition. It was even more satisfying to see him grow, in his job and as a person.

For me, the psychic income was enormous; that was my "profit."

PROFIT AND OUR FELLOW EMPLOYEES

> "What he's done here at NATD is put key people in critical departments and give you free rein to do what you want. It's like having your own business."
>
> *Clare Stevens (die maker)*

"It's like having your own business." Think of the profit that could be generated in your department, division, or corporation if every fellow employee felt—and acted—as though it was his or her "own business."

Our associates at NATD clearly understand the critical necessity of making a profit. They see the link to their job security, personal career growth, and increased pay. However, profit is *not* the primary incentive for our coworkers to work hard. That isn't what motivates them individually.

We created a climate where each employee could do his best. Our associates are treated as equals, as human beings of value—personally, professionally. They earn the freedom to solve problems, to create, and to attain their individual goals at work. That's what motivates them: the opportunity for good people to follow their basic instincts—to do their best and be recognized and rewarded for it. They have control over their jobs rather than the other way around.

The key here is to mesh the goals of the corporation with those of each employee. It may sound complicated or obtuse, but it isn't. In our experience, the personal job specs of our coworkers are the same as yours and mine. We'd like a job where we can make a difference, a job where we can contribute, a job where we have earned the freedom and respect to do it our way—to add human value.

One night while I was CBWA, die maker Russ Church gave me quite a shock:

> "I'm leaving NATD, Tom. It's just me and the Mrs. now and we love to travel. In my new job, we get free airfare anywhere in the world. Besides, the same job in their aircraft maintenance shop pays twelve percent more."

There was little I could say or do to dissuade him. His mind was made up, his reasoning sound.

Three or four months later, Russ sent a message that he wanted to return to his old job at NATD—at the same pay as before. As we visited together later, I was interested to hear the reasons why he wanted to return:

> "All the free airfare's great, Tom. But they made me feel like a dummy. They tell me, 'Russ, do yourself a favor. Just do your job and let the front office come up with the ideas.' I could have saved them a lot of money with just one idea. They sure didn't think much of me.
>
> "Sure, pay and benefits are important. I have to provide for my family. But what I really want is to do my best. Respect me and my ideas. I want to help."

Help them, and in turn they'll help you. Then your goals are in harmony. The results will stun you—year after year after year.

THE KNEE BONE'S CONNECTED TO THE THIGH BONE

I got a phone call this morning from an employee in one division of a $15-billion multinational corporation. He asked me to speak on values at a dealer-customer round table. During our conversation

I innocently asked, "How's business?" His response was startling: "Just great. We're well on our way to achieving our corporate goal of $250 billion in sales by the year 2025." Oh, really? His company—a household name—has gone through four major reorganizations and attendant layoffs in the last five years; their earnings are static at best; and the stock is languishing on the NYSE. And he says, "We're well on our way . . ."

This attitude is typical of a problem prevalent in every big company sprawled across the worldwide business landscape. Some individuals, some departments, even some divisions are figuratively disconnected from their corporate parent. These individuals and/or entities are so "unto themselves" that they've developed a tunnel vision that precludes their seeing overall team performance. They've become so insular that they've lost touch with their corporate parent and its overall performance. There's no linkage. They don't understand that what they do impacts corporate profit.

The solution to this widespread problem is frequent personal contact and repetition of your message about profitability. It's absolutely essential to remind your associates in their terms how their company is faring. In addition, your fellow employees have to be reminded again and again how their individual job performance can affect overall profit. This is certainly true at NATD.

I'm constantly on the lookout for signs that our coworkers are taking our success and profitability for granted. In a meeting once, Larry Curtis in Engineering said to me, "Come on, Tom. What's a measly five hundred dollars?" He was very cavalier about it and that upset me. My response was instinctive:

> "If it's so measly, then I know you personally won't mind giving it to our company. Anybody in this meeting, anybody got a measly five hundred dollars to spare? Let's go outside, on the street. Let's stop everyone and ask for a measly five hundred. Larry, profit is hard to come by. There is no such thing as a measly five hundred dollars."

The message was clear. Watch expenses. It's *our* company. We're in business for a profit—a big profit.

In the rush of daily business at NATD, sometimes we forget the obvious: to remind our customers to pay our bills promptly. Periodically, one of the people in the office will forget the loss of potential NATD profit due to slow bill payment by our customers. As a result, scheduled follow-up calls will be put aside.

The remedy is straightforward. A five-minute math session provides stark proof of the significant amount of our lost profit. Our accounts receivable person makes a clear connection: "If I do my job correctly, NATD will 'earn' X dollars profit. That's important. I can see that now."

Perhaps the most meaningful example of the impact of individual effort on company profit occurs each month when our group analyzes prior-month profit performance by job. Those sessions repeatedly illustrate how one person's individual effort can make or break the profit on the entire job.

As a result, there is repeated reaffirmation of the importance of each person on the production line. It's made clear again and again that what our coworkers do has an immediate financial impact on all of us at NATD. These discussions further reaffirm all coworkers' sense of self-worth, their contributions, and their value to the company. It gives additional meaning to their work.

I JUST LOVE TO GIVE AWAY MONEY

At NATD, people don't work for just money . . . but it sure helps to pay the rent or buy groceries. Money is also a form of personal recognition and another way to say thank you.

If someone at NATD does something special, something new, something better, usually we become more efficient. As a result, our cost of goods is lower and our gross margin increases. If our gross margin increases, our pretax profit goes up. I love to give away money to our coworkers—$100, $500, $1,000. In twelve years, the biggest special award check totaled $3,500.

We do not use these financial awards as an incentive. Instead, they are our way of saying thank you—after the fact. People like using their brains; they enjoy the recognition, the sense of accomplishment. The check is merely one more corroboration of their worth, not an inducement to try.

Perhaps that's why there is never any grousing about who gets the cash awards for these special achievements. People never say, "How come Karl gets these big checks when he's just doing his job?" They know that the contributions he makes benefit everybody. They know we're all working in a New Partnership.

To share the wealth (NATD profit) and further engender our New Partnership, NATD instituted an Employee Stock Ownership Plan (ESOP). We enacted this program about one year after buying the company. Each year a portion of our pretax profit is deposited in the ESOP. These monies are partially used to buy shares of stock in NATD for every employee. In that way, we are all shareholders in NATD. Each of us is devoted to sustained profit improvement. There are two benefits. First, the level of NATD's ESOP contributions is directly dependent upon the amount of profit generated. In addition, the value of each share is directly related to the worth of the company. And that's based on profit.

In an effort to increase the number of shares available to our co-workers each year, I waived my rights to participate in the program. As a result, my existing stock holdings in NATD were diluted each year. The ESOP always received newly issued shares of stock in NATD.

Compensation for our NATD sales group is also closely tied to performance. And it should be. Here's how it works. Our sales associates receive a low base salary—just enough for a sparse lifestyle. Then the fun begins. They earn an ascending commission on the "last" dollar of sales with *no ceiling on total compensation.* You should have seen the fire ignite in the eyes of our sales associates when I outlined that concept for the first time.

Think about it for a minute. The more they sell, the more they make, not only in absolute dollars but in their share of the "last" sales dollar. Here's an example. Joe receives X dollars base pay. In addition, if he sells $2 million worth annually, he earns a certain percentage commission; on the *next* $2 million of sales, he earns an even higher percentage commission, and so on. Why not? The last dollar of sales is incremental volume. If the compensation package is structured correctly, your fixed costs have long since been covered. As a result, a disproportionate amount of that last sales dollar goes right to that little box at the lower right hand corner called profit.

What sense is there to put a limit on a salesman's total earnings? By nature, these people are built to win, to excel, to stand out. In my mind, it seems counterproductive to cap their opportunity to win—big. The more money our sales folk make, the more profit our corporation makes. Since the entire group shares in our total profit, we all win. I love to give away money.

SUBCONTRACT TO INCREASE YOUR PROFIT

The best definition of overhead came from the former owner of NATD: "If it doesn't turn a wheel, it's overhead." It's beautiful. And he's right. So we watch overhead like a hawk.

Where is it written in stone that every necessary business function must be accomplished internally, by company employees?

It isn't, and we don't—at NATD.

We outsource or subcontract wherever possible. Our P&L is my report card. Over time we've found it consistently more profitable to have expert outside vendors. As you know, there are specialists in health insurance, computer software, accounting, legal, engineering, production, and sales. We use them all, reducing fixed payroll and overhead, thereby increasing profit. Besides, these people can often do the job better, faster, and cheaper than we can. That is their only business; they are the experts.

We learned that the hard way when we tried to generate our monthly profit statement on the computer. We had absolutely no in-house experience in our office. After stumbling around as amateurs for far too long, we finally realized our lack of expertise. Rather than hire a resident computer software guru, we contracted for a turnkey operation for the P&L. The wheel had already been invented, so it was cheaper to buy it than to build it—both in dollars and in time. Besides, this subcontracting relieved the added burden on the group in the office. They could then concentrate on their jobs where they were more proficient.

A second area where we subcontracted out a traditional in-house business function is in engineering. Before the advent of CAD (computer-aided design), NATD purchased detailed engineering die design layouts from a number of independent contractors. It just didn't pay to have a full-timer on our payroll. If we had the need to design new dies all week, every week, that would be great. But we didn't. So we subbed it out. Not only did we increase our profit but we also obviated potential additions to overhead.

Whenever we reach capacity in our die construction group, we regularly contract to have entire dies made by outside specialists in the Midwest. Since wage scales are lower in the heartland, their prices often are lower than ours. We guarantee their workmanship to our clients. Why not do that? To hire permanent employees against a projected temporary peak workload is folly.

The same premise holds true in production at NATD. Employee turnover is costly and traumatic—for everyone. As a result, when our production backlog suggests hiring more coworkers, we often subcontract our rote, repetitive, relatively simple assemblies. One of our favorite outsources is the handicapped. If we jointly pick an appropriate job, their quality and delivery are fine. They provide surge capacity to help us handle the overload, and we feel great about being able to send some work their way.

TO MAXIMIZE PROFIT, PLAY FOR THE LONG BALL

We've always adhered to the long-term view. "What's the best course of action today for the future? Don't get drawn into expedient action just to solve today's problems. It will always come back to haunt you." Critics may scoff: "Of course. You can afford to do that; NATD is privately held. You have no public shareholders snapping at your heels for constant quarter-to-quarter profit improvement."

Technically, they're right. Our only other shareholders are fellow employees, through the ESOP plan. Yet NATD's continuing profit pressures were intense. Not unlike most entrepreneurs, we were highly leveraged financially. As a result, NATD had to generate substantial profit consistently just to service an imposing debt load. When it's your money and your personal obligations, believe me, the pressure is uniquely real.

But we were lucky. Again and again during my years in Big Corporate, I saw the lackluster results of expediency—in both financial and human terms. The lesson became clear: Go for the long ball—always. Here's just one illustration at NATD.

It seemed like only yesterday. Clare Stevens was so excited. "Come out and see it run, Tom. Our new electrical discharge machine [EDM] is hooked up and ready to go. It even cuts out die blocks automatically."

Three years later, Tom speaking: "What do you mean, we need a new EDM unit? We just bought one, Clare. How much? Four hundred thousand? That's impossible."

Or is it? The easy course of action would have been to make do with the old unit. It was slower to operate and technologically obsolete. But our existing EDM unit still performed its job. Besides, none of our competitors had anything comparable. We could have postponed that purchase for several years and increased our profit and return on invested capital.

But we didn't. We couldn't delay the purchase—not if we were playing for the long ball. The new EDM further extended our competitive advantage—in delivery time and technical flexibility. We could build more complex dies to meet our customers' needs. In reality, it was an easy decision.

CORPORATE AMERICA AND PROFIT

"Money is the biggest narcotic of all."

A letter to the editor
San Francisco Chronicle, *March 1992.*

Profit is *the* critical motivation for CEOs in most corporations today. But their definition of profit has been increasingly redefined to mean personal gain rather than corporate earnings. Aversion to risk coupled with personal greed typifies many corporate "leaders." Instant gratification of their greed is illustrated again and again in the obscene compensation programs, enacted by their boards of directors who (surprise!) are staffed by fellow CEOs of other major companies. These peers have similar financial aspirations. This story can be corroborated in most proxy statements of Fortune 500 companies.

Accompanying this single-minded preoccupation with profit (their own) is a management style that brooks no impediments, human or otherwise. After all, "Business is business." Do whatever it takes to make a profit. That justifies their manipulation of fellow employees and their stonewalling of the truth.

Another form of profit (compensation) for top executives is power to "manage" events and human beings. Such egotistical use of power is reflected in rigid hierarchies throughout "their" corporations, coupled with commensurate perks—all dispensed by the king, the CEO. It reminds me of King Arthur and the Knights of the Round Table. Pledge undying allegiance to the king, couple this with homage and subservience, and you will be rewarded with a share of the plunder. Fight this system and you'll be an outcast, excommunicated, and ultimately eliminated.

The age-old stereotype of success in big business depicts the ruthless manager who callously steps all over the backs of his "subordinates" in his quest to improve profit and thereby scale the corporate heights. There is little question in my mind that this type of manager will be increasingly ineffective and ultimately outmoded in your lifetime.

It's fascinating to note the emergence of General Electric's chairman, Jack Welch, as an apostle of the demise of autocratic management. Here are his words, from the Chairman's Letter of G.E.'s 1991 Annual Report: "The individual who typically forces performance out of people rather than inspires it, the autocrat, the big shot, the tyrant . . . always delivers [results]—at least in the short term. In an environment where we must have every good idea from every man and woman in the organization, we cannot afford management styles that suppress and intimidate."

Perhaps Anita Roddick, CEO of Body Shop International, expressed this point of view in her book, *Body and Soul* (Crown

Publishers, 1991): "There are no modern day heroes in the business world, no captains of industry who make my blood surge. I have met no corporate executive who values labor and who exhibits a sense of joy, magic, or theater. All the big companies seem to be led by accountants and lawyers and become moribund carbon-copy versions of each other. If there is excitement and adventure in their lives, it is contained in the figures on the profit and loss sheet. What an indictment. Huge corporations are dying of boredom caused by the inertia of their giantism." She goes on to point out: "If companies are in business solely to make money, you can't fully trust whatever else they do or say. The whole sense of fun is lost, the whole sense of play, of derring do" (page 173).

She's right. There has been something missing throughout most of our business life. It's always seemed so rote—so meaningless. Play it safe; don't show any emotion. "Chasing profit doesn't turn me on. They jigger the numbers anyway." Fun? Having fun is not an integral part of business. Fun is emotion. But that's all there is— emotion, human emotion—whether in life, love, friendship, or war. Why not in business to make a profit? And it doesn't cost a cent.

All of us want to succeed in our daily work. The commonly accepted criterion of success is money, power, or both. If that's your motivation, that's your business. What I'm suggesting here is to let your personal values peek through just a bit. You can get ahead, you can achieve success, by helping others succeed. Your success will be the result of sincerely helping your associates to find meaning in their daily work. More than anything else, that's the underlying principle of the New Partnership.

THE *ESSENCE* OF A NEW PARTNERSHIP— PROFIT

1. Increasing profit is an absolutely essential element in business.

2. To most of your fellow employees, corporate profit is not the real motivation for hard work. Their incentive—not unlike yours—comes from an inherent desire to:

    • do their best

    • contribute

    • be recognized as a person of worth

    • control their work and not vice versa

3. Demanding profit at the expense of your coworkers is both stupid and passé.

    • These people create profit.

    • Don't exploit them.

    • Encourage them.

4. The joy of management results from living a basic truth: By helping others in business, you help yourself.

5. Align your business goals with those of your fellow employees and both parties will win.

HOW *YOU* CAN BUILD A NEW PARTNERSHIP TO IMPROVE PROFIT

1. Get your group together to determine the impediments to improving profits in each of their jobs, one by one.

   • Ask for their help in finding solutions.

   • Let them go do it—their way.

2. Have monthly profit reviews and use specific examples to illustrate how one individual's effort can impact the bottom line. Keep on doing it with positive examples.

3. Continually show and tell your coworkers how their individual performance can quickly impact overall profit and thereby the potential well-being of themselves and their associates.

4. Don't personally pledge allegiance to all of the above and then avoid implementation in your area by blaming your boss—who may be from the old school.

   • You can do it without his/her approval.

   • Increase profit and he/she won't care how you accomplish it.

5. Earn an equitable wage and install a group bonus system.

   • Reward all fellow employees at the same rate as profits increase over prior year or a combined year base period.

CHAPTER FIFTEEN

Enthusiasm and Humor

Both Are Key Management Tools

"Nothing great was ever achieved without enthusiasm."

Ralph Waldo Emerson,
Essays: First Series. Circles.

In my experience, enthusiasm and humor are important business tools and integral to successful management. I've often wondered why none of the business schools offer a course on these subjects. One fetching title might be "Lighten Up; enjoy; inspire."

For over twenty years I labored properly—in conformity—amid the offices and conference rooms of big corporations. It's an unwritten rule that there should be no expression of genuine emotion, no enthusiasm, no humor, no frivolity. Proper demeanor mandates a stern and preoccupied countenance. "After all, this is a place of business. As managers, we are burdened with weighty problems. Should the amount of our cents-off coupon be five cents or seven cents?"

If you enjoy your job, show it. But be careful; it's contagious. As a manager you'll be emulated—like it or not. Your fellow employees will see your enthusiasm. It will rub off on them—to everyone's benefit. Business doesn't have to be so serious.

Once again, have a look at your own situation. Don't you like being with people who enjoy life? Each of us knows at least one person who always seems "up," full of vitality and enthusiasm. When you are around such a person, haven't you found yourself smiling, in a more buoyant mood—almost in spite of yourself? It's no different in business. Try it.

Let's smash the Berlin Wall erected by corporate tradition that quarantines enthusiasm. Think of your associates in business, the people on the line, whether you are in a manufacturing or service industry. Many of those fellow employees have daily business lives filled with a deadening monotony from rote and repetitive jobs. Yet they are under ever-increasing pressure to produce more and more—without any errors.

Can you imagine the effect your spirit of enthusiasm will have upon them, and their productivity? Sure, that's the purpose of daily coffee breaks—to pause, to refresh, to return to work reinvigorated. But go beyond that. Live your enthusiasm with your associates. Give them a mental lift, a momentary respite from their daily routine. It's fun, it's productive. And it's appreciated. Besides, it's good business.

The sooner we smash the stilted and self-serving barriers erected by management to distance themselves from "their" workers, the sooner we understand and help each other, the sooner we'll all win—together, in a New Partnership.

I'm not suggesting that we all suddenly become one of the boys or girls and head out for a few beers together every day. Unfortunately, there will always be a thin line that separates management from the employees. For those who need more of an "arm's length" relationship, it's already in place.

Enthusiasm can be such a powerful motivation. Here are several events that occurred at NATD over the years. They were genuine, they came from the heart, and they had a positive cumulative impact.

ENTHUSIASM

I'll never forget the month our sales first topped one million dollars. It was about twenty-four months after buying the company. What an accomplishment, what a thrill, what joy! I was so excited, I wanted to share my exuberance with the ones who had done the real work: our coworkers.

A catered luncheon was set up in the plant—steak and all the trimmings. Guess who won Super Person of the Month? That's right—everyone. And everyone got a fifty-dollar check. We all quit early and went home to celebrate, with full shift pay.

The group knew the source of my enthusiasm; they realized its importance, its significance. They were proud to be an integral part of this accomplishment. They were enthused for weeks afterward.

Your enthusiasm doesn't have to be focused only on business. Sometimes the benefits follow a circuitous route back to it, however. Boating and fishing are a primary sports activity for our coworkers. They just love these hobbies. Often, during the week after work, they go fishing. Weekends are no different. Let's put it this way—this is *the* favorite joke at NATD:

NEWSPAPER WANT AD

Wanted: Good woman with boat and motor

Purpose: Possible matrimony

Next Step: Please send color photo of boat

There was great excitement when David Lopes brought his new Scarab "cigarette" ocean racer to the plant one day. His boat accelerated to over 90 mph in the open ocean. It was as sleek as a Stealth bomber and equally well designed. The plant became a tomb at both coffee breaks and lunch that day. You had to stand clear of our exit doors to avoid being trampled by the horde rushing to the parking lot for inspection.

Believe me, enthusiasm is contagious. Guess who rushed out there along with everyone else? I was equally enthusiastic. It was quite a boat. Unfortunately, my idea of a good conversation is an interrogation. My curiosity is endless. That's just me. Evidently that day was no exception. The group saw my interest, my enthusiasm in "their" hobby. They were pleased.

Now I'm not going to sit here and tell you our productivity increased 2,000 percent because of that one instance. We both know better. Yet I believe my enthusiasm toward my coworker's key outside interest made a difference.

Incidentally, enthusiasm with your customers is also not forbidden. It works exactly the same way. And it's equally contagious. One time Tom Curtis, an engineer at Apple Computer, and I were chatting.

> TOM CURTIS: Of all our suppliers, I don't know of another that performs better than NATD.

> TOM MELOHN: Yee hah! (*Gives a whoop, a cowboy yell, and claps like crazy.*)

Tom Curtis knew—he could tell, see, sense, and feel everyone's sincere exuberance—our desire to win, to be the best of all his suppliers. And that's not a bad place to be in the eyes of your customers.

Or, if you prefer, hear an earlier interchange with the buyer from Apple Computer who first recognized NATD as their leading supplier:

> PAUL ALVAREZ: No, I'm serious, Tom. Your company is truly a world-class vendor. There are very, very few companies in the world that can match your quality and service record.

> TOM MELOHN: I'm stunned. . . . (*Then a holler, followed by a shout of joy.*)

Why not? I love to win, I love to compete—I love my job. Live it. Show it. Not businesslike? Not mature? Fine. But I'll tell you this: It's much more fun to go through life half full than half empty.

Try it—you'll like it. Besides, it's profitably contagious, with your fellow employees, with your customers . . . and in your daily life.

Sincere enthusiasm with both customers and prospects bears great dividends. Everyone likes a winner; everyone wants to be associated with a winner. Share your wins with your customers. Tell them—better yet, show them—the accolades the group has won: letters of commendation, zero rejects reports, award plaques, anything that says "We're number one!" They'll be more inclined to buy from you, a proven winner.

One instance comes to mind. As usual, there was one key prospect whose buyer had seen it all. Nothing we could say by letter or phone made any difference. He just would not buy from NATD. Finally, we hatched a plan. "Give us ten minutes with you—in person. If you're still not interested after that, we'll never bother you again. That's a promise."

When we were ushered into his spacious office, we saw a grim-visaged man, seated behind an imposing walnut desk. His greeting was perfunctory: "I'm a busy man; your ten minutes has begun." Over and over and over and over and over and over and over, we proudly pulled out and put on his desk award after award given NATD by our major customers. This purchasing manager could barely see us over the pile of plaques strewn on his desk. Finally, old stone face slowly cracked a smile. "Okay, we'll at least give you a try. That's impressive." And awa-a-a-ay we went.

HUMOR AT NATD

Humor? In business? That's not the place for jokes. Really? Where is that chiseled in granite?

Again, turn to your own life. Ever been in a difficult situation? You know what I mean. The tension almost crackles across the room. Tempers flare, voices mount . . . and then a joke, a quick quip, and *bang*, it's gone—dissolved in an instant. Then cooler heads prevail.

What's going on here? Is there some alchemy at work? No, it's just human nature. In effect, people who laugh together have created a momentary bond. They have identified with and reacted the same way to a common stimulus—in this case, humor. Remember our discussion earlier about family at NATD: with our colleagues, with our customers. Humor is certainly a great leavening agent in forging this partnership.

This incident is still vivid in my mind. One day a California State franchise tax team arrived unannounced at NATD. They demanded to see all our employee state tax withholding records— right now. They also commandeered all supporting data. This was a big job requiring probably two or three hours for us to complete. They expected our immediate cooperation.

Evidently we did not respond quickly enough. The senior state auditor summoned me to the meeting area. He demanded that I order my underlings to drop everything to do his bidding.

Tempers were flaring; the glares were widespread and unyielding; the tension mounted; the fireworks were about to begin. Nothing I did or said could calm either party. Our coworkers in accounting were livid at the auditor's imperious attitude. He in turn was both suspicious and unyielding. Surely there was a cover-up at NATD.

After listening to the righteous wails of both parties, I got up and went over to the stack of our accounting files piled on the desk. Opening one at random, I suddenly stopped. With growing panic on my face, I whirled around to our accountant and croaked, "I told you never to show *this* set of our financial data to anyone—ever!"

A snicker or two was quickly followed by widespread and relieved peals of laughter. Even the auditors cracked a smile. Happily, the crisis was defused. The auditors agreed to a plant tour while our associates in the office gathered the necessary files. Inadvertently, humor had quelled a possibly ugly incident.

HUMOR WITH OUR CUSTOMERS

In the early days at NATD, we had just received our first orders from a potentially large new customer, Freiden Mailing Corporation. Jim Copeland, the buyer, was an avid fisherman. A budding friendship developed between us primarily by phone. Our daily sessions were necessary to assure proper coordination and delivery of perhaps one hundred different production parts and assemblies, each in quantities of thousands, each with impossible due dates.

Our first shipments were on time and without any rejects. Things were under control. Jim even invited me to a party at his home. Two days before the party, he called. During the conversation, Jim reminded me not to call his office on Friday. He was going salmon fishing on opening day of the season. Small talk followed, with me accusing him of general ineptness as a fisherman and forecasting he would not catch one fish.

The moment I hung up, I got an idea. Buy Jim a whole huge raw salmon, completely intact. Then hide it in the bathtub in his home during the party. Don't ask me why. I just did it—for fun. The next night, with the help of a few fellow party-goers, I filled his bathtub with water and the salmon. On the pretext of having problems with his toilet, we called Jim into the bathroom. The minute he saw the fish floating in his bathtub, I said, "There's your damn salmon, Jim. That's as close as *you'll* ever get to catching one."

Amid raucous laughter and shouts of surprise, Jim's facial expression said it all. Shock, amazement, wonder, and then a broad smile—coupled with laughter. He thought it was hysterical—and so did everyone else. It was fun, it was sincere, it was a bonding of sorts. From that day forward, three things happened: We became fast friends, the story of the incident spread throughout his company, and our business increased.

Ever seen the box inside the box inside the box routine? You start by opening a large box, then you open the somewhat smaller box packed inside, etc. The gift item is finally lifted out of a tiny ring box. Years later, some employees still kidded me about this incident at another major customer.

One day our national sales manager wandered in—somewhat startled. Total NATD sales to Hewlett Packard had just reached a million dollars. Several years earlier, Al Sankey in the Engineering Department at Hewlett Packard in Santa Rosa, California had the courage and conviction to be the first to try out our small fledgling company. There was certainly reason to celebrate. We wanted to thank him personally—and in front of his peers.

A celebration lunch was scheduled. Accompanied by his boss and perhaps ten other engineers, Al joined our sales manager and me for lunch in a roadhouse near their plant. After a pleasant lunch filled with small talk, I rose to give Al his gift from all of us at NATD (knowing that supplier presents were not allowed). The speech went something like this:

> "Al, here's a small gift from NATD. Please go ahead and open it while I'm speaking."
>
> Al starts opening the first box.
>
> "NATD now sells Hewlett Packard well over a million dollars' worth a year—thanks to you."
>
> Al opens the second box.
>
> "Although you receive special cash kickbacks from NATD each month, you have indicated that's not enough."
>
> Al opens the third box—more slowly. Al's boss's eyes start to narrow. Al's peers laugh somewhat nervously.
>
> "Al, you said last week by phone that your wife really would enjoy a fine diamond ring."
>
> Al stops opening the fourth box—the size of a ring box. His eyes dart from face to face—his countenance confused, pleading, yet with a wan smile.
>
> "Al, please open the diamond ring box and enjoy— from NATD."
>
> He finally does—and with a gurgle of relief, takes out two aspirin.
>
> After a moment, pandemonium. Clapping, catcalls, and convivial good humor laced with relief fill the room.

A great moment, a great memory, and again, a bonding of sorts. Humor helped get us closer to our customer.

Here are the last two stories to illustrate the positive impact of humor in business. One day Allan Kemline in Engineering was called over to our then best customer, Xerox Corporation. A design engineer, Gene, wanted Allan's input on one new-part design. I asked to tag along; perhaps I could try once more to learn something about engineering. I also smelled a potential order. Besides, I liked Gene. He was a good guy, a smart engineer. His judgment of suppliers was superb—and he liked NATD.

Sitting in Gene's office after the first few minutes was boring.

Ever listen to two tooling engineers? These guys converse in what I refer to as "funny talk." You can't understand them. It's like a foreign language. Once in a while, I'd hear a familiar word or phrase: tensile strength, parabola, radius. But that was all.

After thirty or forty minutes, the woman who was passing out the weekly company paychecks walked in. The two engineers were so wrapped up in their conversation, they didn't even hear the office door open or my comment, "Thanks. I'll give it to Gene."

I put the envelope with Gene's paycheck into my inside sport coat pocket without a word.

Perhaps fifteen minutes later, a knock on the door brought our two friends out of the ionosphere. and a man entered. Gene said, "Allan, Tom, I'd like you to meet my boss, Mike. These two are from NATD, Mike. We buy a lot from them."

Who knows where the idea came from? Without missing a beat, my response went something like this:

> "Hi, Mike (shaking hands). You're just in time. Gene, here's your special weekly check from NATD for steering all that work our way."
>
> Silence, shock, stupefaction. Then Gene's anguished voice: "My check. It's my paycheck. How did you get my paycheck? Look, Mike . . . look. Please look. It's my own paycheck from our company."

Cruel? Insensitive? Perhaps. Yet both of these practical jokes were graciously received (after a moment or two) in the way they were intended. Humor was a common denominator to bring us together. It worked every time . . . almost.

It was Academy Award time at our then biggest customer, Xerox: their annual Supplier Banquet. Make no mistake, this was big time. Top executives from some of America's best-known companies were in attendance, by invitation only. Only the customer's twenty best vendors—worldwide—were invited. The accolades were nice but the prestige of winning was formidable . . . and quite saleable elsewhere. (Everyone likes to deal with a winner.)

The cocktail area was jammed, all the suppliers jostling for position with the customer's top brass. Hardly noticeable in my fire-engine-red slacks, polo shirt, and blue blazer, I studiously avoided the crush. Top quality and service beat politicking every time. One of the purchasing V.P.'s sycophants suddenly appeared, tense and out of breath. "The V.P. wants to meet you. Come on!" I went over, but after a few minutes of banter with his boss, Bob, about my "costume," I excused myself, suggesting there were many other suppliers eager to meet him.

As with a monarch, evidently a vendor—or anyone else "beneath" the V.P.—simply doesn't excuse himself from "King Customer's" presence. He is the one who dismisses *you*. Later, as we moved into the banquet room, I was summoned once again—this time by a different sycophant. "There's been a change in seating assignments. Bob wants you at his table. Follow me." Since they were paying, I followed.

During dinner our banter continued—before the covey of speechless and dumbfounded assistants. Friendly insults were exchanged, including "Why do I want to sit next to you? You don't even sign our purchase orders."

A few minutes before he got in front of the microphone to present the awards, Bob told me I had to give a speech. NATD had been suddenly chosen to represent all vendors. It was a friendly challenge—but beneath the veneer ran an undercurrent of pressure.

Excusing myself from the table, I went to wash up. When the time came, NATD won two awards: Supplier of the Year, and . . . Worst-Dressed Company President. The audience howled and so did I. It was a humorous touch. I had to respond. Approaching the speaker's rostrum, I noted a quiet commotion just below the dais. There was one of Bob's sycophants crawling around on his hands and knees in a complete panic, unobtrusively trying to fix a faulty sound system.

Here's an approximation of what happened next.

"Dick, Dick—please get up. Begging a supplier on your hands and knees—it really isn't necessary."

The audience howled.

"Bob, thank you for NATD's two awards. Both were well deserved. With the importance of this event, I know you'll understand if I occasionally refer to my notes. Incidentally, this note paper is exactly the same material that you print your blueprints on."

With that, I pulled out a roll of toilet paper and threw it as a streamer across the banquet room.

Several minutes later, the laughter subsided enough for the show to resume.

There's an interesting sequel to this evening. Bob subsequently asked me to chair a vendor advisory board for his company. From time to time, he'd call, wanting a vendor's point of view on some problem. Once I asked him why he kept turning to us for advice. His answer was tragically accurate:

> "You're the only vendor who stands up to me—the only one that levels with me—who tells the truth."

CORPORATE AMERICA AND ENTHUSIASM AND HUMOR

Now let's both have a look at the role of enthusiasm and humor in Big Corporate:

> "Quiet please. Stifling at work."

THE *ESSENCE* OF A NEW PARTNERSHIP— ENTHUSIASM AND HUMOR

1. Sincere enthusiasm is essential to success in business . . . and in life.

2. Enthusiasm is contagious.

3. Everyone likes a winner—to be around them, to do business with.

4. Humor is a universal language.

5. Humor can defuse difficult situations.

6. Humor can be a catalyst, a bonding device to cement human relationships.

7. Companies often suppress the expression of sincere human emotion—including humor.

HOW *YOU* CAN BUILD A NEW PARTNERSHIP BASED ON ENTHUSIASM AND HUMOR

1. Be yourself.

2. Let your inherent enthusiasm shine through. Look around for reasons to be "up" in your business. They're there.

3. Think through specific ways to lighten things up at your place of work. We both know productivity increases when tension and pressure are defused with humor.

4. Share the wins—with your fellow employees, with your customers.

5. Look for the humor in your daily work life. Share this emotion with your associates and customers.

6. Enjoy—the clock's running.

7. Now. Start now.

CHAPTER SIXTEEN

Leadership: From the Head, from the Heart

"All I do is to guide our coworkers in the right direction, and then get out of their way."

Tom Melohn, (head Sweeper)

So much verbiage has been written about leadership today, most of it by social psychologists or self-proclaimed gurus. I've never read any of it. I'm afraid I'd pick up all the jargon, the pithy phrases, the right moves . . . and contaminate my basic beliefs, my gut instincts. But I'm sure of one thing. The true source of leadership is in your heart and in your head. In my judgment, the best leaders have two characteristics. The first is an unswerving, single-minded, utterly all-consuming set of values not unlike the NATD currencies.

The second shared trait of leaders is a similar perception of people. Over and over again, they express their belief in the innate goodness of human beings. All the energies of the best leaders—in fact, their entire lives—are dedicated to helping people achieve their full potential.

So there you have it. A nonnegotiable set of values and a love of humanity—the two characteristics that exemplify the most effective leaders. When you think about it, that's what the New Partnership is all about.

Leadership—at NATD? This subject just never enters our

minds during the working day. We're too busy concentrating on our number one objective—no rejects—to worry about the niceties of management theory. Yet some academics would say, "Leaders have to have a vision. Aha! Quality. There it is—that's your vision." Maybe so. We don't think that way. That's our *job*—no rejects. That's what our customers want; that's what keeps bread on the table. That's why we do it.

You know what *is* in my mind almost every day at NATD? To live my values each day: to be myself and to help others do the same. These things are *vitally* important to me. There is not a doubt in my mind that our success results from that same single-mindedness and caring on the part of our fellow employees. They, too, want to live the same values in their daily lives at NATD.

LEADERS ARE MADE, NOT BORN

If you met Allan Kemline you would not think of him as a leader. Quiet, unassuming and gentle, Allan certainly would never be mistaken for John Wayne—a prototypical Hollywood leader. Yet year after year, Allan successfully leads our Engineering Department with a deft hand.

If you distill the essence of his success, it's deceptively simple. Allan lives his values—consistently. Early on, I was shocked to hear that Allan was a major figure in his religious group, often speaking before eight to twelve thousand people. Our Allan? Our quiet, retiring, unassuming chief engineer? Allan readily acknowledged his stage fright on the podium. He also was quick to add that his strong religious beliefs help him "spread the message" with unshakable confidence.

Another critical attribute of Allan's leadership stems from his love of humanity. I'll never forget the day we were crossing the San Francisco Bay Bridge en route to a customer meeting. While visiting together, I asked Allan what he would rather be doing at that very minute. His answer was immediate: "I'd like to be teaching religion to young people." It is this same caring, giving trait that Allan displays each day at NATD. There are no histrionics in

Allan's leadership style—no fireworks, no leaping over the ramparts—nor does he exude charisma. But he gets the job done, deftly, humbly, graciously—as a leader. Each of us can learn to lead—in our own way.

EVERYONE LEADS HIMSELF

The key here is both conviction and consistency. Put it in your terms. Do you believe someone who lies to you? Of course not. Do you believe someone who says one thing and does another? If your boss compromises her stated beliefs for the sake of the business, how many times can she do that? Once? Twice? At what point do you lose all respect for her? Your fellow employees are no different. Consistency is absolutely critical to living your values—every day.

It may come as a surprise to you to learn that I don't really believe that a leader in the traditional sense is necessary. When you have good people who care, they simply lead themselves.

Good people who care know what to do. They are pros—in their jobs, in their values. My task is to align the direction of the company with the values of these coworkers. Once that is understood, our associates take over. Make no mistake, our single goal needs frequent reinforcement. That's easy. Doing your best and producing super quality are synonymous. Listen to Tom Parrnelli in Quality Control:

> "There are many success stories here. I think the company itself is *our* success story. We've all grown with the company and the company has grown with us. I really feel it's a community success rather than an individual success."

One day the six-year-old daughter of a coworker stopped by NATD with Mom to pick up Daddy. We were chatting and she asked me, "What do *you* do here?" Out of the mouths of babes . . . That episode got me thinking. If everyone runs the place, what in fact do I really do all day?

In retrospect, it seems simple. I have five priorities.

First, to be sure the NATD ship is headed in the right direction, that our business strategy is sound.

Second, to hire only good people who care.

Third, to "stay the course": to be sure we *all* live our values, each day.

Fourth, to cheer every win, big and small.

Fifth, never, ever, to let bureaucracy sneak in.

That's my charter.

TOUGH CHOICES

The charter may be simple, but it isn't always easy. Along the way I've had some tough choices to make, some difficult terrain to navigate. Often leaders appear to glide effortlessly from pinnacle to pinnacle, from success to success. They apparently are never sullied with the grinding realities of everyday life and, more tellingly, with the bitter taste of failure. But as the song so aptly phrased it, "It ain't necessarily so."

At NATD, ours was not a smooth and uninterrupted journey on the "yellow brick road." Instead, our trek was marked by potholes and flat tires; several times we almost ran out of gas. But we expected bumps, detours, and delays. Even so, we always knew we'd get there. There was *never* any doubt of it.

Remember the sign on President Truman's desk? THE BUCK STOPS HERE. As Head Sweeper at NATD, what were the toughest decisions I had to make and why? How did I decide? Are there any regrets? This is not merely a trip down Memory Lane. Instead, through this discussion, my hope is to share the pressures, the loneliness, the personal emotions involved in facing up to the brutal problems of being cast as a leader.

It's easy to be a leader when business is good. The real challenges come in times of adversity. What price are you willing to pay to live your values consistently and to continue to love your fellow man no matter how difficult things get? What did Hemingway call it—"grace under pressure." Not surprisingly, my toughest decisions rarely involve things; they involve people, people I care about a great deal: our coworkers at NATD.

Solving "thing" problems is relatively easy. Should we accept this order? Can we deliver on time? Should we lease more space, hire more people, buy more capital equipment? The "numbers" will get you 90 percent of the way to a decision. No problem.

It's the people problems that are gut-wrenching—at least for me. A cynic may say, "What do you expect? Management should never get emotionally involved with their 'subordinates.' " How can you spend eight or ten hours a day with people you respect and admire without getting emotionally involved? That's all there is. They're family. That's how we won—big—for years. To shut human emotion out of your business life is shortsighted.

Let me share with you the events, emotions, and options involved in several very tough problems at NATD. I'll try to relate accurately and impartially the underlying motivations.

Tough Choice #1

It all began auspiciously when we hired two journeyman die makers at the same time and with grateful relief. NATD was bursting at the seams. New orders were flooding in. Major new customers were seeking us out with their new projects. NATD was on a roll—except for one problem. We didn't have enough qualified die makers to meet our delivery dates.

Die makers are the true artisans of our industry. Our coworkers can be obsessed with quality, but if our dies aren't built perfectly and don't function properly, nothing else matters. Qualified die makers are a vanishing breed.

I knew we had to hire some additional die makers—and fast. A flurry of NATD "help wanted" ads generated little response. I went through each application hopefully, anxiously, reading and rereading them, interviewing candidates even though I knew better. You could tell from their résumés they weren't qualified. But I was increasingly desperate. The clock was ticking away—like a time bomb. The tension was beginning to mount. One day Clare Stevens said to me, "What are we going to do, Tom? We need some pros in here to help—now. I know they are impossible to find, but our group's exhausted. We can't expect them to go fifty-five hours a week much longer. Do something."

Soon after that "Judas" appeared at our door. (Obviously, there's been a name change here. I don't want to hurt people's feelings or embarrass anyone—wherever they are.) His job application was solid, his experience impressive, his prior job tenure satisfactory. Our interview together was uneventful. Although quiet, Judas was of the old school. In his mind, I was management, he was "labor," and that was that. There was no changing his opinion. My only hesitation in hiring him was his manner. Judas was Mr. Rigid. In his life, the choice was always simple; there was never any room for divergent opinion. I thought, "So who's perfect?" and I hired him with no misgivings. We were lucky. I was grateful.

After our interview—on the way out—Judas remarked that his friend and fellow die maker Iscariot (not his real name . . .) was also interested in working at NATD. I jumped at his suggestion. Within a few days, Iscariot was in my office. The same pattern developed: His qualifications were solid, our interview uneventful. Iscariot was also quiet and almost too respectful. I recognized a cynical side to him, but I rationalized, "You can't disqualify someone for that. Besides, both men are old-timers; they'll add maturity to our group." He was hired—on the spot. We were saved! I was grateful.

Both Judas and Iscariot were professional die makers. They went about their work quietly, methodically, with no fuss. All seemed well.

But it wasn't. Always subdued, always in the background, Judas and his friend would "push the envelope" of the front office. They didn't trust "management." I've said overtime was voluntary at NATD. Judas made it perfectly clear he did not work overtime, even in an emergency. That's fine. His attitude was bothersome, but . . . I was still grateful to have him on board. Only later did I finally learn that Judas had told the other die makers they were foolish to work so hard. Nothing overt, nothing dramatic, no confrontation, he and Iscariot worked in the shadows.

As our company expanded, our jobs grew more complicated. Our dies became quite large and very heavy. Judas always found a way to work only on the smaller jobs. Iscariot was never far behind. I gave this annoyance only a passing thought. It was Clare's group. He managed in his own way.

One Monday morning, I discovered that Judas had verbally hassled Joe Rosario in the machine shop over some minor supposed transgression. That annoyed me a bit. Judas's complaint regarding Joe was really none of his business. Besides, Joe worked in an entirely different area. When Clare discussed this incident with me, I told him my feelings but urged him to use his best judgment. This was Clare's responsibility.

I still didn't recognize the growing discord and its sources. Perhaps Clare needed my emotional support to draw the line with the twins. He knew what was going on. But if he did need help, I missed his nonverbal signs completely.

Judas was on the day shift; Iscariot worked nights. The rumblings were soon heard there also. The night-shift pay premium wasn't enough. The work load for the night shift was always too much. The complaints were seemingly sporadic, random, and always anonymous—but debilitating over time.

The feeling of family in the die shop seemed to be disintegrating. Instead of our daily light banter together, there was a deliberate reserve toward me. "How can we help" was replaced by "Do we have to?" or, worse yet, "We can't do that." A new bravado appeared, almost an imperious swagger. "Plain talk" became "no talk." We were in trouble, but I was still oblivious. I didn't want to see. I was still grateful.

Then the confrontation came—sudden, explosive, and unilateral. Clare was the unwitting spokesman—the die makers' emissary. He told me that all of the die makers must have an immediate pay raise—now or else. The tempo of their demand soon accelerated, becoming louder and more insistent. "Ed's interviewing over at . . . They're paying so much per hour more at . . . Better hurry. Better make up your mind."

Frankly, I was stunned. Actually, I was hurt—really hurt. I was also between a rock and a hard place. NATD would be crippled if some key die makers left. But that wasn't the primary issue. I felt betrayed, used, exploited. The "hard ball" they were playing had no place at NATD—ever. Most of us had worked together for ten years, helping others, growing together, sharing our wins. We were family. When there was a slow period—sometimes for months—the die makers were never penalized financially. We even "made work" and "carried" them—always.

Equitable compensation had never been an issue at NATD. We prided ourselves on being competitive in pay. Clare always kept me knowledgeable about wage rates elsewhere. And now this. It just didn't make sense. Clare and I spent hours together discussing the situation. What's going on, why, where's the real problem, why the threatening ultimatum? His answers were sparse.

Over the previous two years, Clare and I had had repeated discussions about reorganizing the die makers' work flow and staffing. The proposed change was dramatic—but increasingly necessary. Clare knew this but couldn't bring himself to effect the change. It would be disruptive. For once in my impatient life, I had waited. Clare had to believe; he had to agree freely. He—not I—had to make the changes.

Then it all came together. Bear Bryant was the catalyst. Remember The Bear? He was the legendary former head coach at Alabama and multiple winner of college football National Championships. There's an apocryphal story about The Bear that I've never forgotten. It goes something like this:

THE SCENE: The Sugar Bowl—27 seconds remaining in the game

AT STAKE: The National College Football Championship

THE SCORE: Alabama is behind by 5 points. First down and eight yards to a touchdown. The last time-out has just begun.

The conversation between The Bear and his quarterback:

QUARTERBACK: Coach, what do we do? No more time-outs. Only time for two or three plays. What do we do? The National Championship's on the line. Thirty million people are watching us on TV. I don't know what plays to call.

THE BEAR: Son—just relax. Take a deep breath. That's it—just relax. Now, let's just think together for a spell. What plays did you call in these last two minutes to drive your team the entire length of this field?

(*Pause.*)

Son, you just trot on back out there. Keep calling them same plays.

TOUCHDOWN!

"Keep calling them same plays. . . ." That's it. Wake up, Melohn; rejoin the real world. You know what's going on in the die area. You've strayed from your own basic beliefs . . . and let others do the same. You've been expedient and "grateful" for too long. That's ridiculous. These two men have taken repeated advantage of our feeling of family. They think me too soft, with mushy values, with no conviction. Here was a milieu ripe for their selfish exploitation.

You're just scared to do what you know has to be done: If the two malcontents are fired, you'll wreck the company. But that's just not true. You know better than anyone: No one is indispensable—ever. Yet you thought they were, and that's why you have stuck your head in the sand all this time. The Bear was right: Just keep doing what you've been doing, what earned success in the first place. Be committed, be consistent.

The final act in this drama was easy. I summoned Clare (yes, that verb was chosen deliberately) to my office along with Judas and Iscariot. The twins were summarily fired. They had no response.

Clare was told rather forcefully to implement the new die making system and restaffing—immediately. Clare was also *ordered* (yes, ordered) to tell all die makers that they were free to leave at any time for another job. That was their prerogative, and I would never stand in their way. The pay demands were never mentioned. Clare and the twins traipsed out, silent and in shock.

Word spread like a prairie fire all across the plant and front offices. You could see our employees clustered in small groups, buzzing conversations flooding the entire plant. This was big news. The implications were clear to everyone.

The next day I called a meeting of all die makers in the training room. I carefully reviewed the entire sordid litany, discussing the mistakes of each party in very plain talk. I told them I had stuck my head in the sand. I had suspended—slipping into corporate talk for a moment—my basic values and done the expedient thing. In a word, I was like a "chameleon," readily changing my colors to adapt to a changing environment. A leader? No way.

When I chastised the die makers for jeopardizing our feeling of family, for trying to leverage their position at the expense of all, Clare interrupted. There was considerable emotion in his voice.

> "No way. This mess is my fault. It's up to me to keep our group on track. I should have fired those two trouble-makers long ago. I knew what they were up to. We also got greedy—at the company's expense. I let the guys down. I let you down. I'm sorry—really sorry."

Then there was complete silence. Nothing else needed to be said. Sometimes silence is a great teacher. She taught us all an unforgettable lesson in those few moments . . . and for years to come.

The denouement was stark in its simplicity and human emotion. Not long thereafter, Ed Rodrigues, a die maker, stopped by.

"Got a minute, Tom?" he said.

"Sure, come on in."

"I'd like to apologize. I'm really embarrassed to have been a part of all that." A sigh. "I was a fool." A long pause. "We have a great company here. I don't know what I was even thinking of."

Ed stood up with moist eyes, his hand extended: "I'm sorry. Shake?"

Shake.

TOUGH CHOICE #2

From time to time, major customers would come to us with tempting proposals for our expansion. Here's just one example. Micropolis, a large multinational corporation, made us an offer: "Open a plant in Thailand. We'll guarantee at least 50 percent capacity utilization for the first three years from the manufacture of our parts. We need your quality in our overseas markets."

This proposed expansion would have provided NATD with three significant benefits: guaranteed and substantial growth in sales and profit, more management opportunities for the group, and greater geographic balance in earnings. Yet measured against our values, the offer didn't have much appeal. Increased profit per se was not a primary motivation. Besides, most of our coworkers weren't interested in living in the Far East—even with a promotion.

In the final analysis, I decided it just wasn't worth the personal price of spending one week a month logging 20,000 air miles to work in a developing country, away from my family. I had endured that kind of physical and mental hara-kiri in big corporations for far too many years.

I turned them down.

TOUGH CHOICE #3

I saw it coming. I let it happen. I failed . . . and NATD paid for it for a long time. Bea Bloomquist caught "me fever." The lady was good. When we were small, Bea handled shipping and receiving. She was a real pro—buttoned up, aggressive, eager to help, a doer. Over the years, she assumed increasing responsibility: production control, warehousing, even purchasing.

As we continued to grow, it didn't take a genius to see this lady was badly overloaded. Everyone turned to Bea. She had all the answers; she knew where everything was. When she went on vacation, her absence was felt throughout the company.

After her annual holiday, her coworkers always (and sincerely) told Bea how much her business acumen was missed, how indispensable she was, how she seemed to know everything. Over time, these accolades became heady music to her ears.

Sure enough, Bea started believing her press clippings. The resulting symptoms of "me fever" were easy to recognize (remember, I worked with vice presidents for years): Bea became aloof, too busy to stop and help, or even to answer a question. Her criticisms of others became more and more strident, even condescending. She was the smartest, the most knowledgeable, always correct—*always*. You could see her attitude; it was scarcely veiled. Her coworkers were all dummies, beneath her.

When fellow employees came to me with complaints about her attitude, I calmed them down, ascribing Bea's mood to "just pressure from her job. It'll change." It didn't . . . I knew it wouldn't. Hers was a severely swollen head.

Our business continued to grow; so did the pressures, so did her ego. It was inevitable. Mistakes occurred. Shipments were misdirected. Purchases were fouled up. Her operation started to come apart. Then she lied to cover up her mistakes. It cost NATD about $13,000 to remedy the situation. But that's not the point.

At NATD, lying is cause for immediate dismissal. No exceptions. Now what? The lady had lied—there was no doubt of that— in addition to an almost terminal case of "me fever." She was coming apart under undue pressure. And this Head Sweeper sat by and let it happen. Who should be reprimanded, Bea or me?

There is a potentially fatal flaw in this New Partnership. Managing this way makes you enormously vulnerable emotionally. If you'll pardon a graphic analogy, sometimes you feel like you're walking around in the midst of your own open-heart surgery. Your heart is exposed, unprotected, vulnerable as can be.

If you're not surrounded by good people who care, who have the same values, you can be severely wounded emotionally. In my life at NATD, this was never a consideration. There was no way I was going to lead the rest of my business life the old Big Corporate way: distant, impersonal, dispassionate. The multiple joys far outweighed the few inevitable emotional wounds. Unfortunately, the Bea incident hurt—a lot. I felt I had failed as a leader and as a manager.

I finally took three steps. I did not fire Bea; I gave her a one-week suspension without pay. I hired two additional people for purchasing and production control. After a series of difficult "plain talk" sessions, her "me fever" sharply subsided. We lurched back toward a feeling of family again—together.

CORPORATE AMERICA AND LEADERSHIP

I'm ashamed to write about leadership today in most corporations. Throughout this book, toward the close of each chapter we've stated the reasons for the paucity of true business leaders today in Big Corporate. There's little sense in reciting them again here. The honor roll is desperately thin—and getting progressively thinner. Perhaps my definition of leadership is wrong. Leadership is made up of two elements: unflagging commitment to a just cause and love of mankind. Using those criteria to measure the current business landscape, Sam Walton was one true leader in business; Mike Walsh is another. I'm sure there are a few more names—but not many. That's just the point.

I'm confident that, when queried about his corporation's financial success, Sam Walton quickly would have shifted credit from himself to the employees. So would Mike Walsh.

More important, the people within both organizations would be quick to point out that their CEO was a people person who understood them, cared about them, and listened to them. He walked his talk.

Profit can go hand in hand with the two key attributes of a leader. In truth, sincere "love" of humanity enhances it.

THE *ESSENCE* OF A NEW PARTNERSHIP— LEADERSHIP

1. The best leaders all have two traits: single-minded conviction of a just cause and love of humanity.

2. Leaders live their values every day in every situation, particularly when under great stress—the moment of truth.

3. Leaders have an overriding goal in mind—one that they've committed themselves to wholeheartedly, unabashedly.

4. The attainment of this primary goal is achieved by fellow employees—particularly if it's in harmony with the values of the group.

5. Good people who care are leaders—inherently. They know what to do, and how to get there.

6. Profit is generated *by* your fellow employees—not *in spite of* them. You *can* reach people with human emotion—not just money. People are motivated more by recognition than by money.

HOW *YOU* CAN BUILD A NEW PARTNERSHIP BASED ON LEADERSHIP

Here are questions asked of me again and again from the podium after my talks. Perhaps it would be helpful if we set forth the Q&A dialogue here.

Question: Can everyone be a leader?

Answer: No. Everyone is a leader already in his or her own way. Good people who care have just been repressed for the greater corporate good (???)—for far too long.

Question: How do I go about being a leader?

Answer: First, be yourself.

Second, hire only good people who care. Treat them just the way you want to be treated.

Third, identify your one or two key objectives.

Fourth, ask your coworkers how best to get there. Listen . . . hard.

Fifth, get out of their way. Cheer them on, and count the gains.

Sixth, start Right Now.

A guy named Einstein said it pretty well:

"Try not to become a man of success but rather try to become a man of value."

CHAPTER SEVENTEEN

Tomorrow and Tomorrow

"How many times can a man turn his head and pretend that
　he just doesn't see?
The answer, my friend, is blowin' in the wind. . . ."

Bob Dylan,
"Blowin' in the Wind"

Well, we've come a long way together in this narrative journey. We've tried to share our beliefs, experiences, actions,
and results over twelve joyous years here at NATD. I hope that
you've "lived" with us and found reaffirmation that this is indeed a successful way to live—both in business and in your
personal life.

In the final analysis, what North American Tool & Die sold
was not precision metal stampings and subassemblies. We sold

- hope to our fellow employees

- peace of mind to our customers

- profit to our bank

- psychic income to me, seeing our coworkers grow in so
  many wonderful ways

But now it's up to you. Sure, there are specific action steps outlined in each chapter. Yet the decision is still yours alone. You can put this chronicle aside and go about your life in the same old way. From time to time, specific incidents in this book may come to mind—particularly when you're faced with a tough situation. Perhaps you'll let the moment of positive action pass—frustrated yet safely mute.

YOU ARE NOT ALONE

You *do* have a choice. Down deep in your gut you know that. You *can* change your life. Let me share a final story with you.

> Tom Peters was kind enough to invite me to his first ever Skunk Camp. All the legends of American industry in his first book, *In Search of Excellence*, were there. I felt like a fly on the wall, watching and listening in slack-jawed amazement as these almost mythical heroes shared their stories of success.
>
> Over and over again, the underlying theme was the same. "I didn't do it, the people did." Sure, the words, the phrasing, the sounds were different, but the underlying message was crystal clear. "The people, the employees, the folk, my associates were responsible for our success."
>
> Several days later, a friend and close business associate asked me what my feelings were while I was at this history-making meeting.
>
> My response was immediate and unthinking: "I realized that I'm not alone."

And you're not alone either. We share the same values. You wouldn't be still reading this book otherwise. We're together in another way, too. There's a good chance that you know first hand the pain and frustration resulting from our silent and long-term servitude to the senseless and outmoded ways of Big Corporate. Yet we're not the only employees who feel that way.

All across this country—in fact, all across the world—there are literally millions of good human beings who share our values. They also live with or have friends who endure the same tragic and rote compliance. And that's the key—*we are not alone*. Together we can change the rigid and sadly dated system of Big Corporate. There are just too many of us to ignore, to stifle, and to punish—anymore. We just won't stand for it.

QUESTION AUTHORITY

Stop for a minute and consider what's going on right now and what the portents of the future hold.

Here's what intelligent corporate CEOs are faced with today. First, they know, down deep in their gut, that something's changing, something really big, something basic. It's more than the threat of offshore competition. That's already dealt with by heartlessly slashing millions of jobs. It's something else—something even bigger.

The old corporate order is changing. Platitudes, deception, and obfuscation are not working anymore. Their time-proven charades are becoming almost counterproductive. Big Corporate managers are hearing: No more!

The same thing's happening in politics, too, both nationally or on the local level. It's painfully apparent that there is an ominous dearth of candidates who honestly represent our values at all levels of politics. Few of them stand for anything.

We've lost faith in our leaders in both government and corporations. (Hard to tell the difference, isn't it?). We've lost faith in the workings of *our* system, which no longer serves us, the "silent majority." Our corporate and governmental leaders have lost touch with those they are supposed to *serve*: the general public, you and me. They have yet to realize that we the people have changed—a lot. We simply don't believe them anymore. They've lied to us too many times. They've made too many empty promises.

What was that pithy bumper sticker so prevalent during the 1960s—QUESTION AUTHORITY. That's even more necessary today than it was then.

Yet the most salient change has occurred within ourselves. Simply stated, we've had enough. No more sham. No more lies. No more self-aggrandizement. There's also a growing realization that we do in fact have the power to make the necessary changes ourselves. We know that we have to—no one else will.

QUIET REVOLUTION

There is mounting evidence that this quiet revolution is "blowin' in the wind." The same young people who questioned the workings of the system during the 1960s are now in mid- and upper management. Because of downsizing, their instincts and feelings may be momentarily sheathed, but they're still in place. Now that corporations have shattered the implicit lifetime employment contract, our younger friends have come to a stark realization that Big Corporate is no different than big politics. The implications and portents are increasingly clear. The system isn't working. It's up to us to change it.

Unwittingly, countless companies have taken the first step in this quiet revolution with the acceptance of worker involvement and self-directed work teams. Make no mistake, this movement is not fueled by any altruistic feelings of top management. Their sole motivation is profit, big corporate profit.

If you really think it through, our corporate moguls had no choice but to let us "do our thing." They've decimated the work force so severely, the old hierarchy is almost inoperative. There simply aren't enough supervisors around anymore to rule in the traditional rigid hierarchical way. Now it's up to us. Business has finally recognized that we have a brain, that our professional competence can impact the bottom line, that we can provide significant added value to the business.

Now the door is open. Let's flood through—quietly, discreetly—broadening and extending the spheres of our competence and influence. Companies will readily acquiesce, as long as the profits roll in. And they will, for a very simple reason. We know the best way. We should, after all. We've done the job for years. We also know how to unravel the convoluted and inefficient systems imposed from on high—generally several thousand miles away.

Gently, softly, with little apparent effort, we can change our lives in business. Together, with the countless others there with us who care, we can make a difference. We can effect massive change, first, by living our values every day, and second, by ruthlessly firing those who persist in lying, politicking, and not doing an honest day's work. Simply by being ourselves and living our values, we'll increase profit dramatically. Corporate management can no longer resist the flood of coworkers who at last are finally controlling their own work lives.

AN UNLIKELY ALLY FOR CHANGE

Help is also on the way, albeit from a strange source. In a way, it's poetic justice. It's coming from us—from our money. With ever-increasing pressure, the huge pension funds—which have billions in assets invested in the stock market—are sending a clear message to the CEOs of Big Corporate:

> "Enough. Stop the empty words, the hollow promises, the blatant self-entrenchment and enrichment.
>
> "Serve your owners—your shareholders.
>
> "Revitalize. In some cases, redirect the corporation to maximize shareholder value over time."

Make no mistake. This is just the beginning. The initial foray of these pension funds has been directed toward excessive compensation in Big Corporate. Now their charter is expanding—and properly so. High on the current agenda is the issue of successful corporate governance itself. When CALPERS (the California Public Employees Retirement System) voted against the proposed slate of corporate directors at Sears, they took the first step in "defrocking the self-anointed" at major corporations.

The first stirrings by corporate boards of directors to exercise their moral and fiduciary duties recently occurred at General Motors, IBM, and Kodak. You can argue that it was tragically overdue. But that's not the point. It's a highly visible start, not only in other Big Corporate board rooms, but throughout America and the world. You can be sure this episode is just the first of many quiet revolutions we'll see in the months and years to come. Sooner or later, these enlightened Big Corporate board members will realize that the real key to rejuvenation, to renewed and sustained success, is to return to the basic human values that were the underpinning of their success years ago: honesty, respect for the individual, teamwork, equality—and caring.

The reason for my belief that more and more corporate boards will enact positive change is simple. Big Corporate board members are predictably alike in two key areas. They are enormously skilled as survivors. They also are acutely aware of their potential legal and financial liability if they continue to ignore their fiduciary responsibility as stewards of the corporation's "health." Even though "protected" by board member insurance, their personal concerns are real and growing. Here, too, is a potent ally in our quiet revolution.

There's another groundswell in public opinion that's working in our behalf. As you well know, our mood in America today isn't "right"—it hasn't been for some time. We all have this gnawing sense of uneasiness, of concern. We know in our gut there's something wrong—structurally wrong—with our country. This goes far beyond any recession and its attendant ills. America is badly off-track and has been for years: in the economy, education, R&D investment, law and order, morality, health, and our government—at all levels. There's a growing sense of hopelessness, almost despair. We're alone—all alone to face a dismal and scary future. It would seem that we've lost our way in business, in politics, in government, and perhaps even in our own personal lives. The old traditional values—our anchors to the past, our moral platform to face the future—have been eroded. Many of our role models have been found wanting. So we wander almost aimlessly, searching for security, meaning, and perhaps even a new moral order. We're engulfed in an ever-widening sense of powerlessness, of vulnerability, of fear. There's no leader at the helm or even on the horizon to guide us out of this morass—from any station in our society.

At the same time, there is an enormous opportunity to "take charge," to provide leadership, in order to rekindle our faith in ourselves, each other, and our country. This may sound ridiculous, but you can do it. You can make a difference in the daily lives of your coworkers in your department, division, or corporation.

These longings, these desires are so deep-seated, so universal that your fellow workers will relatively quickly align themselves with your business goals. But your goals must be the result of living the basic values of decent human beings. All of us are desperately seeking a home, a safe place, a place where human values are lived, where people can escape the world's never-ending and senseless strife.

Your fellow employees can find their new home at your company. It happened with us. It can happen again with you. Just go back to what made this country great. Things like:

- Honesty

- Trust

- Plain talk

- Respect for the individual

- Teamwork

The end result of this New Partnership will absolutely astound you.

This book suggests one answer to our problems. By returning to those beliefs, those values that made America great, everyone at NATD proved that success in business can be achieved without sacrificing those beliefs. In fact, the success of NATD was because of these values.

Success in business (and in life) does not have to be at the expense of our personal beliefs.

> The real lesson of North American Tool & Die is simple. If you reach out and care—genuinely care—for your fellow employee, there's no limit to what you can achieve.

> North American Tool & Die is restoring fundamental human values to the work place . . . and in the process, it's teaching all of us that quality of product and quality of work life go hand in hand.*

That's it. That's the essential essence of what we did, together, at NATD.

In the final analysis, it's up to you.

> They did not yet see, and thousands of young men . . . now crowding to the barriers of their careers, could not see that if a single man plant himself on his convictions and then abide, the huge world will come round to him.

> *Ralph Waldo Emerson*
> *An American Scholar*

Just go do it!
For your sake . . .
for your kids . . .
for their kids. . . .

---

* *The New Partnership* (video training film), Enterprise Media. Cambridge, Mass.

Afterword

For something like twenty-five years Tom Melohn toiled successfully and valiantly in the fields of Corporate America. But, I must quickly add, not happily. As he put it, with a low bow to Thoreau, he was, like untold thousands of others, leading a life of quiet desperation. Well paid, but not well used. And he kept dreaming of a vivid utopia: "A company where individual performance would be the primary yardstick, where politics was outlawed, where people could work together towards a common goal." Well, who doesn't share that dream? I mean, don't we all have something like that in mind? Haven't we reams of paper written about this new paradigm? I've even written a number of reams on this hallowed future myself.

What makes Tom Melohn unusual, if not unique, is that he went out and bought a company, depleting his entire life's savings, and actually created and nurtured this vivid utopia. He's invented the future and it works. Glory be to God!

I won't try to summarize his book since I presume you've already read it. I will, however, tell you two things that I won't say I learned solely from reading this inspiring book, but which reinforces and confirms just about everything I've learned about organizations and leadership over the past forty-five years or so.

First, Tom Melohn understands that the central issue facing our organizations today—an issue that must be addressed—is how to release the brain power, the know-how of the work force. Companies are going to fall or rise on whether or not they recognize that it's going to take brains, ideas, knowledge that will create innovation, re-invention and result in successful performance.

Second, he understands that you're not going to unblock that talent with whips and chains, that you're going to have to create an environment of respect, caring, integrity, high standards and, above all, trust.

Its that *trust factor* which Tom not only understands but translates into the day-to-day operations of NATD. We all talk about trust, but Tom's found the common-sense way to make it a living source of empowerment. As far as I can tell, he bases trust on five factors: competence, candor, congruity (call it integrity), constancy, and caring. Five Big C's. Easy to remember and excruciatingly difficult to live by and implement. But that's the way he does it and I sit back in awe and admiration of how the performance of NATD reflects his basic convictions, his view of persons.

I was perhaps unduly impressed with *The New Partnership* because it so clearly rhymes with my mentor's book, *The Human Side of Enterprise*, written almost thirty years ago by Doug McGregor. They also had one other thing in common. Both knew, first hand, what it was to lead, to be in the arena. And in this hazardous age of fast change, it is especially important that leaders and managers think carefully for themselves. In the words of Robert Graves:

> Experts ranked in serried rows
> Filled the enormous plaza full.
> But only one is there who knows
> And he's the man who fights the bull.

The man who fights the bull (no pun intended) does not live in the breezy world of journalists or gurus. The successful person who fights the bull lives in the real world, a world that requires real work, and it doesn't get done with rhetoric or shortcuts or group think. It gets done with leaders like Melohn who know how to translate purpose into action and to sustain it. OLE to Tom Melohn.

WARREN BENNIS
Distinguished Professor of Business Administration,
University of Southern California
and author of *An Invented Life* and
Reflections on Leadership and Change

Index

A

Absenteeism, phoney, 12–13
Accounting firm, for year-end
  audit, 9
Accounting operation, quality
  and, 178
Act, latitude to
  in corporate America, 166
  at NATD, 162–63
Adam, Karl, 51, 80, 109, 110,
  112–13
Administrators, elimination of,
  141
Age, hiring considering, 95
Alcoholic, employee as, 146–47
Alexander & Alexander, 179
Alvarez, Paul, 25, 216
Apple Computer
  NATD and, 87, 162, 175–76,
  185, 193–94, 216
  TV commercial of, 164–65
Assembly line work, front office
  women sharing, 78–79
"Assistant to" jobs, elimination
  of, 141
Audit, "big six" accounting firm
  for, 9

Authority, need to question,
  243–44
  see also Power

B

Bathrooms, equality and
  cleanliness regarding, 46
Bega, Gloria, 9, 79, 178
Beliefs, living one's, 21
  see also Values
Bettencourt, Teresa, 17, 20, 50,
  61, 64, 71, 83, 114–15, 127,
  172
Big Corporate, see Corporate
  America
Blasques, Frank, 37, 65–66, 70,
  77, 80, 111, 130–31, 133–
  34, 161
Bloomquist, Bea, 192, 235–37
Bloomquist, Levi, 130
Body and Soul (Roddick), 209–
  10
Body Shop International,
  Roddick and, 209–10

Bonus, equality regarding, 47
Boss, employees as, 79–80
Brown, Bob, 158
Brown, Dave, 114
Buddy system, for new hires, 105
Bureaucracy, small management structure minimizing, 139–41
Burros, Marion, 41
Business plan, elimination of, 140–41
Business units, *see* Profit centers

C

Cabral, Tony, 50, 156, 172
CALPERS, 245
Cannon, David, 25
Capital equipment, employees involved with purchasing, 53
Car show, visiting, 67–68
Career paths of employees, small size allowing involvement with, 146–47
Caring, 4
  see also "Caring by walking around"
"Caring by walking around" (CBWA), 147, 202
  Corporate America and, 27
  creativity noted in, 113
  huddles observed by, 82–83
  learning about employees by, 67–68, 133–34
  new employees evaluated by, 102–3
  Super Person suggested from, 128, 129
  trust from, 20–21

Cars
  equality regarding, 47
  expenses for personal, 8
  round-trip travel between home and offices in, 8
Cash payments, stopping unaccounted, 8
CBWA, *see* "Caring by walking around"
CEO, involvement of in hiring process, 105–6
Chabot Community College, 158
Change
  aimless society and, 246–47
  authority questioned for, 243–44
  corporate boards and, 245–46
  many aspiring for, 242–43
  pension funds and, 245–46
  quiet revolution for, 244–45, 246
  values and, 247–48
Christmas, company celebrating, 66–67
Church, Russ, 202
Cleanliness
  Corporate America and, 58
  employees having responsibility for, 46
Clothing
  Corporate America versus NATD and, 69–70
  freedom in choice of, 110–11
Coach, Head Sweeper as, 80
Commitment, for creativity, 122
Communications, in Corporate America, 71
  see also Plain talk
Commute, hiring considering, 95
Companionship, family at work fostering, 64–67
Company car
  equality regarding, 47
  for sales calls, 8

Compensation, *see* Pay
Competence
  power and, 155, 157–59
  trust in coworkers', 17–18
Computer
  quality and, 178
  working at home and, 27
Conformity, in Corporate
    America, 164–65, 213
Conscience, trust in coworkers',
    18–19
Consistency
  in actions, 8
  values and, 227
Copeland, Jim, 218–19
Corporate America
  broken up into profit centers,
    145, 147–50
  caring for employees and, 27
  conformity and, 164–65, 213
  creativity and, 123–24
  customers and, 191
  decision making and, 165
  do unto others and, 56–59
  employee empowerment and,
    124
  employment anniversaries
    and, 135
  enthusiasm and humor and,
    223
  family and, 71–74
  gainsharing programs and,
    135
  having latitude to act and, 166
  hiring and, 103–6
  honesty and, 14–15
  information gaining and, 165–
    66
  layoffs and, 137
  leadership and, 237
  movement against, *see* Change
  organization chart and, 163
  pay and, 163
  perks and, 163
  plain talk and, 39–42

power and, 154, 163–66
profit and, 208–10
quality and, 179–81
resource allocation and, 164–
    65
self-directed work teams and,
    124
size and, 148–50
staff jobs and, 149
teamwork and, 88
thank you and, 135–37
time and, 68–69
trust and, 26–27
working at home and, 27
Corporate boards, change and,
    245–46
Cost increases, plain talk on,
    37–38
Courage, for creativity, 117–
    18
Coworkers
  employees as, 45
  plain talk of on "no rejects,"
    32
  trusting, 24–25
  trusting competence of, 17–18
  trusting conscience of, 18–19
  see also Employees
Creativity, 109–25
  being yourself for, 110–11
  believing in yourself for, 111–
    13, 120–21
  commitment for, 122
  Corporate America and, 123–
    24
  courage needed for, 117–18
  definition of, 109–10
  initiative for, 113–15
  mistakes allowed with, 118–
    20
  New Partnership built on,
    124–25
Currencies, 4
  see also Caring; Dignity;
    Equality; Honesty; Mutual

Currencies (*continued*)
  respect; Recognition; Self-
  worth; Teamwork; Trust;
  Values
Curtis, Larry, 36–37, 188
Curtis, Tom, 87, 175–76, 185, 216
Customer service, 189–90
Customer(s), 185–98
  Corporate America and, 191–
    97
  customer service and, 189–90
  decency and values of, 186
  dignity from, 52
  emotional involvement with,
    195–96
  employees informing, 54–55
  enthusiasm with, 216–17
  as family, 186–89, 191
  growth of, 185–86
  humor with, 218–23
  information shared with, 191–
    92, 196
  New Partnership built on,
    197–98
  obstacles to partnership with,
    185, 191–96
  partnering with, 190
  plain talk with, 37–39, 86, 190
  power shared with, 193–94
  quality and, 175–77
  selection criteria for, 185–86
  at Super Person meeting,
    195–96
  teamwork with, 86–87
  trust in, 25–26

D

Data Products, 116–17
Decision making
  in Corporate America, 165
  at NATD, 161

Delivery
  plain talk on, 39
  quality and, 178
  trust defined by, 25–26
DeSerpa, Emilia, 48
Die construction,
  subcontracting, 207
Die makers, leadership problem
  with, 229–35
Digital Equipment Corporation
  (DEC)
  employment anniversaries
    celebrated at, 135
  NATD and, 86, 192
Dignity, 4
  Corporate America and, 56
  do unto others and, 50–52,
    54–55
Dinner
  NATD treating employee to, 51
  thank you to employees said
    by buying, 134–35
Do unto others, 45–60
  beginning at NATD and, 54–
    56
  Corporate America and, 56–
    59
  dignity and, 50–52, 54–55
  equality and, 46–47
  mutual respect and, 48–50
  New Partnership built on, 60
  self-worth and, 52–55
Doughnuts, celebrating with
  employees with, 63–64
Dress, *see* Clothing
Duk, Kim, 63
Dylan, Bob, 241

E

Earnings loss, gobbledygook on,
  39–40

Eastman Kodak, change by
board of, 246
EDS, General Motors versus,
149
Education
"help wanted" ads avoiding,
94
quality and, 173–74
technical competence
through, 157–59
Efficiency, in small management
style, 141–43
Einstein, Albert, 239
Emergencies, pay lent in, 64
Emotional involvement, with
customers, 195–96
Emotional security, work
fostering, 62–64
Employee empowerment
in Corporate America, 124
failure of, 155–56
Employee evaluations
in first month of employment,
102–3, 105
plain talk and, 33–35
Employee involvement, as step
towards change, 244
Employee profile, developing, 92
Employee Stock Ownership
Plan (ESOP), at NATD, 47,
94, 205
Employee suggestion box,
Corporate America having,
123–24
Employee(s)
as alcoholic, 146–47
as boss, 79–80
as buddy for new hires, 105
building trust among, 21–23
celebrating with, 63–64
competence of, 157–59
in control, 82–83
as coworkers, 45
customers informed by, 54–55
firing, 34–35

honesty of, 12–13
honoring each other, 52
motivation of, 12
plain talk from, 36–37
power shared by, 154–56
profit created by, 200, 201–4
quality achieved by, 170–75
rewarding, 56
technical competence of, 157–
59
see also Coworkers; Hiring
Employment anniversaries,
celebrating
by Corporate America, 135
at Super Person meetings,
130
Employment tenure, hiring
considering, 95
Engineering, subcontracting,
207
Enthusiasm, 213–18
in corporate America, 223
with customers, 216–17
New Partnership built on,
224
over hobbies, 215–16
over sales, 215
see also Humor
Equality, 4
Corporate America and, 57–
58
do unto others and, 46–47
Equipment, employees painting,
70
Esmark, staff department at,
149
ESOP, *see* Employee Stock
Ownership Plan
Evaluations, *see* Employee
evaluations
Expansion, NATD's offer of,
235
Expense accounts, accuracy of, 8
Extracurricular activities, hiring
considering, 96

F

Family, 61–76
   being yourself fostering, 68–71
   companionship from, 64–67
   Corporate America and, 71–74
   customers as, 186–89, 191
   encouraging, 67–68
   New Partnership built on, 75–76
   security from, 62–64
   Super Person award for encouraging sense of, 129
Feedback, for huddles, 81
Ferrari, Fred, 79, 115, 161
Field sales, quality and, 178
Financial security, concern for that of employees, 63
Firing, policy on, 34–35
Freiden Mailing Corporation, NATD and, 218–19
Front office employees, assembly line tasks shared by, 78–79
Full day's work, employees doing, 12
Fun
   sense of family built through, 69–70
   with small management style, 146–47
Future, profit maximization and, 207–8
   see also Change

G

Gainsharing programs, in Corporate America, 135, 181

General Electric, 105
   entrepreneurial business units at, 145
   Welch and, 209
General Motors
   change by board of, 246
   EDS versus, 149
   Nummi and, 131
Gilbert, Betty, 187
Giving, employees and, 71
Gloves, as quality symbol, 176–77
Golden rule, 60
Goyenche, Art, 111
Growth
   of customers, 185–86
   quality and, 170

H

Handicapped, outsourcing with, 207
Hawk, Jack, 67–68
Head Sweeper, role of, 80
Health, concern for that of employees, 63
Health insurance, low cost of, 178–79
"Help wanted" ads
   of Corporate America, 104
   hiring from, 93–94
Hewlett Packard, 3, 47, 73–74
   NATD and, 87, 114, 175, 176–77, 185–87, 200–1, 219–20
   profit centers at, 148
Hiring, 91–107
   age as factor in, 95
   commute as factor in, 95
   Corporate America and, 103–6

Hiring (*continued*)
  employee evaluation and, 102–3
  employee profile developed for, 92
  extracurricular activities as factor in, 96
  finding good people for, 93
  half- or whole-day job trial for, 101–2
  from "help wanted" ads, 93–94
  importance placed in, 54–55
  job application as factor in, 95–96
  job interview for, 96–100
  New Partnership built on, 90–91
  pay cutting as factor in, 95
  prior job tenure as factor in, 95
  references checked for, 101–2
  from referrals, 93
  selection process for, 95–96
  values of prospective employees important in, 98, 99
  see also Pay
Hobbies, enthusiasm over, 215–16
Home, *see* Working at home
Honesty, 4, 7–16
  Corporate America and, 14–15
  in employees, 12–13
  establishing climate of, 7–12
  of management, 7–12
  New Partnership built on, 15–16
  working both ways, 12–13
Honor, *see* Dignity
Hospital, employees in, 64
Hostetter, Rich, 113, 159, 200
Hot sheet meeting, 142–43
Huddles, with teamwork, 81–83

Humanity, leadership's love of, 225, 226–27, 237
Humor, 217–23
  in Corporate America, 223
  with customers, 218–23
  at NATD, 217–18
  New Partnership built on, 224

I

IBM
  change by board of, 246
  NATD and, 122
  profit centers at, 150
In-line manufacturing, at NATD, 162
In Search of Excellence (Peters), 242
Information gaining
  in Corporate America, 165–66
  at NATD, 161–62
Information sharing
  customers and, 191–92, 196
  for huddles, 81
Initiative, for creativity, 113–15
Intelligence, quality and, 173–74
Interview, *see* Job interview
Iverson, Ken, 71

J

JIT, *see* Just-in-time delivery
Job, employees having choice of, 98–99, 104–5
Job application, hiring considering, 95–96

Job costing analyses meeting, 143
Job interview, 96–100
    of Corporate America, 104
Job performance, evaluations of,
    33–35
Job rotation, teamwork
    increased by, 83–85
Job tenure, *see* Employment
    tenure
Job trial, in hiring process, 101–2
Johnson & Johnson, profit
    centers at, 148
Johnson, Janie, 79, 140
Just-in-time (JIT) delivery
    with Digital Equipment
    Corporation, 192
    in small management style,
    141

K

Karlsson, Eric, 3–4, 64–65, 92,
    119–20, 146–47
Kautz, Peter, 179
Kemline, Allan, 18–19, 33–34,
    35–36, 87, 161, 193, 220–
    21, 226–27
Knittle, Wayne, 25
Kronheimer, Al, 47

L

Lam, Joddy, 49, 172, 188–89
Layoffs
    in Corporate America, 137
    honesty in dealing with, 10–
    11

Leadership, 225–39
    in Corporate America, 237
    die makers challenging, 229–
    35
    love of humanity of, 225, 226–
    27, 237
    making of, 226–27
    New Partnership built on,
    238–39
    priorities of, 228
    toughest choices for, 229–
    37
    traits of, 225–26
    values of, 225, 226, 237
Leave of absence, granting, 64
Lee, Bill, 86, 87
Less is more, *see* Management,
    small style of
Lockheed
    profit centers at, 150
    Skunk Works at, 150
Lombardi, Vince, 77
Long ball
    profit maximization and,
    207–8
    time and, 69
Lopes, Dave, 52, 66, 78, 82,
    116–17, 120, 161
Louis, Joe, 144
Low-cal, low-fat, low- cholesterol,
    gobbledygook on, 40–41
Lying, by employees, 13

M

MacMillan, Ken, 86, 129
McPherson, Rene, 22
Magna International, 148
Maintenance, Corporate
    America and, 58
Malveda, Edwin, 200–201

Management
 helping others as joy of, 199–201
 honesty of, 7–12
Management, small style of, 139–51
 administrators eliminated in, 141
 "assistant to" jobs eliminated in, 141
 bureaucracy minimized by, 139–41
 business plan eliminated in, 140–41
 efficiency in, 141–43
 employees challenged to do more in, 140
 fun with, 146–47
 just-in-time delivery and production in, 141
 meetings eliminated in, 142
 memos eliminated in, 142
 organization chart eliminated in, 143, 156
 profitability of, 144–45
 reports eliminated in, 142
 secretaries eliminated in, 141–42
 size of, 147–48
 speed from, 143–44
 staff jobs eliminated in, 140–41
 "work cells" in, 141
 work groups and, 143
Marriage, of employees, 64
Meetings
 in Corporate America, 148–49
 eliminating, 142
 hot sheet, 142–43
 job costing analyses, 143
 see also Super Person meetings
Memos, eliminating, 142
Merit, Super Person award based on, 128, 130

Merit pay increases, plain talk on ending, 32–33
Micropolis Corporation, NATD and, 190, 235
Milan, Bob, 174–75
Mistakes, permission to make, 118–20
Motivation, of employees, 12
Mudge, Ken, 7, 25, 116
Mutual respect, 4
 Corporate America and, 56
 do unto others and, 48–50

N

"NATD University," 158–59
Nationality, quality and, 173–74
New Partnership, 4–5, 7
 creativity as basis of, 124–25
 do unto others as basis of, 60
 family as basis of, 75–76
 hiring as basis of, 90–91
 honesty as basis of, 15–16
 humor and enthusiasm as basis of, 224
 leadership as basis of, 238–39
 plain talk as basis of, 43–44
 power as basis of, 167–68
 profit as basis of, 211–12
 quality as basis of, 181–82
 small size enhancing, 146
 teamwork as basis of, 89–90
 thank you as basis of, 137–38
 trust as basis of, 24, 26, 28–29
Newspaper ads, see "Help wanted" ads
Nikeshin, Alex, 187
No rejects
 employees working toward, 78
 in "help wanted" ads, 94

No rejects (*continued*)
  leadership theory
    overshadowed by, 226
  as objective, 31–32, 71, 79
  plain talk on, 31–32
  profits and, 170
  quality and, 169–70, 171,
    172–73
  specialists supporting, 84
  Super Person award for
    aiming for, 129
  see also Quality
Nonfraternization, with
  customers, 195–96
Nordhausen, Ed, 55, 178
Norsworthy, Jim, 162–63
NuCor Steel, 71
Nummi
  NATD and, 143–44, 185–86,
    187
  "thank you" said by, 131–32
Nunes, Lydia, 63, 65

O

Objective
  employees sharing, 78
  specialists supporting, 84
  see also No rejects
Office
  Corporate America and, 58
  equality in choice of, 46, 47
Olson, Ken, 135
Oneself, *see* Yourself, being
"Open door" policy, on plant
  floor, 20–21
Organization chart
  in Corporate America, 163
  elimination of, 156
  at NATD, 143
Ornellas, Vera, 91, 103, 173

Ortiz, Manny, 96
Outsourcing, *see* Subcontracting
Overtime
  compensation for, 23–24
  volunteers for, 78–79

P

Packing, respect for employees
  in, 48
Park, Ku, 174
Parking
  Corporate America and, 57
  equality regarding, 47
Parrnelli, Tom, 33, 45, 143–44,
  172, 227
Partnering, with customers, 190
Pay
  in Corporate America, 163
  cut in as selection criterion, 96
  determining, 100
  employees earning part of
    coworkers', 85–86
  equality regarding, 47
  hand-delivered, 85–86
  job interview dealing with,
    100
  plain talk and, 32–33
  quality and, 173–74
  to sales associates, 205–6
  Super Person meetings
    distributing, 85
  see also Rewards
Payment terms, plain talk on, 38
Peck, M. Scott, 136
Pension funds, change from,
  245–46
Perks, in Corporate America,
  163
Perot, Ross, 149
Peters, Tom, 242

Plain talk, 31–44
  company objectives and, 31–32
  company politics and, 35–36
  Corporate America and, 39–42
  with customers, 37–39, 86, 190
  delivery and, 39
  employee evaluations and, 33–35
  job interview dealing with, 99–100
  New Partnership built on, 43–44
  pay and, 32–33
  price and, 37–38
  in Super Person meetings, 130
  terms and, 38
  working both ways, 36–37
Planning, profit maximization and, 207–8
Plant layout, employees responsible for, 53
Policy manuals
  in Corporate America, 148
  elimination of, 143
Politicking, plain talk and, 35–36
Power, 153–68
  competence and, 155, 157–59
  Corporate America and, 57, 154, 163–66, 209
  as customer/vendor partnering barrier, 193–94
  of decision making, 161, 165
  elements of, 159–63
  employees sharing, 154–56
  of information gaining, 161–62, 165–66
  of latitude to act, 162–63, 166
  New Partnership built on, 167–68
  "promotion syndrome" and, 154

  of resource allocation, 160–61, 164–65
  responsibility and, 155–56
  see also Authority
Price, plain talk on, 37–38
Problem-solving, at NATD, 82
Problems
  employees solving, 22–23
  leadership handling, 229–37
Production, subcontracting, 207
Productivity, small size increasing, 146
Products, of NATD, 241
Profit, 199–212
  corporate America and, 208–10
  Employee Stock Ownership Plan sharing, 205
  employees creating, 200, 201–2
  future planning for, 207–8
  helping others as, 199–201
  individual's impact on, 202–4
  joy of management and, 199–201
  New Partnership built on, 211–12
  no rejects and, 170
  sales associates and, 205–6
  small management style and, 144–45
  subcontracting increasing, 206–7
  values and being yourself maximizing, 245
Profit centers, large companies divided into, 145, 147–50
Profit statement, subcontracting generating, 206
"Promotion syndrome," 154
Purchase orders, verbal, 25

Q

Quality, 169–83
  Corporate America and, 179–81
  customers and, 175–77
  education and, 173–74
  employees achieving, 170–75, 181
  New Partnership built on, 182–83
  no rejects and, 169–70, 171, 172–73
  service and, 177–79
  Super Person meeting stressing, 172–73, 175
  see also No rejects

R

Recognition, 4
  of employees, 65–66
  sharing with employees, 73–74
  see also Rewards; Super Person meetings; Thank you
Recruiting, *see* Hiring
Reengineering, quality improvement in Corporate America and, 180
References, checking in hiring process, 101–2
Referrals, hiring from, 93
Reports, eliminating, 142
Resource allocation
  in Corporate America, 164–65
  at NATD, 160–61
Respect, *see* Mutual respect

Responsibility, power and, 155–56
Retirement, celebrating, 65–66
Retirement home, visiting that of employee, 68
Rewards, for good work, 56
  see also Pay; Recognition; Super Person meetings
Roddick, Anita, 209–10
Rodrigues, Ed, 122, 234–35
Rosario, Joe, 9, 113, 117–18, 200, 231
Rosas, Raphael, 113
Roses, thank you said to women with, 133
Ruiz, Hilda, 129
Ruiz, Ruben, 82–83

S

Sales, enthusiasm over, 215
Sales associates
  commission to, 205–6
  quality and, 178
  trusting, 19
Sankey, Al, 219–20
Sears, 245
Secretaries, eliminating, 141–42
Security, family at work fostering, 62–64
Self-directed work teams
  in Corporate America, 124, 180–81
  as step towards change, 244
Self-worth, 4
  Corporate America and, 56
  do unto others and, 52–55
Service, quality and, 177–79
Shifts, employees having choice of, 99, 104–5

Shipping, respect for employees
in, 48
Sick leave, as additional
vacation, 13
Sickness, of employees, 64
Sigma, quality improvement in
Corporate America and,
180
Silva, Pee Wee, 147
Simmons, Dave, 201
Small management style, see
Management, small style of
SPC, see Statistical process
control
Staff jobs
in Corporate America, 149
elimination of, 140–41
Statistical process control (SPC),
quality improvement in
Corporate America and,
180
Stevens, Clare, 68, 70, 85, 86,
114, 121, 187, 201, 230,
231, 232, 233–34
Subcontracting, profit increased
by, 206–7
Sun Microcomputer, NATD
and, 38, 188
Supelario, Ling, 52
Super Person meetings, 127,
128–31
customers at, 195–96
employment anniversaries
celebrated at, 130
enthusiasm shown at, 215
pay distributed at, 85
plain talk at, 130
quality stressed at, 172–73, 175
retirement recognized at, 66
see also Super Person of the
Month award
Super Person of the Month award,
127, 128–29, 130–31
everyone winning, 215

for having latitude to act,
162–63
Suppliers, relations with, 188–89

T

Taylor-Weber, Jeff, 173–74
Teamwork, 4, 77–90
beliefs on, 77–78
Corporate America and, 88
with customers, 86–87
employees earning part of
coworkers' pay in, 85–86
employees in control in, 82–83
entire company encompassed
by, 78–79
everyone as boss in, 79–80
honesty building, 13
huddles and, 81–83
job rotation increasing, 83–85
New Partnership built on, 89–
90
trust building, 23
see also Self-directed work
teams
Telephones, honesty in dealing
with, 11
Tenure, see Employment tenure
Terms, plain talk on, 38
Thank you, 127–38
buying dinner for employees
saying, 134–35
Corporate America and, 135–
37
financial awards saying, 204–5
New Partnership built on,
137–38
Nummi saying, 131–32
"old school" against saying,
132

Thank you (*continued*)
random gifts and gestures
saying, 133–34
size as excuse for not saying,
132–33
Super Person meetings saying,
127, 128–31
in union shop, 131–32
Third shift, compensation for,
23–24
Thomasy, Laurie, 79, 188
Time
Corporate America and, 68–
69
family developed by giving of,
67–68
at NATD, 69
Total quality management
(TQM), quality
improvement in Corporate
America and, 180
Toyota, Nummi and, 131
TQM, *see* Total quality
management
Trust, 4, 17–29
building, 21–23
from "caring by walking
around," 20–21
in Corporate America, 26–
27
in coworkers' competence,
17–18
in coworkers' conscience, 18–
19
in customers, 25–26
job interview dealing with,
100
New Partnership built on, 24,
26, 28–29
in sales associates, 19
working both ways, 23–25
Truth
employees telling the, 13
honesty established by telling,
9–11

U

Uniform, *see* Clothing
Union Pacific, sense of family at,
72
Union shop, thank you in, 131–
32

V

Valente, Mark, 86
Values
change and, 247–48
consistency and, 227
of customer, 186
hiring considering, 98, 99
leadership and, 225, 226, 237
living one's, 7, 12, 28, 175,
245
teamwork facilitated by same,
78
see also Currencies
Vitti, John, 31, 32, 48–49, 50,
62
Vosner, Larry, 18, 25, 84, 144–
45

W

Wal-Mart, sense of family at,
71–72
Walsh, Mike, 71, 237
Walton, Sam, 71–72, 237
Want ads, *see* "Help wanted"
ads
Watson, Greg, 73–74, 87, 186

Weiser, Fred, 20, 82–83, 131, 155
Welch, Jack, 105, 209
Whitman, Pete, 63
Work cells, in small management style, 141
Work groups, at NATD, 143
Working at home, 19
  Corporate America on, 27
Workman's compensation, low cost of, 178–79
World Waiting to Be Born (Peck), 136
Wright, Joan, 11

X

Xerox Corporation, 69
  NATD and, 174–75, 220–23

Y

Yourself, being
  for creativity, 110–11
  profit maximization by, 245
  sense of family from, 68–71

About the Author

Born and raised in the Chicago area, Tom Melohn graduated cum laude from Princeton University and served two years in the U.S. Navy.

Tom's marketing career started at Procter & Gamble, followed by Leo Burnett Advertising, Pet Milk, Swift & Company, and C & H Sugar—where he was senior vice president. He then became a co-owner and Head Sweeper at the North American Tool & Die Company (NATD).

NATD has been written up in a number of best-selling business books, including *Passion for Excellence, Thriving On Chaos, The Leadership Challenge, Winner Take All, Teaching The Elephant to Dance, Breakpoint & Beyond, The New Paradigm in Business, Marketing Myths,* and *Credibility.*

NATD was one of seven companies featured in the PBS-TV documentary "In Search of Excellence." Numerous newspaper and magazine articles, as well as CNBC-TV, have also highlighted NATD's accomplishments.

Tom has written articles for the *Harvard Business Review* and *Inc* magazine. He and his wife, Holly, live in the San Francisco Bay area.

You can also see Tom Melohn in his training video: *The New Partnership: Managing for Excellence with Tom Melohn.*

This program was filmed on location at North American Tool & Die and at two of their customers, Nummi and Apple Computer. You can see footage of Tom in action with his employees and customers.

For information contact:

Enterprise Media, Inc.
91 Harvey Street
Cambridge, MA 02140

PHONE: 1-800-423-6021
FAX: 1-617-354-1637

The characteristics of NATD's environment include a notable absence of complicated paperwork or layers of management; trust and respect at all levels; devotion to quality of product and dedication to customer service; self-management and decision-making authority on the front line, managers who act as facilitators rather than bosses; and an abundance of reward and recognition for employees doing "something smart."

"[The New Partnership] is a motivational video, a representative response to the plea for excellence in American business issued by Tom Peters, the video's spokesman advocate of this method of turning the traditional corporate hierarchy on its head."

"This video is appropriate, and in fact recommended for corporate management training and for graduate and undergraduate management classes.

***** Video Rating Guide for Librarians; Vol. 2 No. 1